WELCOME TO CLUB SCUD!

Doonesbury Books by G.B. Trudeau

Still a Few Bugs in the System
The President Is a Lot Smarter Than You Think
But This War Had Such Promise
Call Me When You Find America
Guilty, Guilty, Guilty!
"What Do We Have for the Witnesses, Johnnie?"
Dare to Be Great, Ms. Caucus
Wouldn't a Gremlin Have Been More Sensible?
"Speaking of Inalienable Rights, Amy..."
You're Never Too Old for Nuts and Berries
An Especially Tricky People
As the Kid Goes for Broke
Stalking the Perfect Tan
"Any Grooming Hints for Your Fans, Rollie?"
But the Pension Fund Was Just Sitting There
We're Not Out of the Woods Yet
A Tad Overweight, But Violet Eyes to Die For
And That's My Final Offer!
He's Never Heard of You, Either
In Search of Reagan's Brain
Ask for May, Settle for June
Unfortunately, She Was Also Wired for Sound
The Wreck of the "Rusty Nail"
You Give Great Meeting, Sid
Doonesbury: A Musical Comedy
Check Your Egos at the Door
That's Doctor Sinatra, You Little Bimbo!
Death of a Party Animal
Downtown Doonesbury
Calling Dr. Whoopee
Talkin' About My G-G-Generation
We're Eating More Beets!
Read My Lips, Make My Day, Eat Quiche and Die!
Give Those Nymphs Some Hooters!
You're Smokin' Now, Mr. Butts!
I'd Go With the Helmet, Ray

In Large Format

The Doonesbury Chronicles
Doonesbury's Greatest Hits
The People's Doonesbury
Doonesbury Dossier: The Reagan Years
Doonesbury Deluxe: Selected Glances Askance
Recycled Doonesbury: Second Thoughts on a Gilded Age

A DOONESBURY BOOK

by G. B. TRUDEAU

WELCOME TO CLUB SCUD!

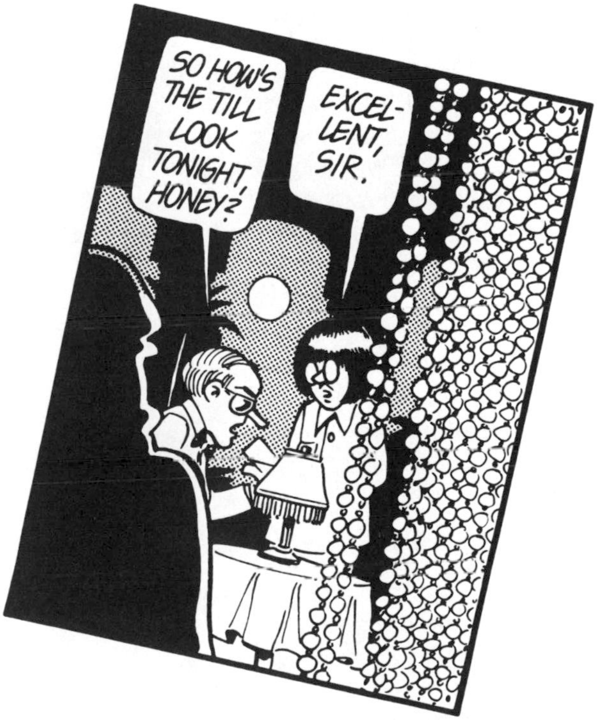
SO HOW'S THE TILL LOOK TONIGHT, HONEY?
EXCEL-LENT, SIR.

ANDREWS and McMEEL A UNIVERSAL PRESS SYNDICATE COMPANY KANSAS CITY

DOONESBURY is distributed internationally by Universal Press Syndicate.

 For information write Andrews and McMeel, a Universal Press Syndicate Company, 4900 Main Street, Kansas City, Missouri 64112.

ISBN: 0-8362-1882-5

Library of Congress Catalog Card Number: 91-73169

"It was like going to a movie: we paid our money, we went to the theater, we laughed, we cried, the movie ended and an hour later we had forgotten about it."

—Saudi financier Adnan Khashoggi

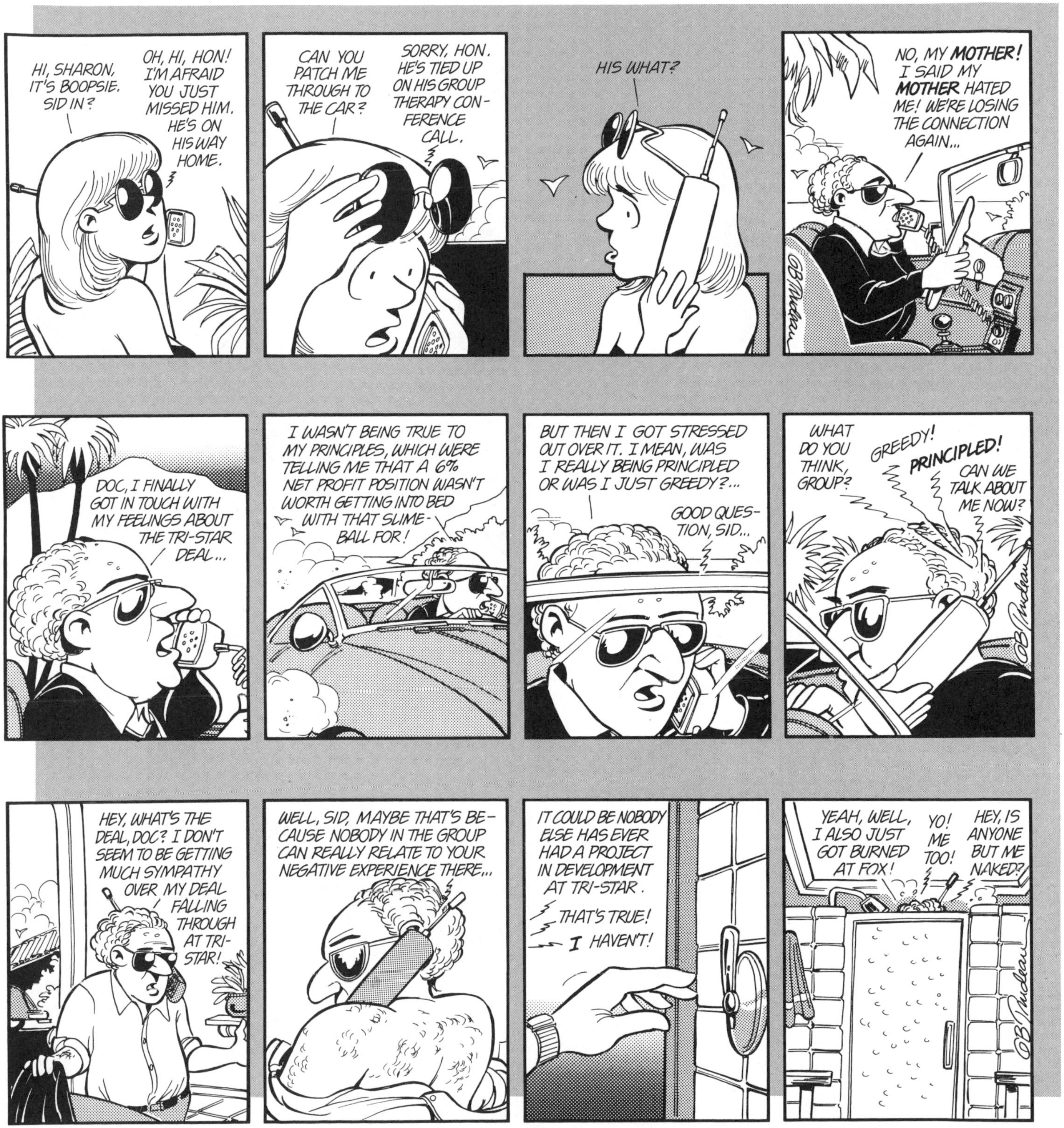
HI, SHARON, IT'S BOOPSIE. SID IN?
OH, HI, HON! I'M AFRAID YOU JUST MISSED HIM. HE'S ON HIS WAY HOME.
CAN YOU PATCH ME THROUGH TO THE CAR?
SORRY, HON. HE'S TIED UP ON HIS GROUP THERAPY CONFERENCE CALL.
HIS WHAT?
NO, MY **MOTHER**! I SAID MY **MOTHER** HATED ME! WE'RE LOSING THE CONNECTION AGAIN...
DOC, I FINALLY GOT IN TOUCH WITH MY FEELINGS ABOUT THE TRI-STAR DEAL...
I WASN'T BEING TRUE TO MY PRINCIPLES, WHICH WERE TELLING ME THAT A 6% NET PROFIT POSITION WASN'T WORTH GETTING INTO BED WITH THAT SLIMEBALL FOR!
BUT THEN I GOT STRESSED OUT OVER IT. I MEAN, WAS I REALLY BEING PRINCIPLED OR WAS I JUST GREEDY?...
GOOD QUESTION, SID...
WHAT DO YOU THINK, GROUP?
GREEDY!
PRINCIPLED!
CAN WE TALK ABOUT ME NOW?
HEY, WHAT'S THE DEAL, DOC? I DON'T SEEM TO BE GETTING MUCH SYMPATHY OVER MY DEAL FALLING THROUGH AT TRI-STAR!
WELL, SID, MAYBE THAT'S BECAUSE NOBODY IN THE GROUP CAN REALLY RELATE TO YOUR NEGATIVE EXPERIENCE THERE...
IT COULD BE NOBODY ELSE HAS EVER HAD A PROJECT IN DEVELOPMENT AT TRI-STAR.
THAT'S TRUE!
I HAVEN'T!
YEAH, WELL, I ALSO JUST GOT BURNED AT FOX!
YO! ME TOO!
HEY, IS ANYONE BUT ME NAKED?

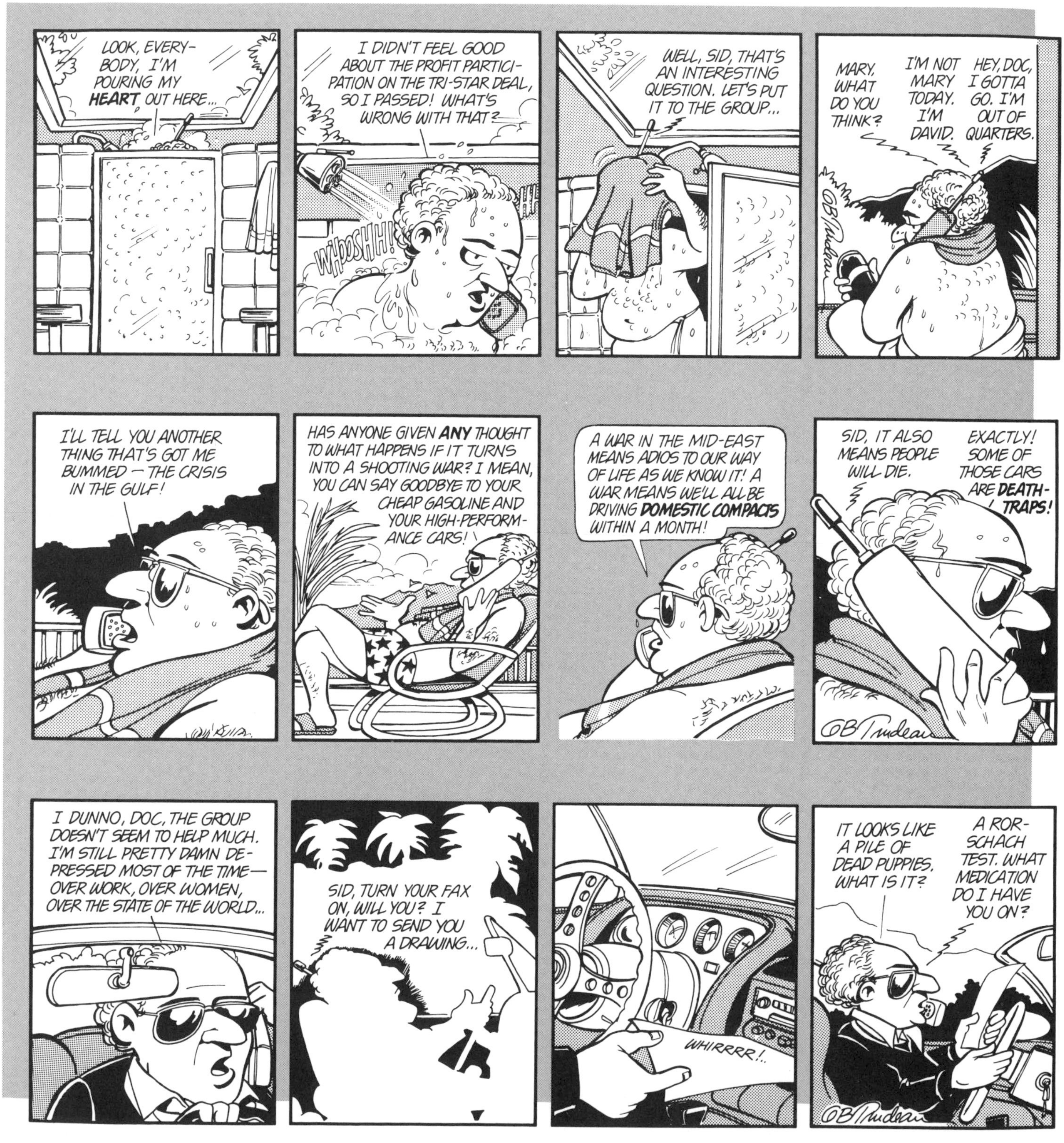
LOOK, EVERYBODY, I'M POURING MY **HEART** OUT HERE...
I DIDN'T FEEL GOOD ABOUT THE PROFIT PARTICIPATION ON THE TRI-STAR DEAL, SO I PASSED! WHAT'S WRONG WITH THAT?
WHOOSHH!
WELL, SID, THAT'S AN INTERESTING QUESTION. LET'S PUT IT TO THE GROUP...
MARY, WHAT DO YOU THINK?
I'M NOT MARY TODAY. I'M DAVID.
HEY, DOC, I GOTTA GO. I'M OUT OF QUARTERS.
I'LL TELL YOU ANOTHER THING THAT'S GOT ME BUMMED — THE CRISIS IN THE GULF!
HAS ANYONE GIVEN **ANY** THOUGHT TO WHAT HAPPENS IF IT TURNS INTO A SHOOTING WAR? I MEAN, YOU CAN SAY GOODBYE TO YOUR CHEAP GASOLINE AND YOUR HIGH-PERFORMANCE CARS!
A WAR IN THE MID-EAST MEANS ADIOS TO OUR WAY OF LIFE AS WE KNOW IT! A WAR MEANS WE'LL ALL BE DRIVING **DOMESTIC COMPACTS** WITHIN A MONTH!
SID, IT ALSO MEANS PEOPLE WILL DIE.
EXACTLY! SOME OF THOSE CARS ARE **DEATH-TRAPS!**
I DUNNO, DOC, THE GROUP DOESN'T SEEM TO HELP MUCH. I'M STILL PRETTY DAMN DEPRESSED MOST OF THE TIME— OVER WORK, OVER WOMEN, OVER THE STATE OF THE WORLD...
SID, TURN YOUR FAX ON, WILL YOU? I WANT TO SEND YOU A DRAWING...
WHIRRRR!
IT LOOKS LIKE A PILE OF DEAD PUPPIES. WHAT IS IT?
A RORSCHACH TEST. WHAT MEDICATION DO I HAVE YOU ON?

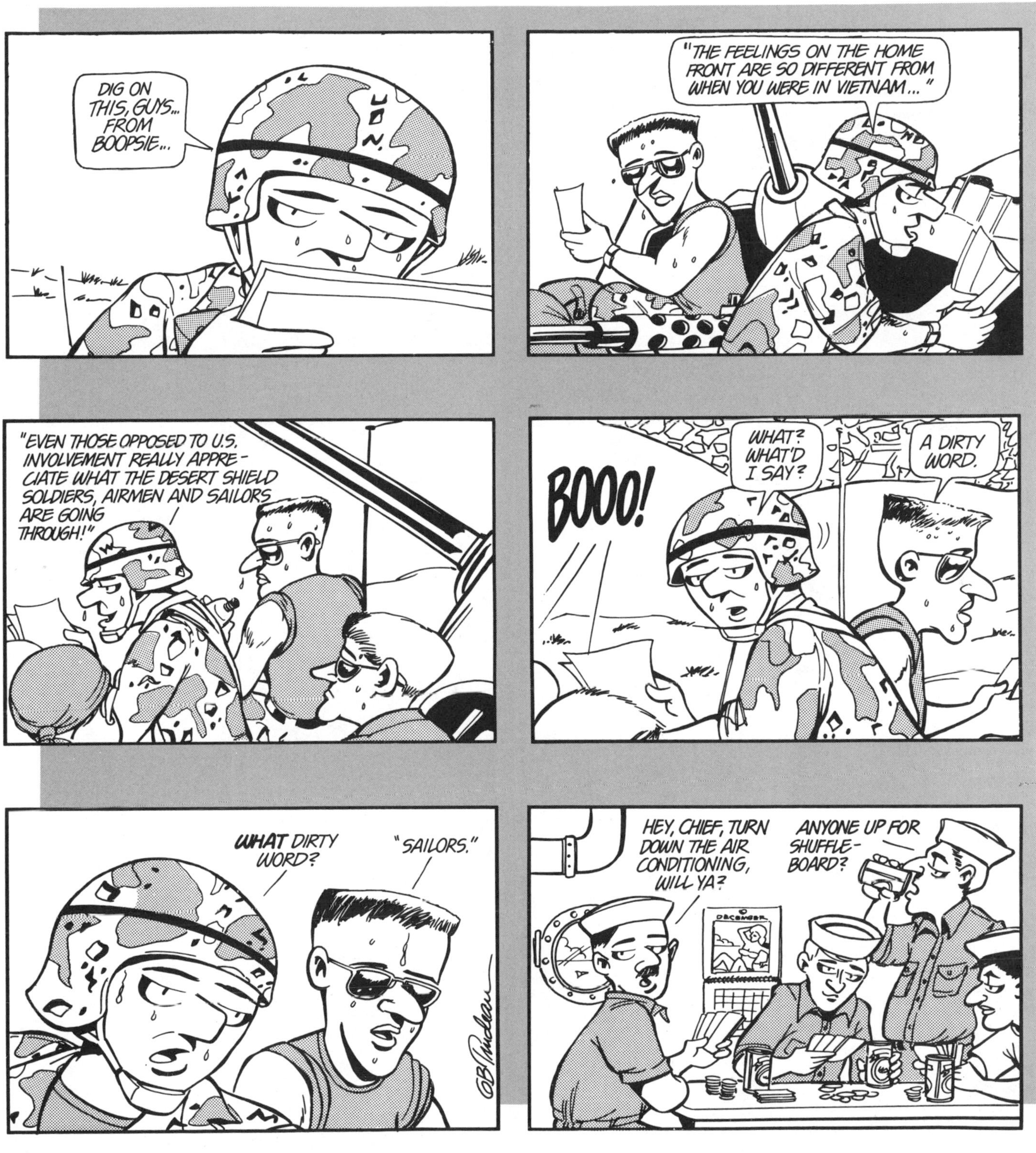
DIG ON THIS, GUYS... FROM BOOPSIE...
"THE FEELINGS ON THE HOME FRONT ARE SO DIFFERENT FROM WHEN YOU WERE IN VIETNAM..."
"EVEN THOSE OPPOSED TO U.S. INVOLVEMENT REALLY APPRE-CIATE WHAT THE DESERT SHIELD SOLDIERS, AIRMEN AND SAILORS ARE GOING THROUGH!"
BOOO!
WHAT? WHAT'D I SAY?
A DIRTY WORD.
WHAT DIRTY WORD?
"SAILORS."
HEY, CHIEF, TURN DOWN THE AIR CONDITIONING, WILL YA?
ANYONE UP FOR SHUFFLE-BOARD?

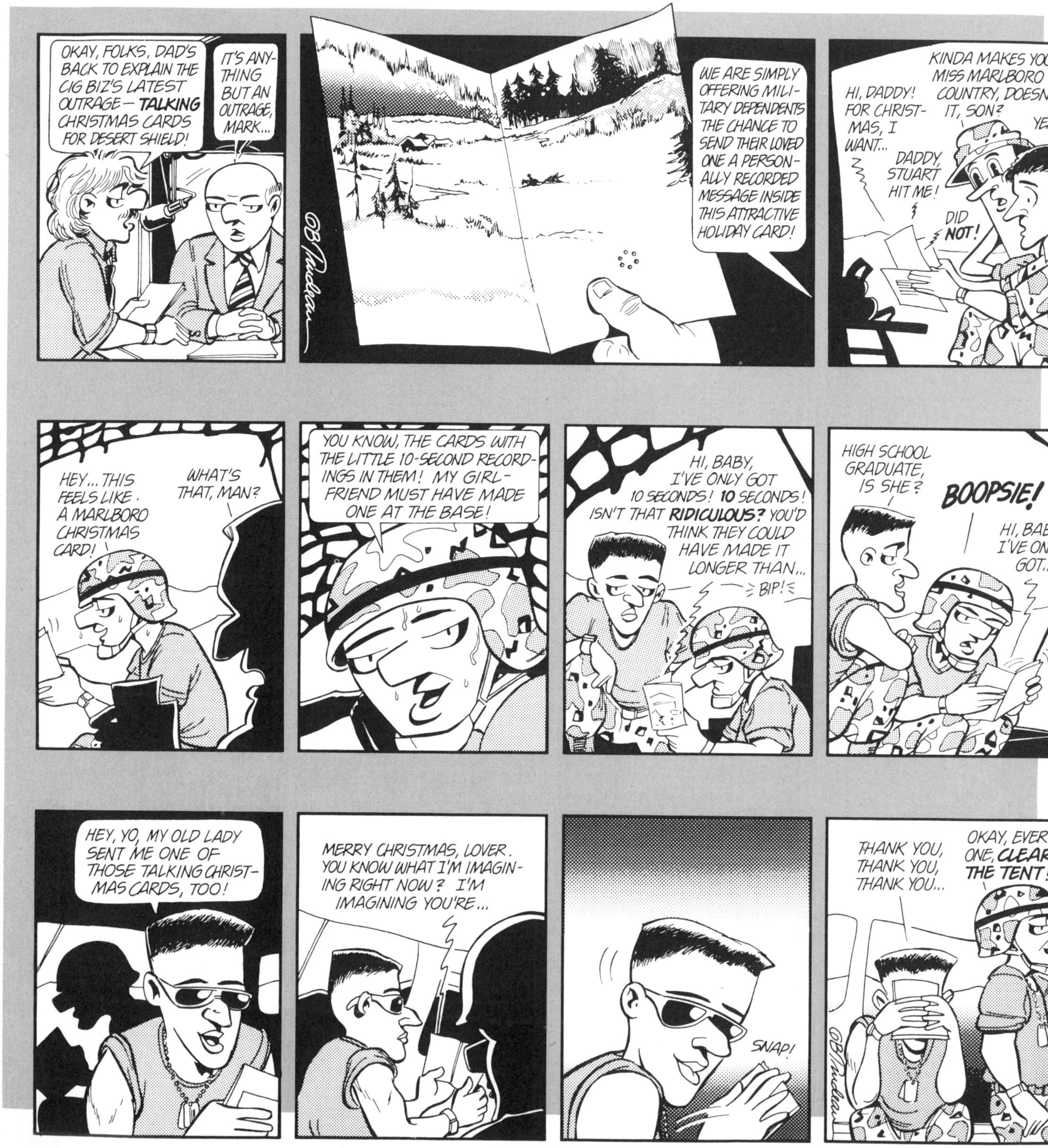
OKAY, FOLKS, DAD'S BACK TO EXPLAIN THE CIG BIZ'S LATEST OUTRAGE — TALKING CHRISTMAS CARDS FOR DESERT SHIELD!
IT'S ANYTHING BUT AN OUTRAGE, MARK...
WE ARE SIMPLY OFFERING MILITARY DEPENDENTS THE CHANCE TO SEND THEIR LOVED ONE A PERSONALLY RECORDED MESSAGE INSIDE THIS ATTRACTIVE HOLIDAY CARD!
HI, DADDY! FOR CHRISTMAS, I WANT...
DADDY, STUART HIT ME!
DID NOT!
KINDA MAKES YOU MISS MARLBORO COUNTRY, DOESN'T IT, SON?
YEAH...
HEY... THIS FEELS LIKE A MARLBORO CHRISTMAS CARD!
WHAT'S THAT, MAN?
YOU KNOW, THE CARDS WITH THE LITTLE 10-SECOND RECORDINGS IN THEM! MY GIRLFRIEND MUST HAVE MADE ONE AT THE BASE!
HI, BABY, I'VE ONLY GOT 10 SECONDS! 10 SECONDS! ISN'T THAT RIDICULOUS? YOU'D THINK THEY COULD HAVE MADE IT LONGER THAN...
BIP!
HIGH SCHOOL GRADUATE, IS SHE?
BOOPSIE!
HI, BABY, I'VE ONLY GOT...
HEY, YO, MY OLD LADY SENT ME ONE OF THOSE TALKING CHRISTMAS CARDS, TOO!
MERRY CHRISTMAS, LOVER. YOU KNOW WHAT I'M IMAGINING RIGHT NOW? I'M IMAGINING YOU'RE...
SNAP!
THANK YOU, THANK YOU, THANK YOU...
OKAY, EVERYONE, CLEAR THE TENT!

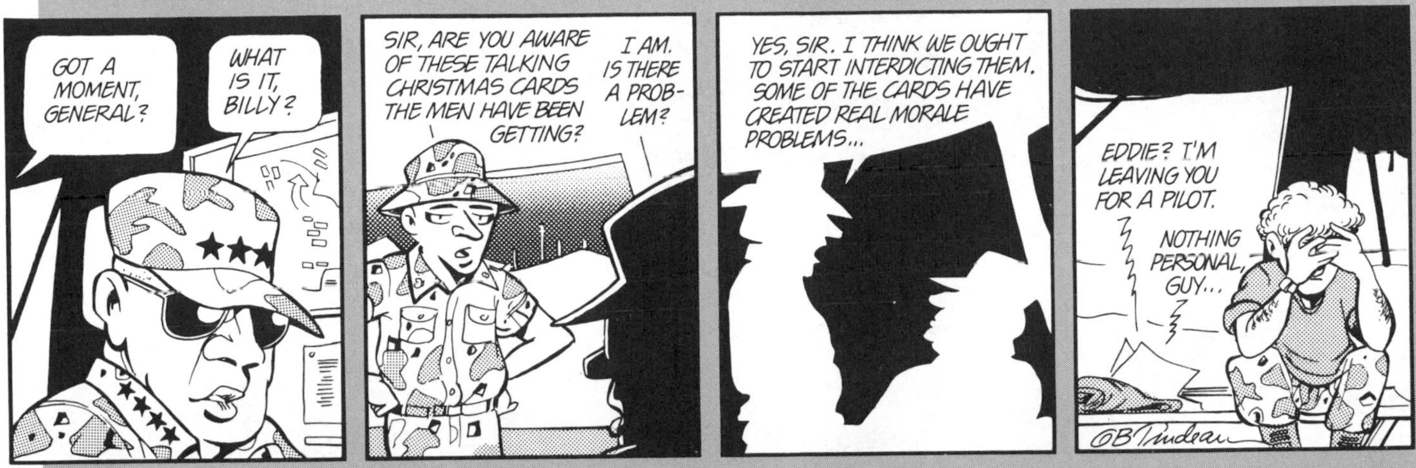
GOT A MOMENT, GENERAL?
WHAT IS IT, BILLY?
SIR, ARE YOU AWARE OF THESE TALKING CHRISTMAS CARDS THE MEN HAVE BEEN GETTING?
I AM. IS THERE A PROBLEM?
YES, SIR. I THINK WE OUGHT TO START INTERDICTING THEM. SOME OF THE CARDS HAVE CREATED REAL MORALE PROBLEMS...
EDDIE? I'M LEAVING YOU FOR A PILOT.
NOTHING PERSONAL, GUY...
©B Trudeau

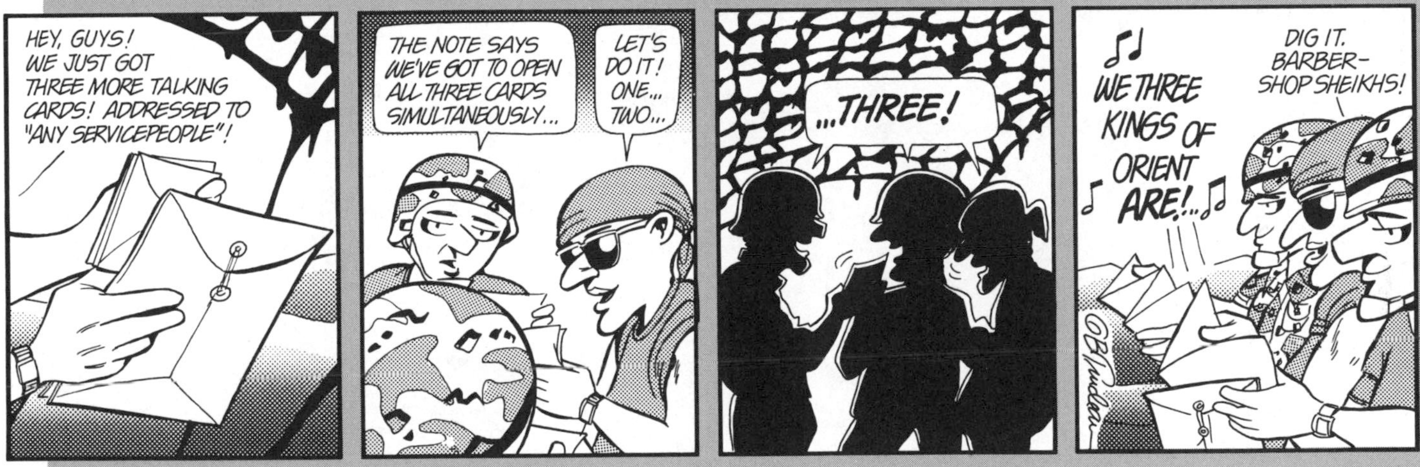
HEY, GUYS! WE JUST GOT THREE MORE TALKING CARDS! ADDRESSED TO "ANY SERVICEPEOPLE"!
THE NOTE SAYS WE'VE GOT TO OPEN ALL THREE CARDS SIMULTANEOUSLY...
LET'S DO IT! ONE... TWO...
...THREE!
WE THREE KINGS OF ORIENT ARE!...
DIG IT. BARBER-SHOP SHEIKHS!
©B Trudeau

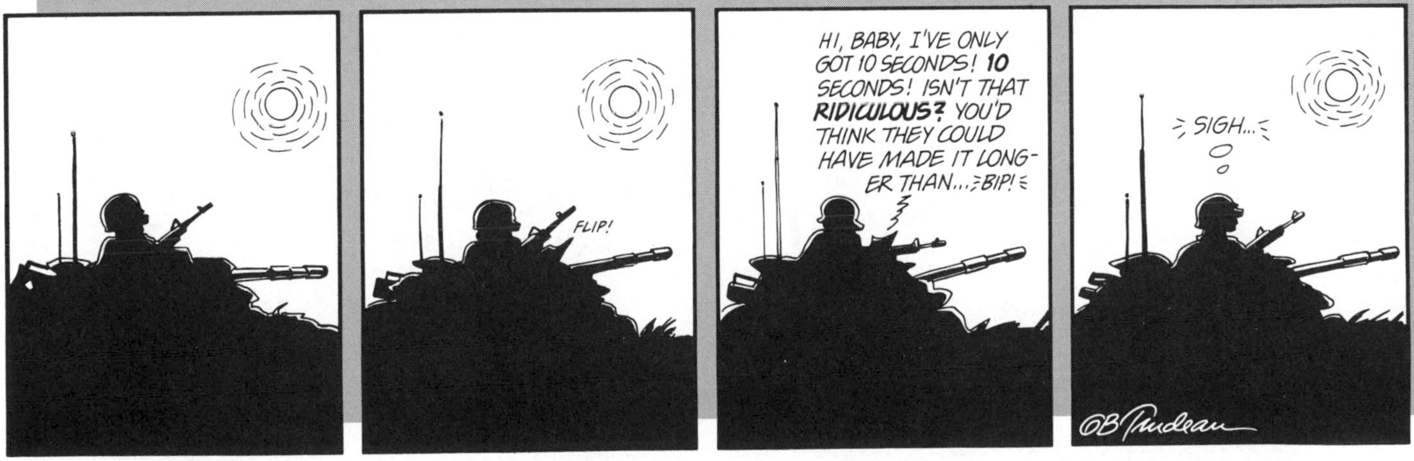
FLIP!
HI, BABY, I'VE ONLY GOT 10 SECONDS! 10 SECONDS! ISN'T THAT RIDICULOUS? YOU'D THINK THEY COULD HAVE MADE IT LONGER THAN...
BIP!
SIGH...
©B Trudeau

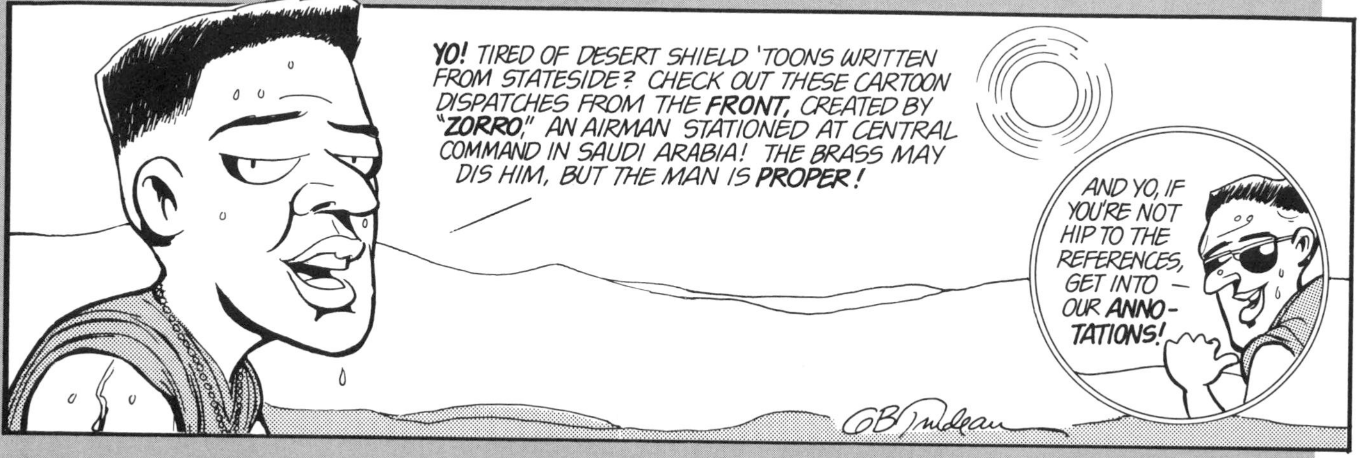
YO! TIRED OF DESERT SHIELD 'TOONS WRITTEN FROM STATESIDE? CHECK OUT THESE CARTOON DISPATCHES FROM THE FRONT, CREATED BY "ZORRO," AN AIRMAN STATIONED AT CENTRAL COMMAND IN SAUDI ARABIA! THE BRASS MAY DIS HIM, BUT THE MAN IS PROPER!
AND YO, IF YOU'RE NOT HIP TO THE REFERENCES, GET INTO OUR ANNOTATIONS!
GB Trudeau

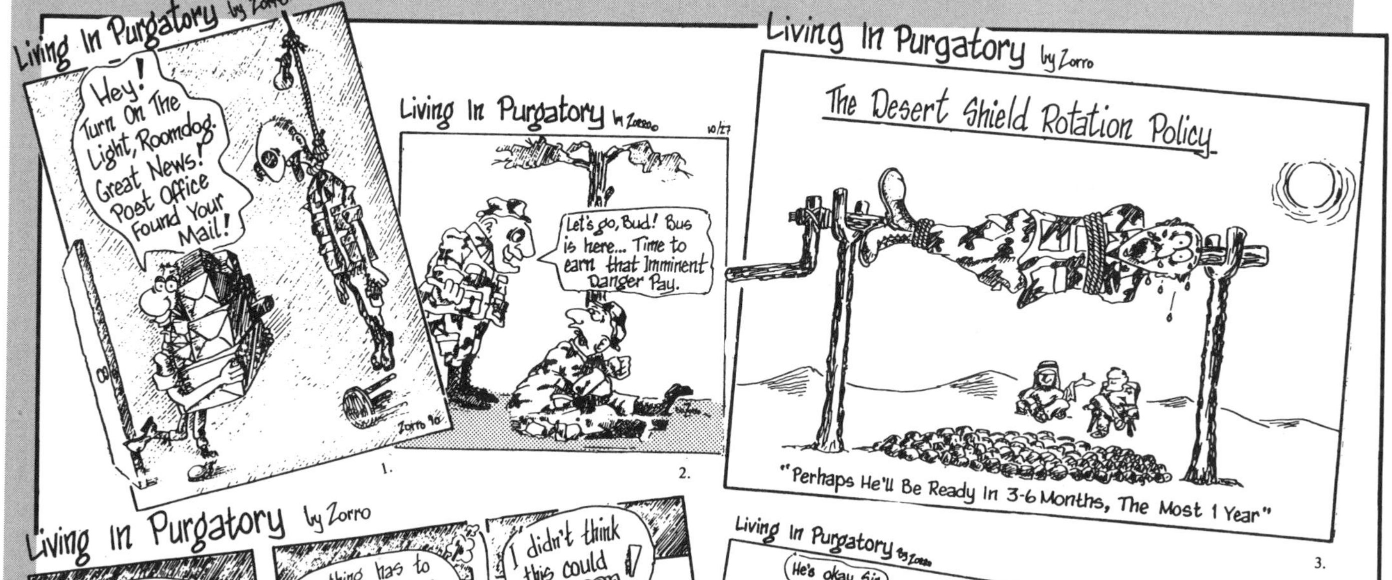
Living In Purgatory by Zorro
Hey! Turn On The Light, Roomdog. Great News! Post Office Found Your Mail!
Zorro '90
1.
Living In Purgatory by Zorro
10/27
Let's go, Bud! Bus is here... Time to earn that Imminent Danger Pay.
2.
Living In Purgatory by Zorro
The Desert Shield Rotation Policy
"Perhaps He'll Be Ready In 3-6 Months, The Most 1 Year"
3.

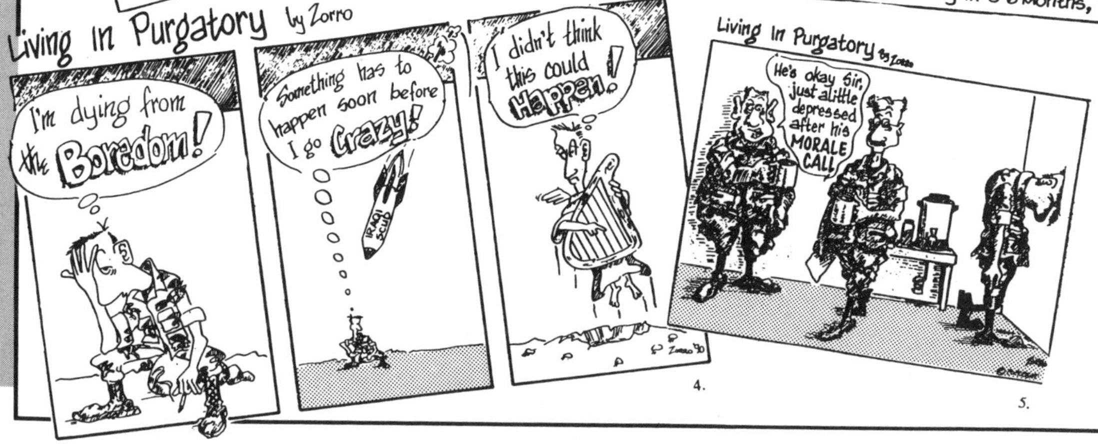
Living In Purgatory by Zorro
I'm dying from the Boredom!
Something has to happen soon before I go Crazy!
IRAQI SCUD
I didn't think this could Happen!
Zorro '90
4.
Living In Purgatory by Zorro
He's okay Sir, just a little depressed after his MORALE CALL
5.

ANNOTATIONS:

1. The huge volume of mail has meant frustrating delivery delays.

2. The bus to and from Cent Com is said to average one accident a week.

3. The Pentagon's no-rotation policy has been a morale-buster.

4. Iraq's decision to test-fire SCUD missiles unnerves the troops.

5. Phone calls home can be difficult. Too often, there's bad news.

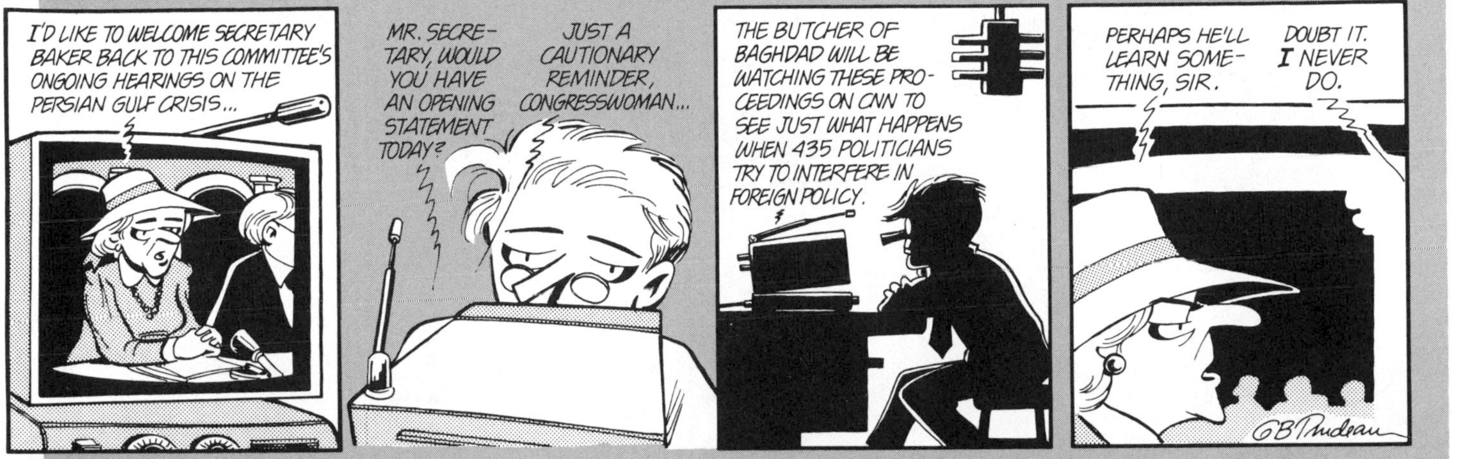
I'D LIKE TO WELCOME SECRETARY BAKER BACK TO THIS COMMITTEE'S ONGOING HEARINGS ON THE PERSIAN GULF CRISIS...
MR. SECRETARY, WOULD YOU HAVE AN OPENING STATEMENT TODAY?
JUST A CAUTIONARY REMINDER, CONGRESSWOMAN...
THE BUTCHER OF BAGHDAD WILL BE WATCHING THESE PROCEEDINGS ON CNN TO SEE JUST WHAT HAPPENS WHEN 435 POLITICIANS TRY TO INTERFERE IN FOREIGN POLICY.
PERHAPS HE'LL LEARN SOMETHING, SIR.
DOUBT IT. **I** NEVER DO.
GB Trudeau

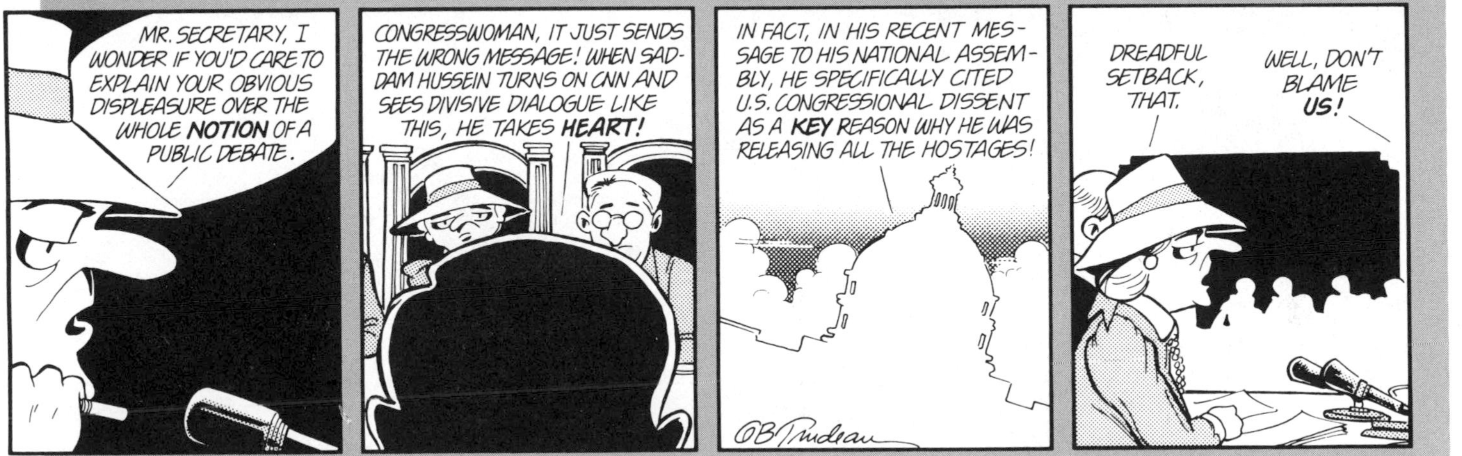
MR. SECRETARY, I WONDER IF YOU'D CARE TO EXPLAIN YOUR OBVIOUS DISPLEASURE OVER THE WHOLE **NOTION** OF A PUBLIC DEBATE.
CONGRESSWOMAN, IT JUST SENDS THE WRONG MESSAGE! WHEN SADDAM HUSSEIN TURNS ON CNN AND SEES DIVISIVE DIALOGUE LIKE THIS, HE TAKES **HEART!**
IN FACT, IN HIS RECENT MESSAGE TO HIS NATIONAL ASSEMBLY, HE SPECIFICALLY CITED U.S. CONGRESSIONAL DISSENT AS A **KEY** REASON WHY HE WAS RELEASING ALL THE HOSTAGES!
GB Trudeau
DREADFUL SETBACK, THAT.
WELL, DON'T BLAME **US!**

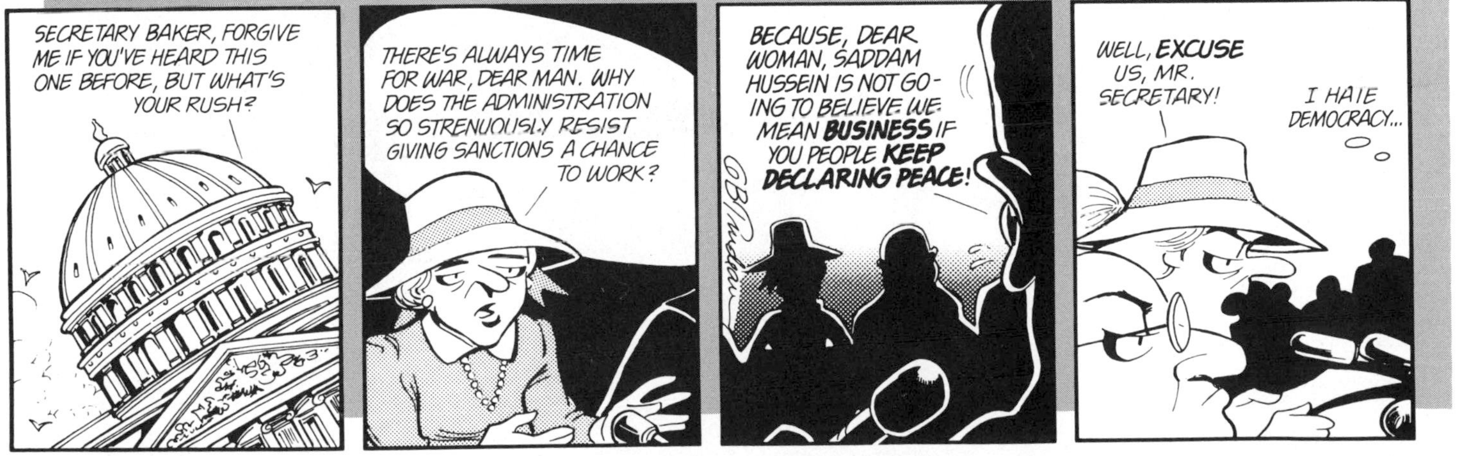
SECRETARY BAKER, FORGIVE ME IF YOU'VE HEARD THIS ONE BEFORE, BUT WHAT'S YOUR RUSH?
THERE'S ALWAYS TIME FOR WAR, DEAR MAN. WHY DOES THE ADMINISTRATION SO STRENUOUSLY RESIST GIVING SANCTIONS A CHANCE TO WORK?
BECAUSE, DEAR WOMAN, SADDAM HUSSEIN IS NOT GOING TO BELIEVE WE MEAN **BUSINESS** IF YOU PEOPLE **KEEP DECLARING PEACE!**
GB Trudeau
WELL, **EXCUSE** US, MR. SECRETARY!
I HATE DEMOCRACY...

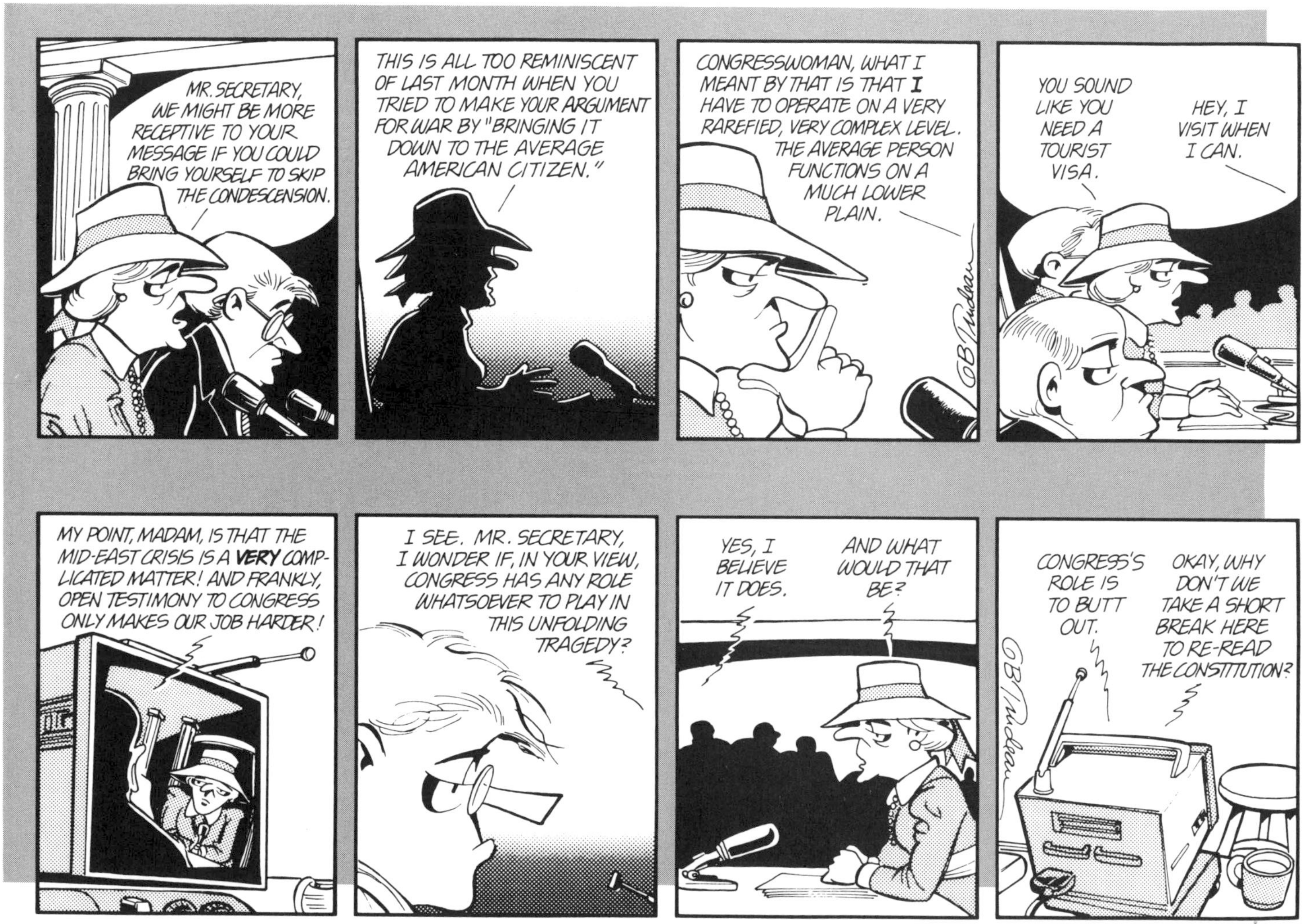
MR. SECRETARY, WE MIGHT BE MORE RECEPTIVE TO YOUR MESSAGE IF YOU COULD BRING YOURSELF TO SKIP THE CONDESCENSION.
THIS IS ALL TOO REMINISCENT OF LAST MONTH WHEN YOU TRIED TO MAKE YOUR ARGUMENT FOR WAR BY "BRINGING IT DOWN TO THE AVERAGE AMERICAN CITIZEN."
CONGRESSWOMAN, WHAT I MEANT BY THAT IS THAT I HAVE TO OPERATE ON A VERY RAREFIED, VERY COMPLEX LEVEL. THE AVERAGE PERSON FUNCTIONS ON A MUCH LOWER PLAIN.
YOU SOUND LIKE YOU NEED A TOURIST VISA.
HEY, I VISIT WHEN I CAN.
MY POINT, MADAM, IS THAT THE MID-EAST CRISIS IS A VERY COMPLICATED MATTER! AND FRANKLY, OPEN TESTIMONY TO CONGRESS ONLY MAKES OUR JOB HARDER!
I SEE. MR. SECRETARY, I WONDER IF, IN YOUR VIEW, CONGRESS HAS ANY ROLE WHATSOEVER TO PLAY IN THIS UNFOLDING TRAGEDY?
YES, I BELIEVE IT DOES.
AND WHAT WOULD THAT BE?
CONGRESS'S ROLE IS TO BUTT OUT.
OKAY, WHY DON'T WE TAKE A SHORT BREAK HERE TO RE-READ THE CONSTITUTION?

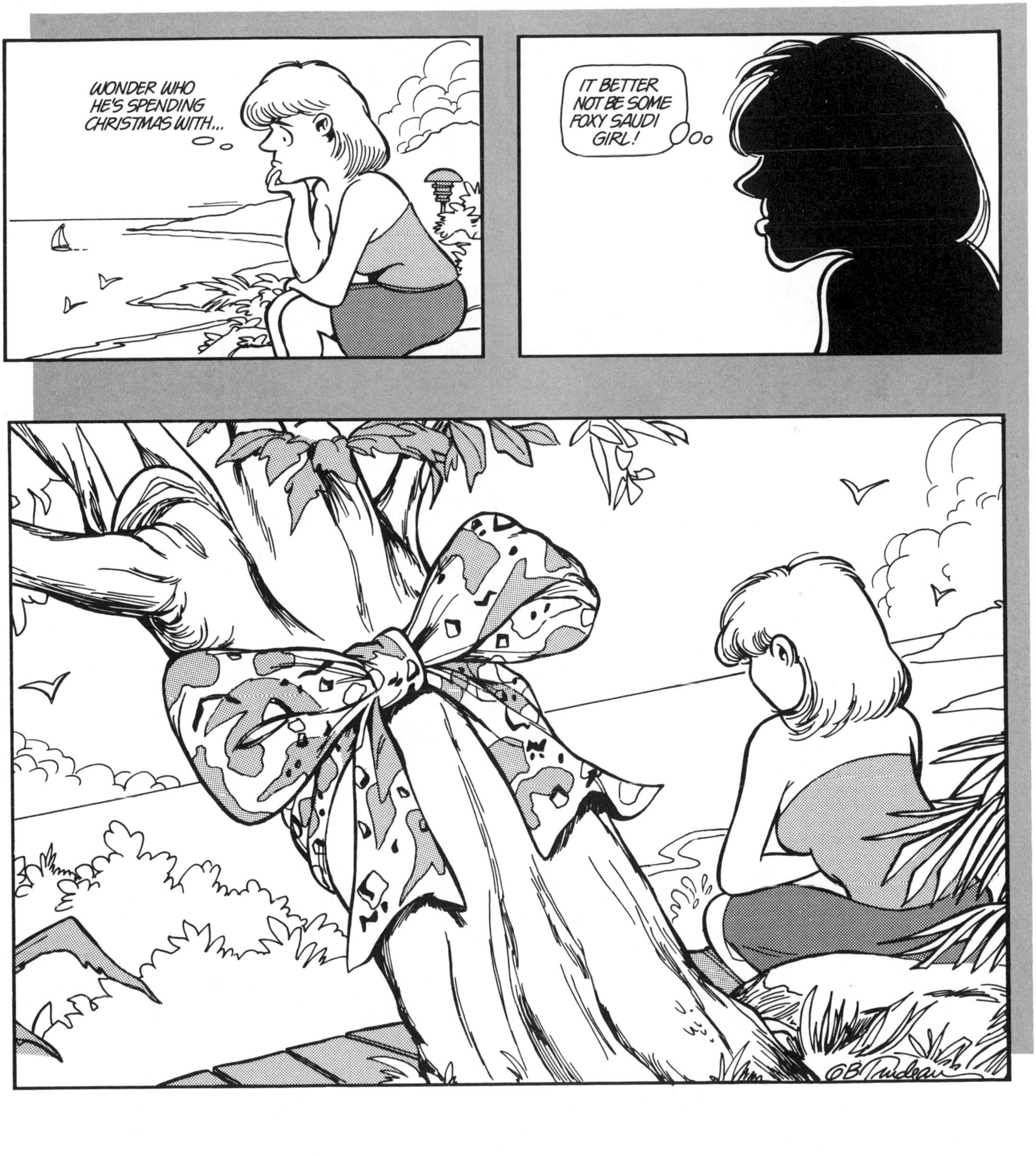
WONDER WHO HE'S SPENDING CHRISTMAS WITH...
IT BETTER NOT BE SOME FOXY SAUDI GIRL!
©B. Trudeau

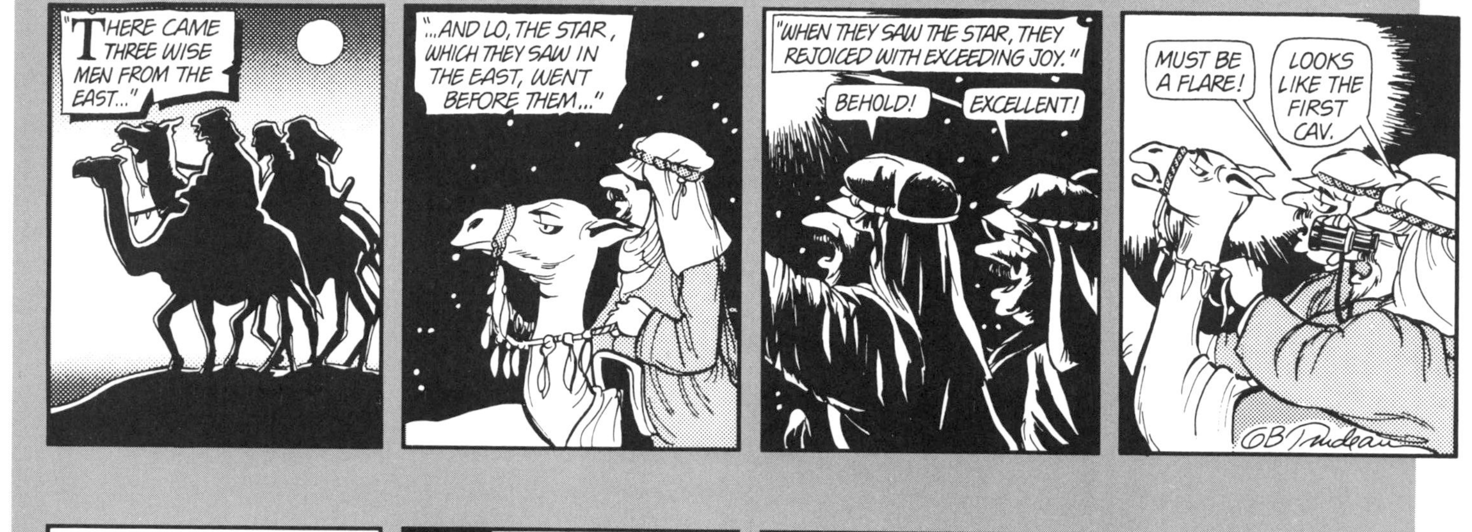
"THERE CAME THREE WISE MEN FROM THE EAST..."
"...AND LO, THE STAR, WHICH THEY SAW IN THE EAST, WENT BEFORE THEM..."
"WHEN THEY SAW THE STAR, THEY REJOICED WITH EXCEEDING JOY."
BEHOLD!
EXCELLENT!
MUST BE A FLARE!
LOOKS LIKE THE FIRST CAV.
©B Trudeau

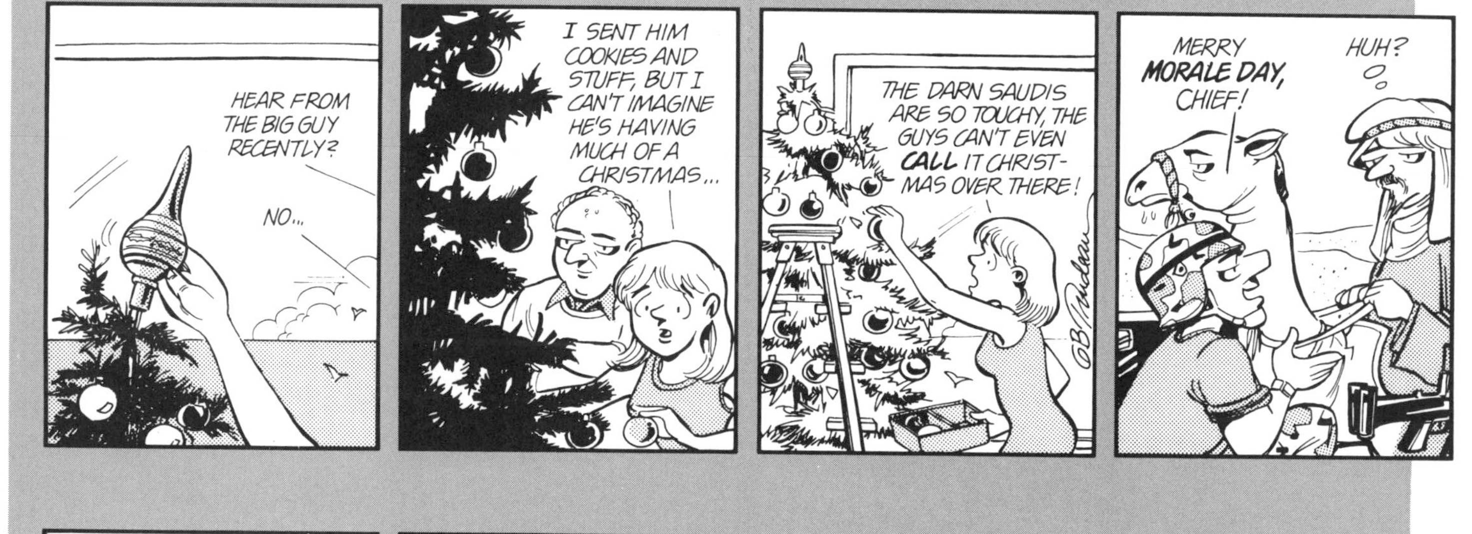
HEAR FROM THE BIG GUY RECENTLY?
NO...
I SENT HIM COOKIES AND STUFF, BUT I CAN'T IMAGINE HE'S HAVING MUCH OF A CHRISTMAS...
THE DARN SAUDIS ARE SO TOUCHY, THE GUYS CAN'T EVEN CALL IT CHRISTMAS OVER THERE!
©B Trudeau
MERRY MORALE DAY, CHIEF!
HUH?

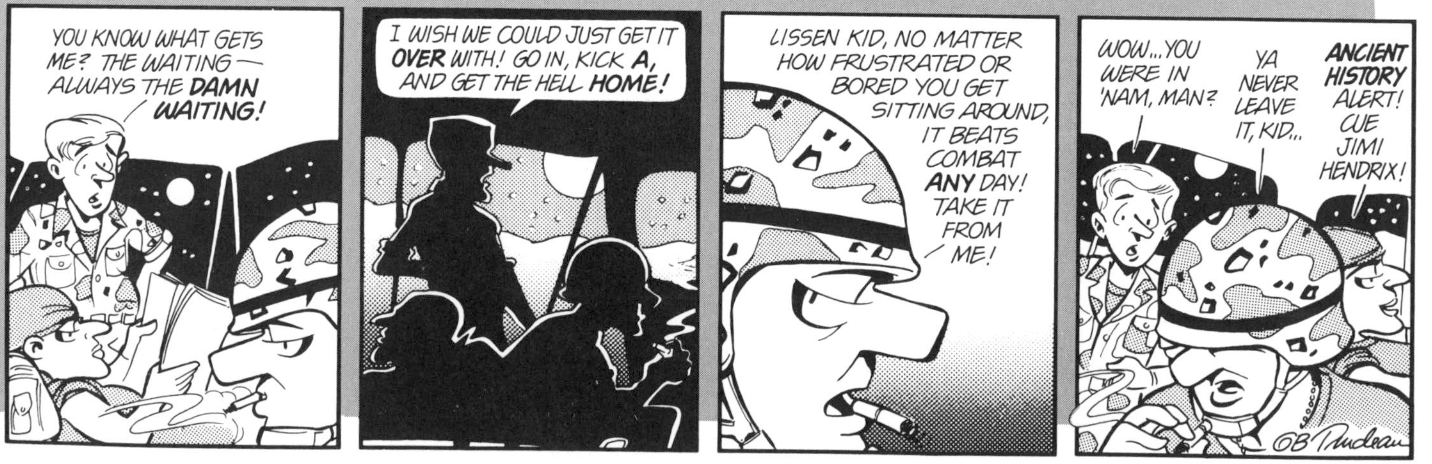
YOU KNOW WHAT GETS ME? THE WAITING — ALWAYS THE DAMN WAITING!
I WISH WE COULD JUST GET IT OVER WITH! GO IN, KICK A, AND GET THE HELL HOME!
LISSEN KID, NO MATTER HOW FRUSTRATED OR BORED YOU GET SITTING AROUND, IT BEATS COMBAT ANY DAY! TAKE IT FROM ME!
WOW... YOU WERE IN 'NAM, MAN?
YA NEVER LEAVE IT, KID...
ANCIENT HISTORY ALERT! CUE JIMI HENDRIX!
©B Trudeau

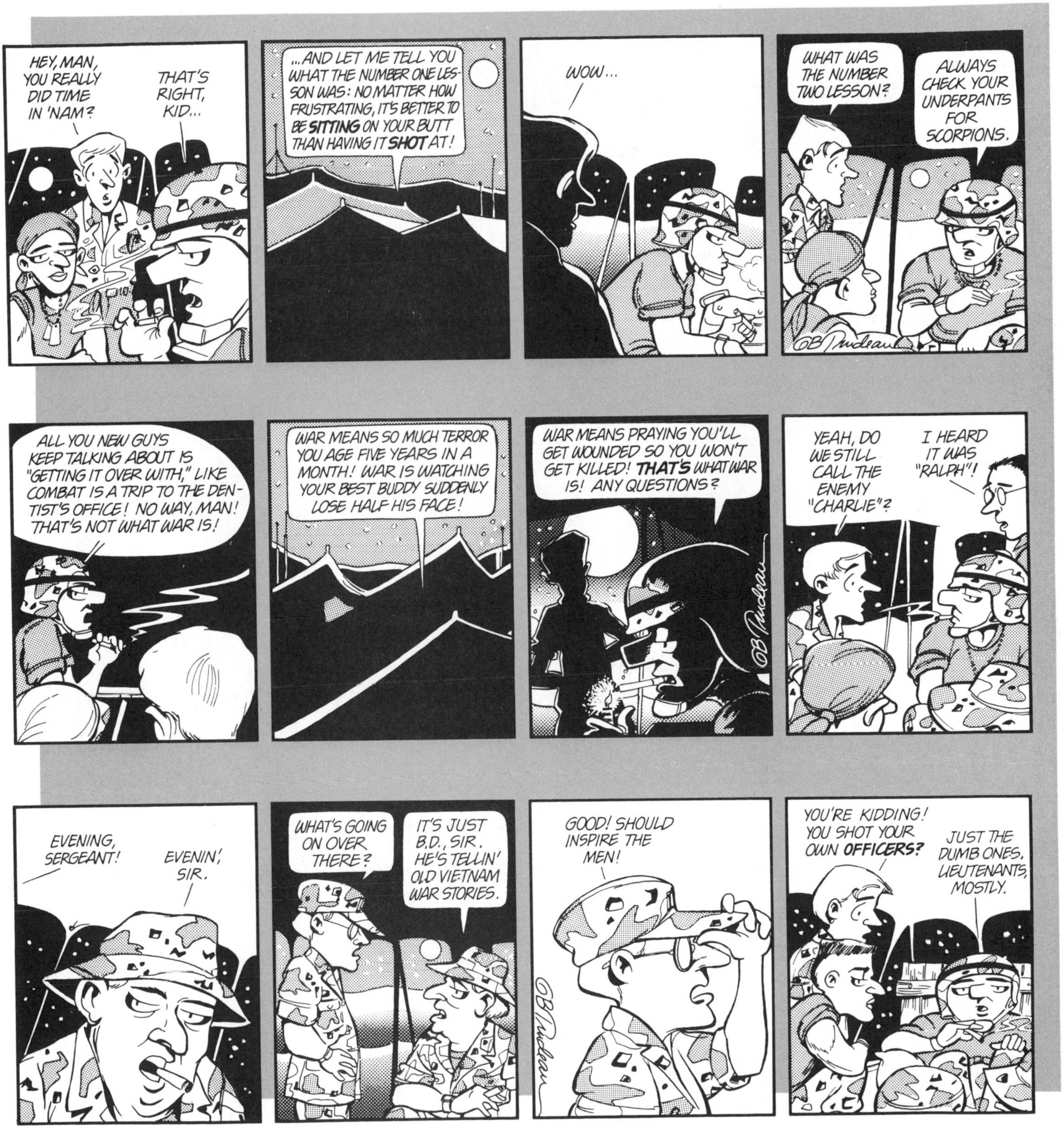
HEY, MAN, YOU REALLY DID TIME IN 'NAM?
THAT'S RIGHT, KID...
...AND LET ME TELL YOU WHAT THE NUMBER ONE LESSON WAS: NO MATTER HOW FRUSTRATING, IT'S BETTER TO BE **SITTING** ON YOUR BUTT THAN HAVING IT **SHOT** AT!
WOW...
WHAT WAS THE NUMBER TWO LESSON?
ALWAYS CHECK YOUR UNDERPANTS FOR SCORPIONS.
©B Trudeau
ALL YOU NEW GUYS KEEP TALKING ABOUT IS "GETTING IT OVER WITH," LIKE COMBAT IS A TRIP TO THE DENTIST'S OFFICE! NO WAY, MAN! THAT'S NOT WHAT WAR IS!
WAR MEANS SO MUCH TERROR YOU AGE FIVE YEARS IN A MONTH! WAR IS WATCHING YOUR BEST BUDDY SUDDENLY LOSE HALF HIS FACE!
WAR MEANS PRAYING YOU'LL GET WOUNDED SO YOU WON'T GET KILLED! **THAT'S** WHAT WAR IS! ANY QUESTIONS?
©B Trudeau
YEAH, DO WE STILL CALL THE ENEMY "CHARLIE"?
I HEARD IT WAS "RALPH"!
EVENING, SERGEANT!
EVENIN', SIR.
WHAT'S GOING ON OVER THERE?
IT'S JUST B.D., SIR. HE'S TELLIN' OLD VIETNAM WAR STORIES.
GOOD! SHOULD INSPIRE THE MEN!
©B Trudeau
YOU'RE KIDDING! YOU SHOT YOUR OWN **OFFICERS?**
JUST THE DUMB ONES. LIEUTENANTS, MOSTLY.

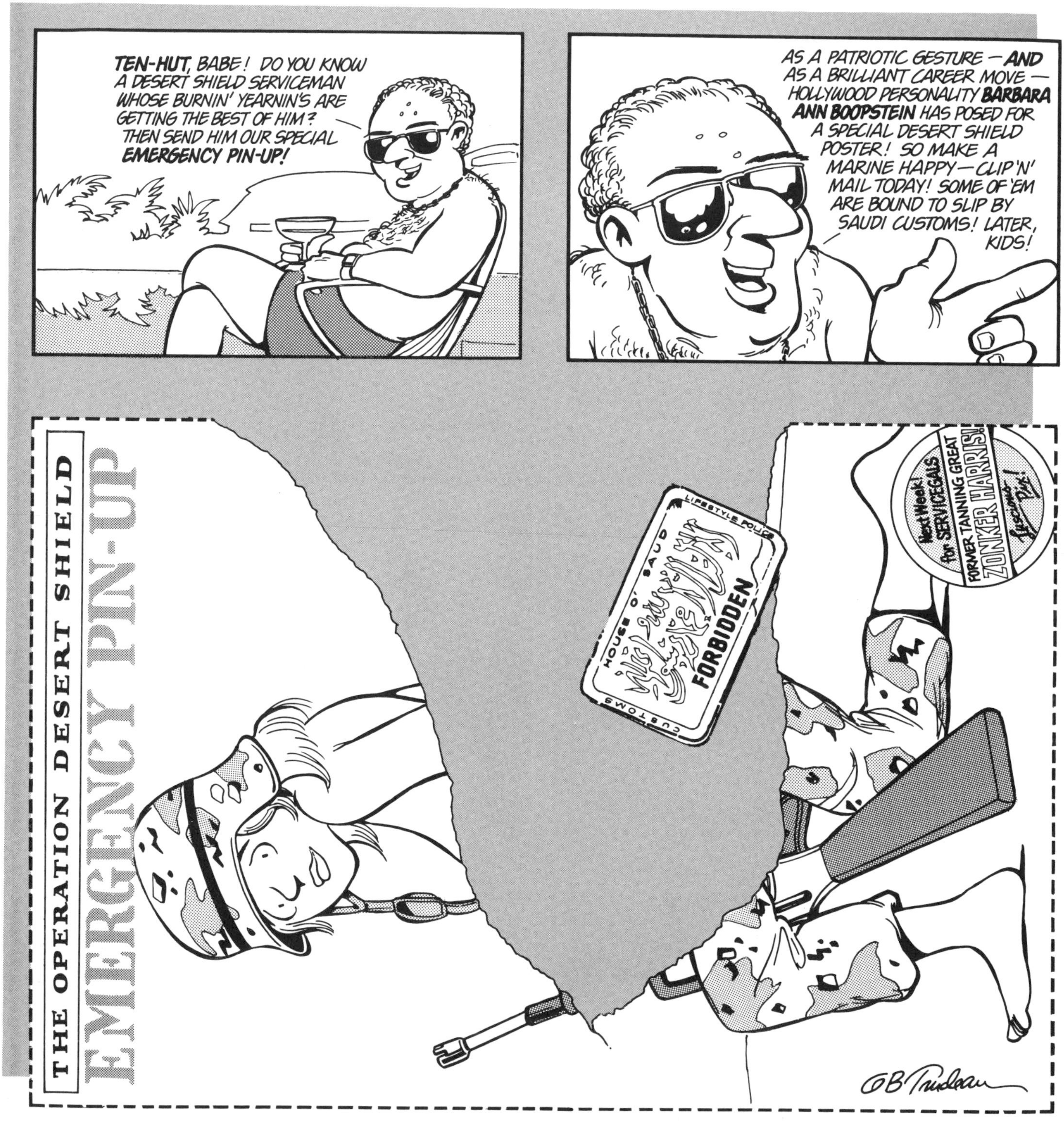
TEN-HUT, BABE! DO YOU KNOW A DESERT SHIELD SERVICEMAN WHOSE BURNIN' YEARNIN'S ARE GETTING THE BEST OF HIM? THEN SEND HIM OUR SPECIAL EMERGENCY PIN-UP!
AS A PATRIOTIC GESTURE — AND AS A BRILLIANT CAREER MOVE — HOLLYWOOD PERSONALITY BARBARA ANN BOOPSTEIN HAS POSED FOR A SPECIAL DESERT SHIELD POSTER! SO MAKE A MARINE HAPPY — CLIP 'N' MAIL TODAY! SOME OF 'EM ARE BOUND TO SLIP BY SAUDI CUSTOMS! LATER, KIDS!
THE OPERATION DESERT SHIELD
EMERGENCY PIN-UP
LIFESTYLE POLICE
HOUSE O' SAUD
CUSTOMS
FORBIDDEN
Next Week! For SERVICEGALS
FORMER TANNING GREAT
ZONKER HARRIS!
Luscious Pix!
GB Trudeau

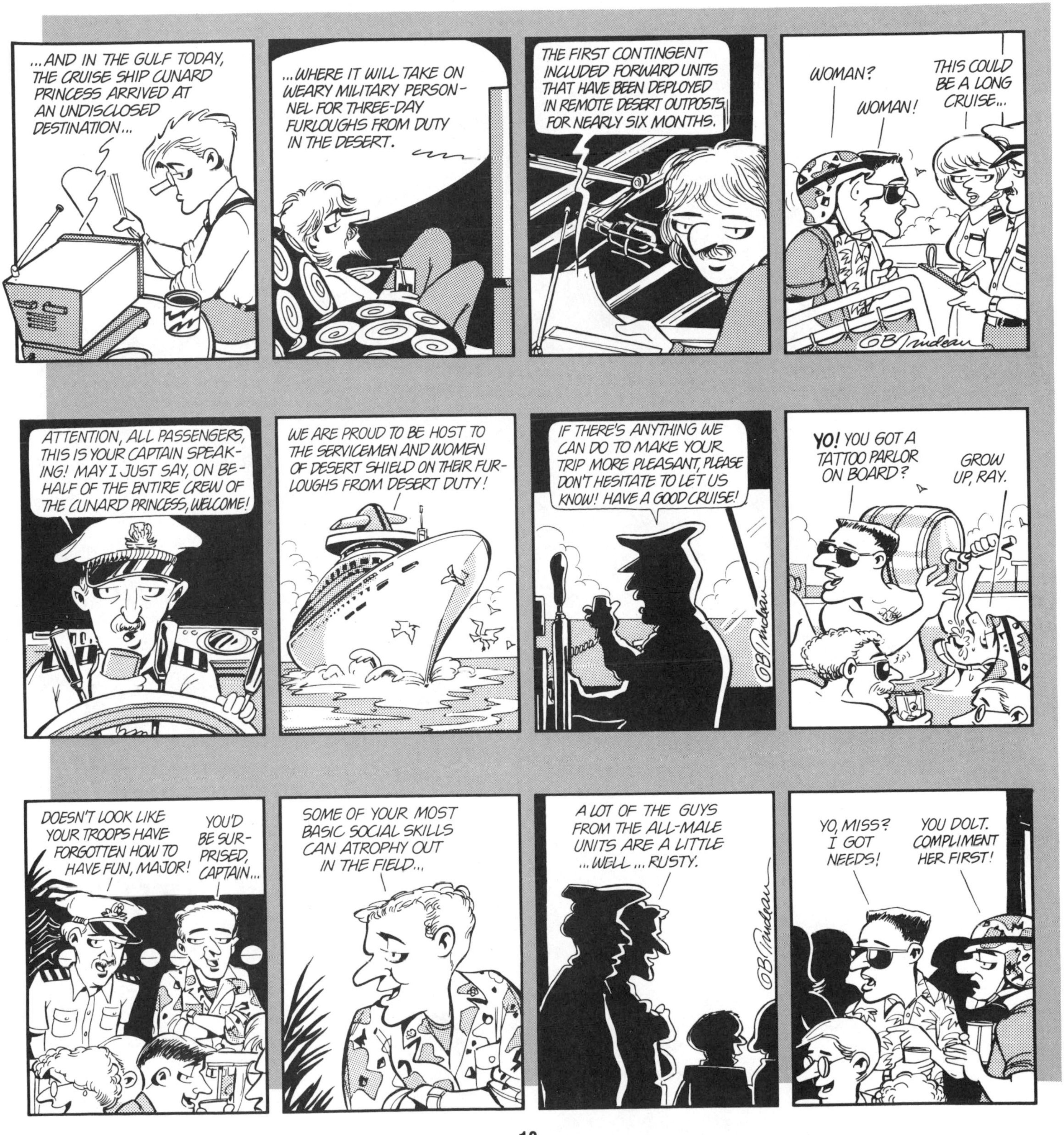
...AND IN THE GULF TODAY, THE CRUISE SHIP CUNARD PRINCESS ARRIVED AT AN UNDISCLOSED DESTINATION...
...WHERE IT WILL TAKE ON WEARY MILITARY PERSON-NEL FOR THREE-DAY FURLOUGHS FROM DUTY IN THE DESERT.
THE FIRST CONTINGENT INCLUDED FORWARD UNITS THAT HAVE BEEN DEPLOYED IN REMOTE DESERT OUTPOSTS FOR NEARLY SIX MONTHS.
WOMAN?
WOMAN!
THIS COULD BE A LONG CRUISE...
ATTENTION, ALL PASSENGERS, THIS IS YOUR CAPTAIN SPEAK-ING! MAY I JUST SAY, ON BE-HALF OF THE ENTIRE CREW OF THE CUNARD PRINCESS, WELCOME!
WE ARE PROUD TO BE HOST TO THE SERVICEMEN AND WOMEN OF DESERT SHIELD ON THEIR FUR-LOUGHS FROM DESERT DUTY!
IF THERE'S ANYTHING WE CAN DO TO MAKE YOUR TRIP MORE PLEASANT, PLEASE DON'T HESITATE TO LET US KNOW! HAVE A GOOD CRUISE!
YO! YOU GOT A TATTOO PARLOR ON BOARD?
GROW UP, RAY.
DOESN'T LOOK LIKE YOUR TROOPS HAVE FORGOTTEN HOW TO HAVE FUN, MAJOR!
YOU'D BE SUR-PRISED, CAPTAIN...
SOME OF YOUR MOST BASIC SOCIAL SKILLS CAN ATROPHY OUT IN THE FIELD...
A LOT OF THE GUYS FROM THE ALL-MALE UNITS ARE A LITTLE ...WELL ... RUSTY.
YO, MISS? I GOT NEEDS!
YOU DOLT. COMPLIMENT HER FIRST!

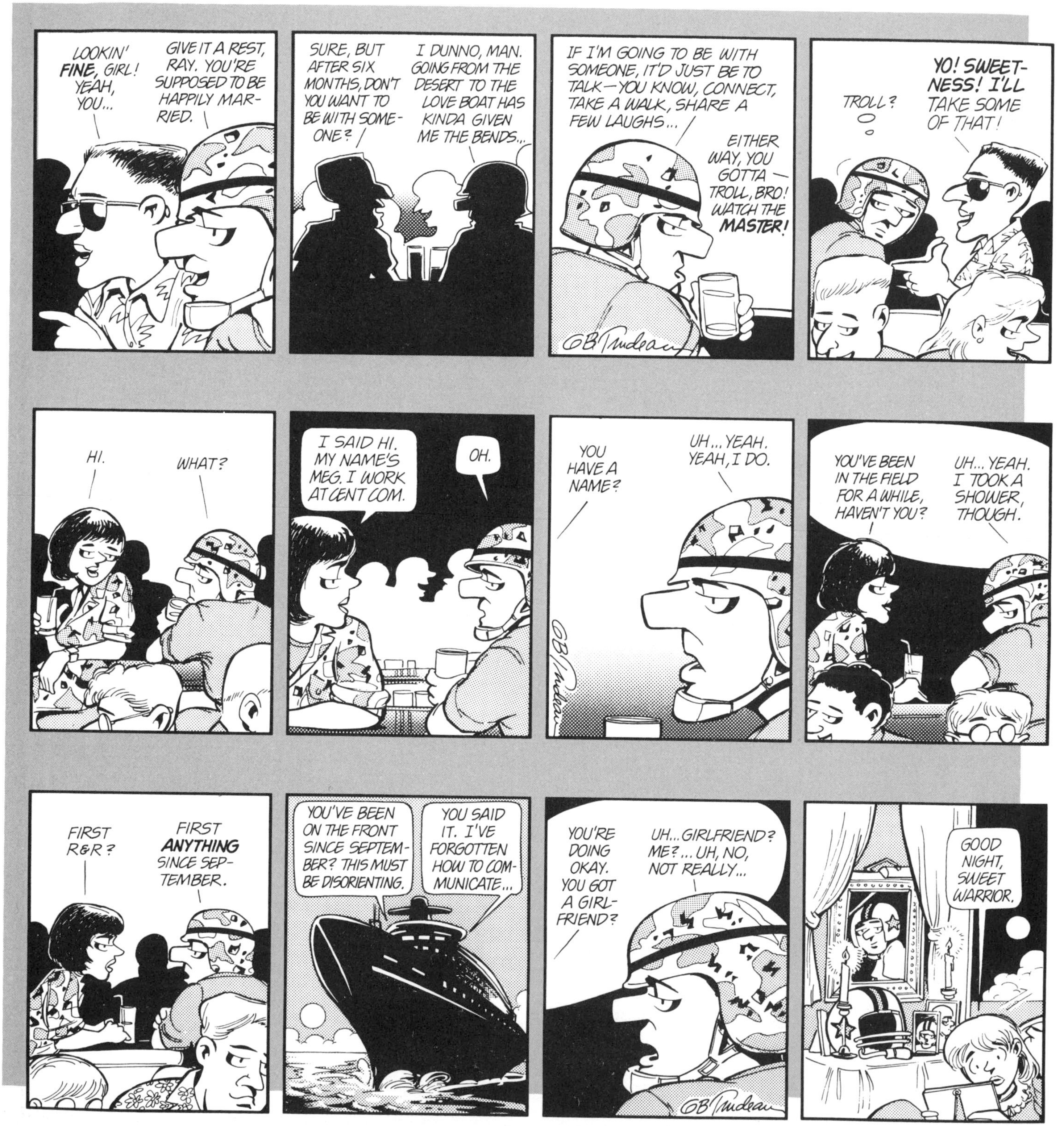
LOOKIN' **FINE,** GIRL! YEAH, YOU...
GIVE IT A REST, RAY. YOU'RE SUPPOSED TO BE HAPPILY MARRIED.
SURE, BUT AFTER SIX MONTHS, DON'T YOU WANT TO BE WITH SOMEONE?
I DUNNO, MAN. GOING FROM THE DESERT TO THE LOVE BOAT HAS KINDA GIVEN ME THE BENDS...
IF I'M GOING TO BE WITH SOMEONE, IT'D JUST BE TO TALK—YOU KNOW, CONNECT, TAKE A WALK, SHARE A FEW LAUGHS...
EITHER WAY, YOU GOTTA TROLL, BRO! WATCH THE **MASTER!**
TROLL?
YO! SWEETNESS! I'LL TAKE SOME OF THAT!
HI.
WHAT?
I SAID HI. MY NAME'S MEG. I WORK AT CENT COM.
OH.
YOU HAVE A NAME?
UH... YEAH. YEAH, I DO.
YOU'VE BEEN IN THE FIELD FOR A WHILE, HAVEN'T YOU?
UH... YEAH. I TOOK A SHOWER, THOUGH.
FIRST R&R?
FIRST **ANYTHING** SINCE SEPTEMBER.
YOU'VE BEEN ON THE FRONT SINCE SEPTEMBER? THIS MUST BE DISORIENTING.
YOU SAID IT. I'VE FORGOTTEN HOW TO COMMUNICATE...
YOU'RE DOING OKAY. YOU GOT A GIRLFRIEND?
UH... GIRLFRIEND? ME? ... UH, NO, NOT REALLY...
GOOD NIGHT, SWEET WARRIOR.

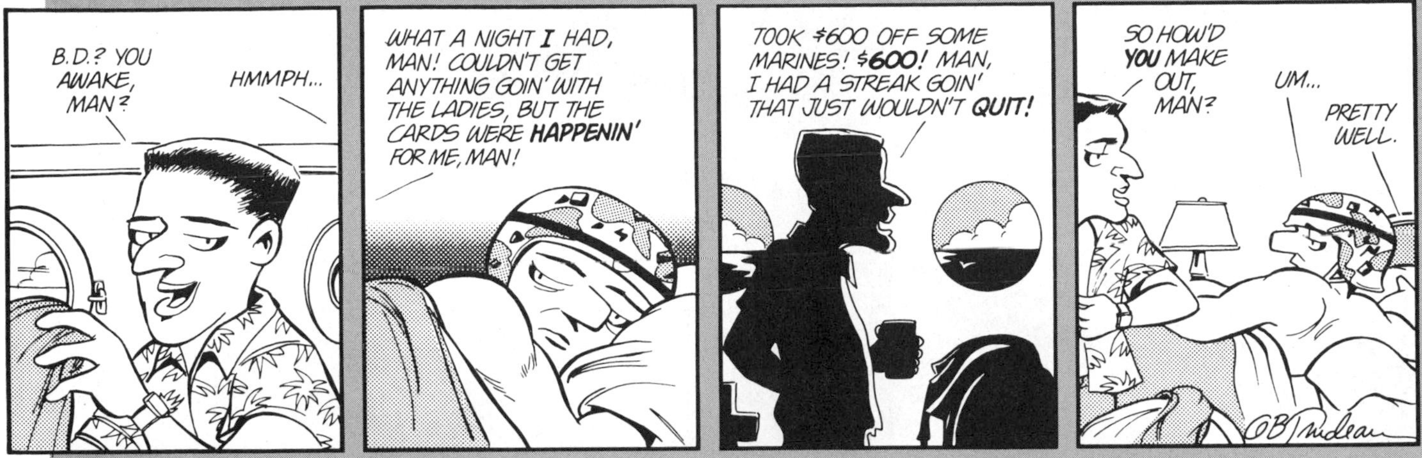
B.D.? YOU AWAKE, MAN?
HMMPH...
WHAT A NIGHT I HAD, MAN! COULDN'T GET ANYTHING GOIN' WITH THE LADIES, BUT THE CARDS WERE HAPPENIN' FOR ME, MAN!
TOOK $600 OFF SOME MARINES! $600! MAN, I HAD A STREAK GOIN' THAT JUST WOULDN'T QUIT!
SO HOW'D YOU MAKE OUT, MAN?
UM...
PRETTY WELL.
GBTrudeau

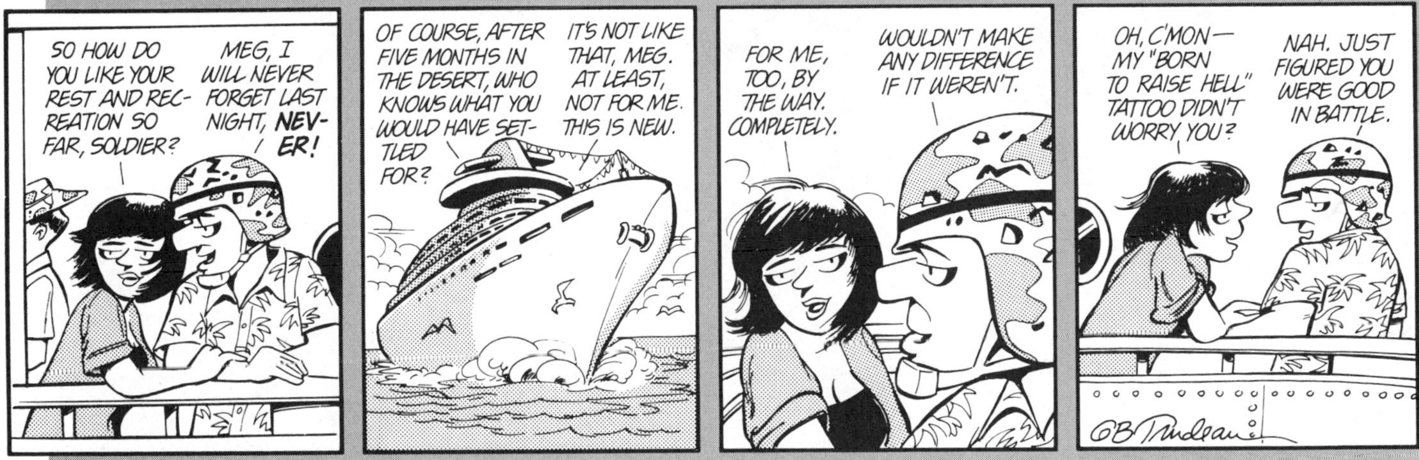
SO HOW DO YOU LIKE YOUR REST AND RECREATION SO FAR, SOLDIER?
MEG, I WILL NEVER FORGET LAST NIGHT, NEVER!
OF COURSE, AFTER FIVE MONTHS IN THE DESERT, WHO KNOWS WHAT YOU WOULD HAVE SETTLED FOR?
IT'S NOT LIKE THAT, MEG. AT LEAST, NOT FOR ME. THIS IS NEW.
FOR ME, TOO, BY THE WAY. COMPLETELY.
WOULDN'T MAKE ANY DIFFERENCE IF IT WEREN'T.
OH, C'MON— MY "BORN TO RAISE HELL" TATTOO DIDN'T WORRY YOU?
NAH. JUST FIGURED YOU WERE GOOD IN BATTLE.
GBTrudeau

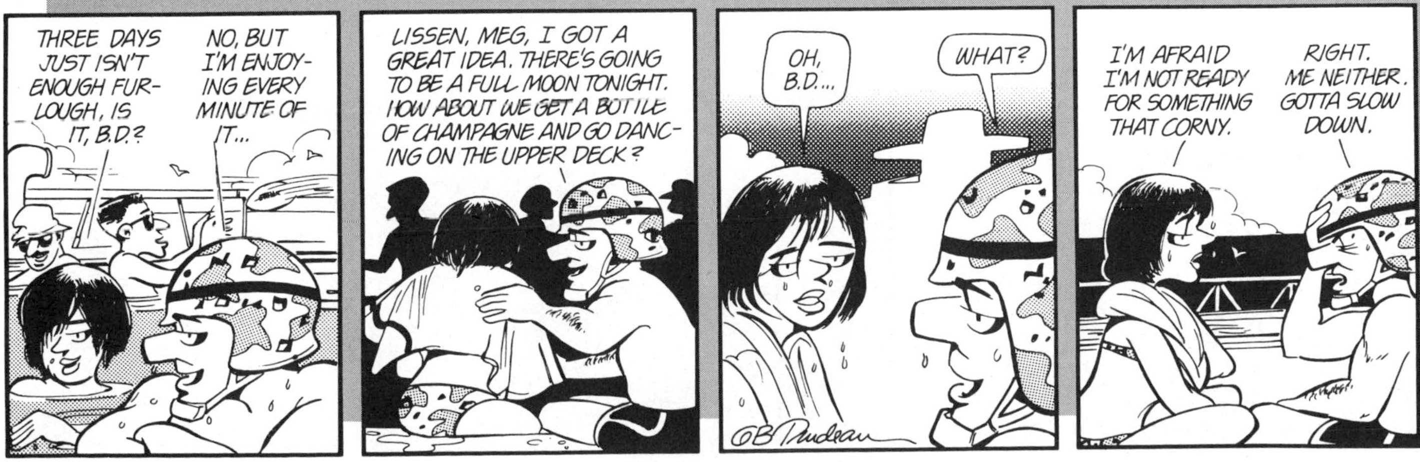
THREE DAYS JUST ISN'T ENOUGH FURLOUGH, IS IT, B.D.?
NO, BUT I'M ENJOYING EVERY MINUTE OF IT...
LISSEN, MEG, I GOT A GREAT IDEA. THERE'S GOING TO BE A FULL MOON TONIGHT. HOW ABOUT WE GET A BOTTLE OF CHAMPAGNE AND GO DANCING ON THE UPPER DECK?
OH, B.D....
WHAT?
GBTrudeau
I'M AFRAID I'M NOT READY FOR SOMETHING THAT CORNY.
RIGHT. ME NEITHER. GOTTA SLOW DOWN.

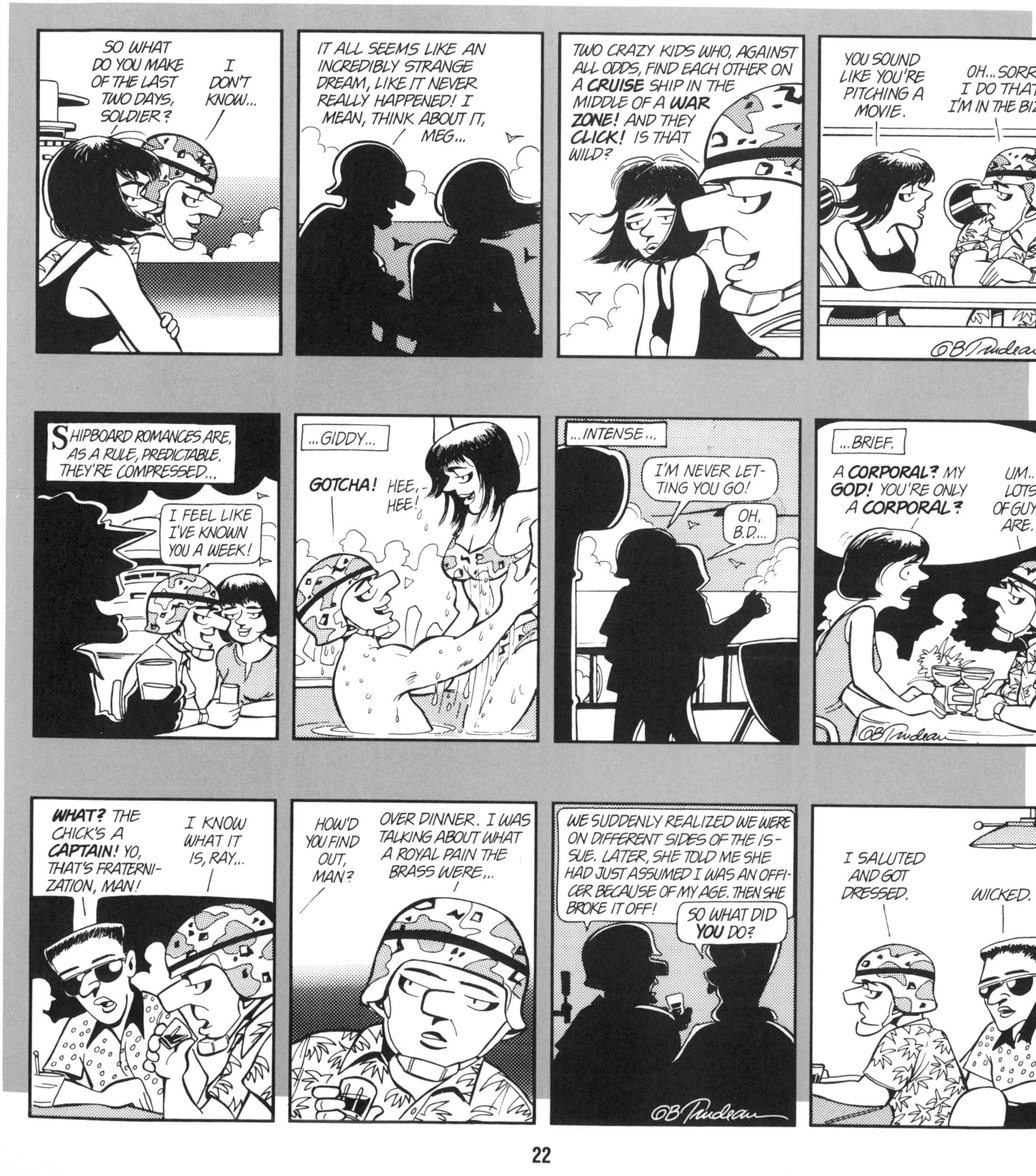
SO WHAT DO YOU MAKE OF THE LAST TWO DAYS, SOLDIER?
I DON'T KNOW...
IT ALL SEEMS LIKE AN INCREDIBLY STRANGE DREAM, LIKE IT NEVER REALLY HAPPENED! I MEAN, THINK ABOUT IT, MEG...
TWO CRAZY KIDS WHO, AGAINST ALL ODDS, FIND EACH OTHER ON A CRUISE SHIP IN THE MIDDLE OF A WAR ZONE! AND THEY CLICK! IS THAT WILD?
YOU SOUND LIKE YOU'RE PITCHING A MOVIE.
OH... SORRY. I DO THAT. I'M IN THE BIZ.
©B Trudeau
SHIPBOARD ROMANCES ARE, AS A RULE, PREDICTABLE. THEY'RE COMPRESSED...
I FEEL LIKE I'VE KNOWN YOU A WEEK!
...GIDDY...
GOTCHA!
HEE, HEE!
...INTENSE...
I'M NEVER LETTING YOU GO!
OH, B.D...
...BRIEF.
A CORPORAL? MY GOD! YOU'RE ONLY A CORPORAL?
UM... LOTS OF GUYS ARE.
©B Trudeau
WHAT? THE CHICK'S A CAPTAIN! YO, THAT'S FRATERNIZATION, MAN!
I KNOW WHAT IT IS, RAY...
HOW'D YOU FIND OUT, MAN?
OVER DINNER. I WAS TALKING ABOUT WHAT A ROYAL PAIN THE BRASS WERE...
WE SUDDENLY REALIZED WE WERE ON DIFFERENT SIDES OF THE ISSUE. LATER, SHE TOLD ME SHE HAD JUST ASSUMED I WAS AN OFFICER BECAUSE OF MY AGE. THEN SHE BROKE IT OFF!
SO WHAT DID YOU DO?
I SALUTED AND GOT DRESSED.
WICKED.
©B Trudeau

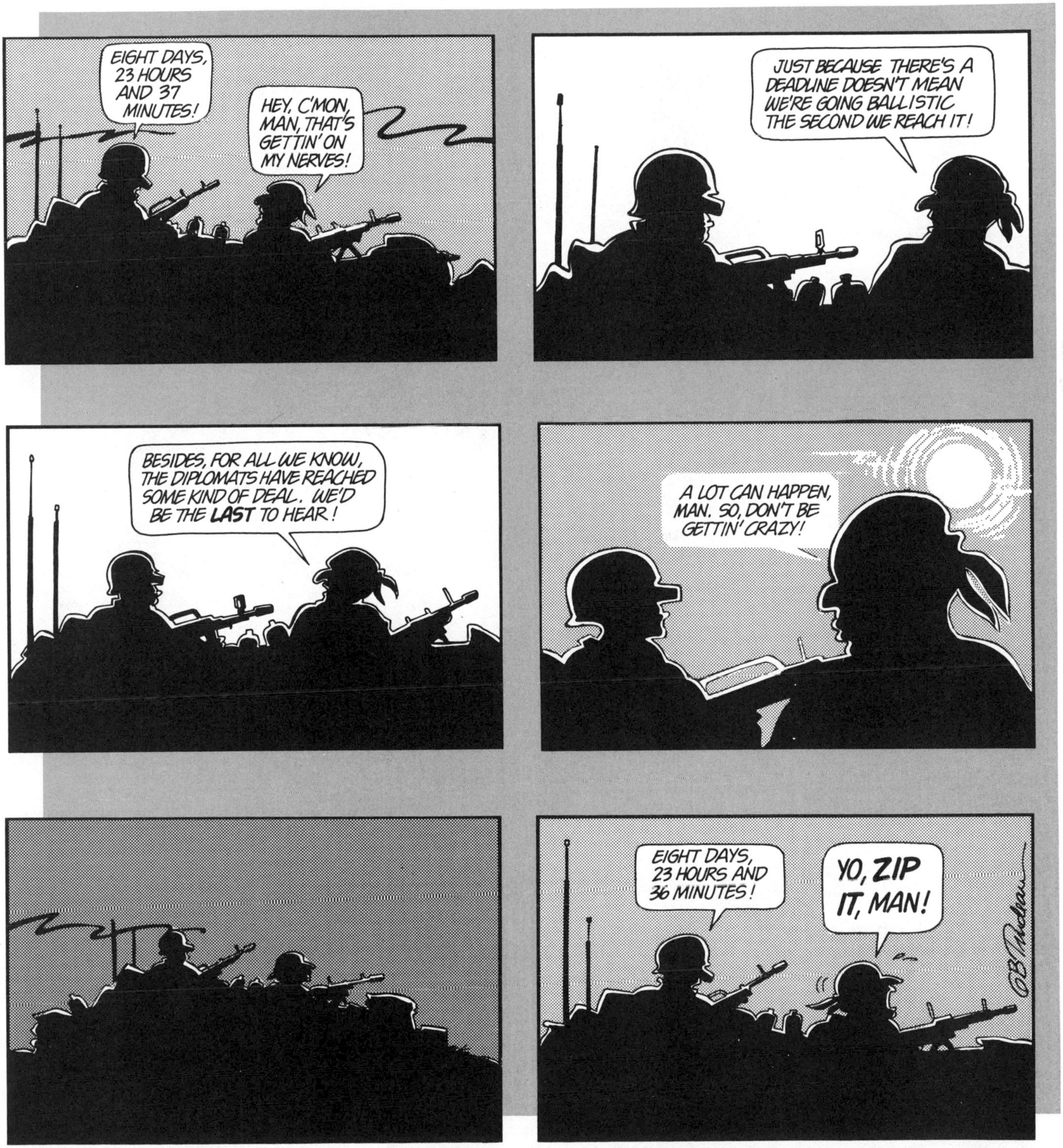
EIGHT DAYS, 23 HOURS AND 37 MINUTES!
HEY, C'MON, MAN, THAT'S GETTIN' ON MY NERVES!
JUST BECAUSE THERE'S A DEADLINE DOESN'T MEAN WE'RE GOING BALLISTIC THE SECOND WE REACH IT!
BESIDES, FOR ALL WE KNOW, THE DIPLOMATS HAVE REACHED SOME KIND OF DEAL. WE'D BE THE **LAST** TO HEAR!
A LOT CAN HAPPEN, MAN. SO, DON'T BE GETTIN' CRAZY!
EIGHT DAYS, 23 HOURS AND 36 MINUTES!
YO, **ZIP** IT, MAN!

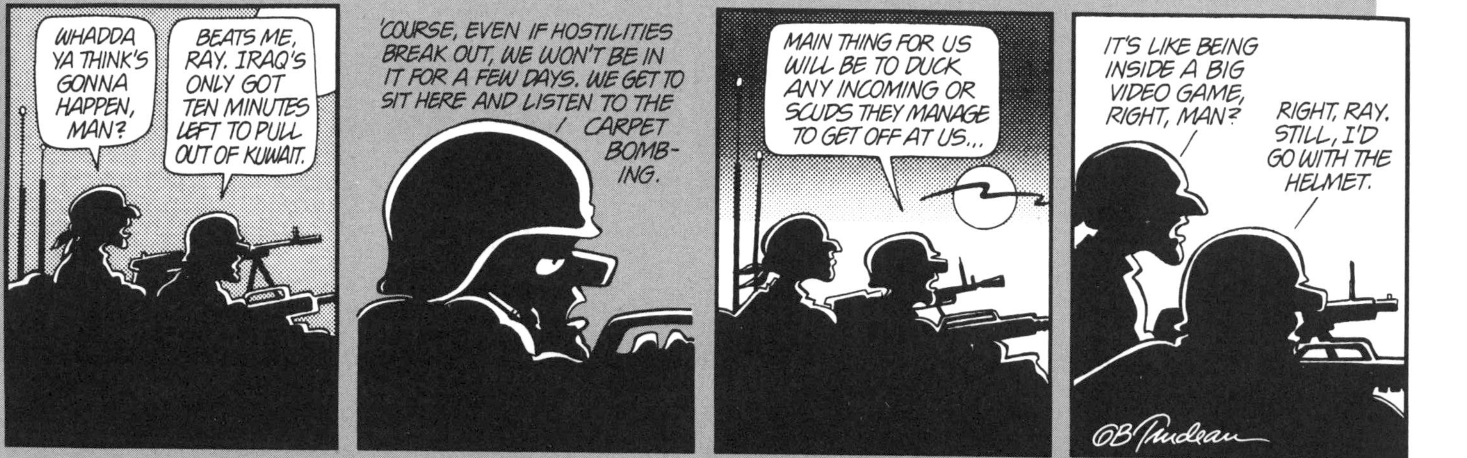
WHADDA YA THINK'S GONNA HAPPEN, MAN?
BEATS ME, RAY. IRAQ'S ONLY GOT TEN MINUTES LEFT TO PULL OUT OF KUWAIT.
'COURSE, EVEN IF HOSTILITIES BREAK OUT, WE WON'T BE IN IT FOR A FEW DAYS. WE GET TO SIT HERE AND LISTEN TO THE CARPET BOMB-ING.
MAIN THING FOR US WILL BE TO DUCK ANY INCOMING OR SCUDS THEY MANAGE TO GET OFF AT US...
IT'S LIKE BEING INSIDE A BIG VIDEO GAME, RIGHT, MAN?
RIGHT, RAY. STILL, I'D GO WITH THE HELMET.
©B Trudeau

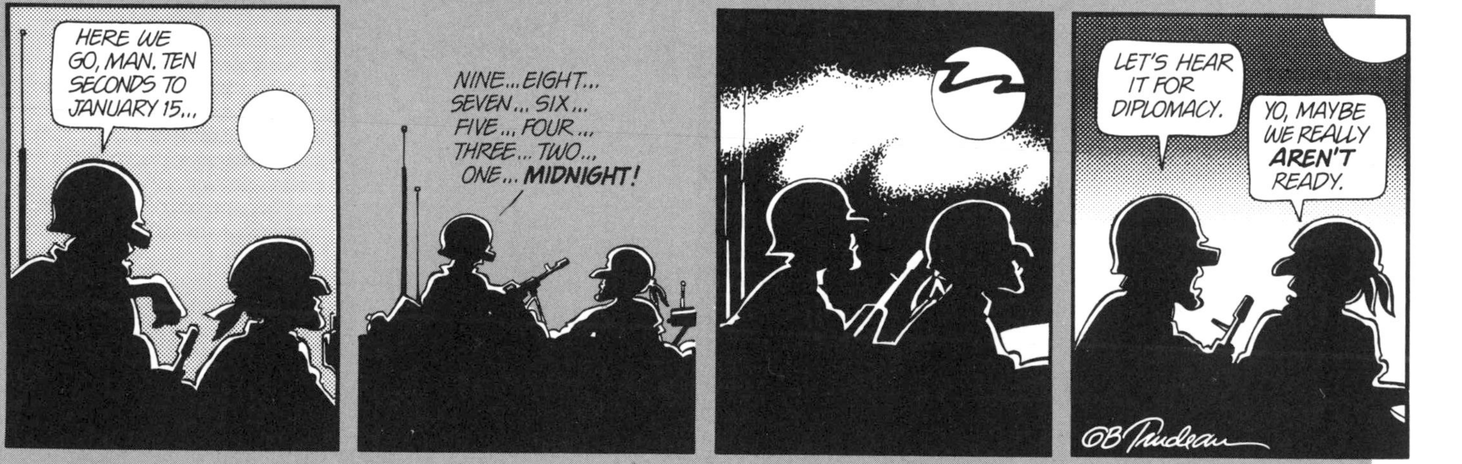
HERE WE GO, MAN. TEN SECONDS TO JANUARY 15...
NINE... EIGHT... SEVEN... SIX... FIVE... FOUR... THREE... TWO... ONE... **MIDNIGHT!**
LET'S HEAR IT FOR DIPLOMACY.
YO, MAYBE WE REALLY **AREN'T** READY.
©B Trudeau

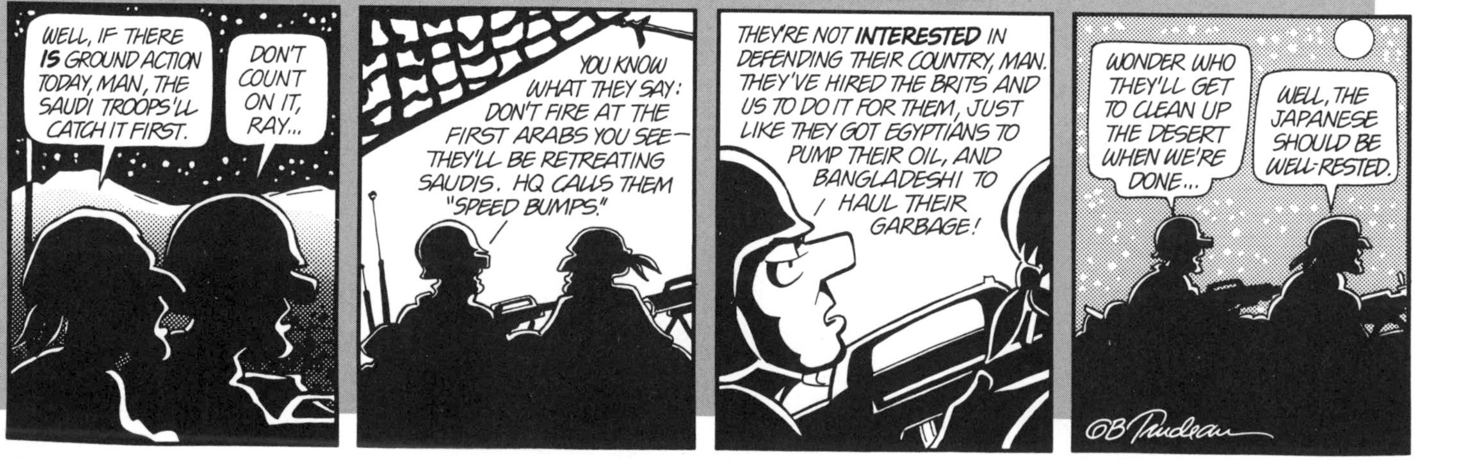
WELL, IF THERE **IS** GROUND ACTION TODAY, MAN, THE SAUDI TROOPS'LL CATCH IT FIRST.
DON'T COUNT ON IT, RAY...
YOU KNOW WHAT THEY SAY: DON'T FIRE AT THE FIRST ARABS YOU SEE— THEY'LL BE RETREATING SAUDIS. HQ CALLS THEM "SPEED BUMPS."
THEY'RE NOT **INTERESTED** IN DEFENDING THEIR COUNTRY, MAN. THEY'VE HIRED THE BRITS AND US TO DO IT FOR THEM, JUST LIKE THEY GOT EGYPTIANS TO PUMP THEIR OIL, AND BANGLADESHI TO HAUL THEIR GARBAGE!
WONDER WHO THEY'LL GET TO CLEAN UP THE DESERT WHEN WE'RE DONE...
WELL, THE JAPANESE SHOULD BE WELL-RESTED.
©B Trudeau

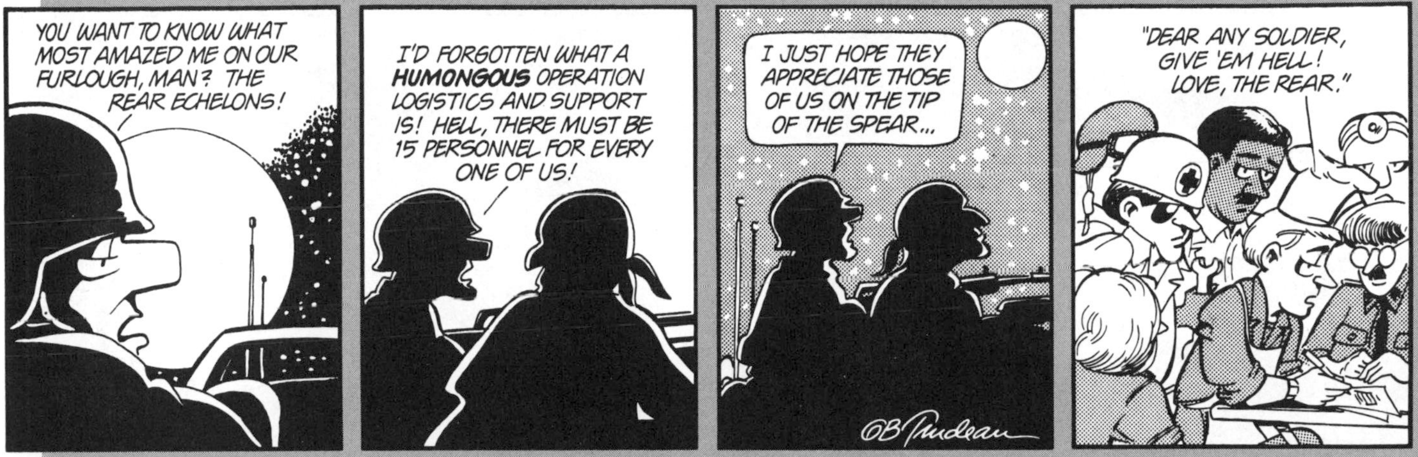
YOU WANT TO KNOW WHAT MOST AMAZED ME ON OUR FURLOUGH, MAN? THE REAR ECHELONS!
I'D FORGOTTEN WHAT A HUMONGOUS OPERATION LOGISTICS AND SUPPORT IS! HELL, THERE MUST BE 15 PERSONNEL FOR EVERY ONE OF US!
I JUST HOPE THEY APPRECIATE THOSE OF US ON THE TIP OF THE SPEAR...
"DEAR ANY SOLDIER, GIVE 'EM HELL! LOVE, THE REAR."

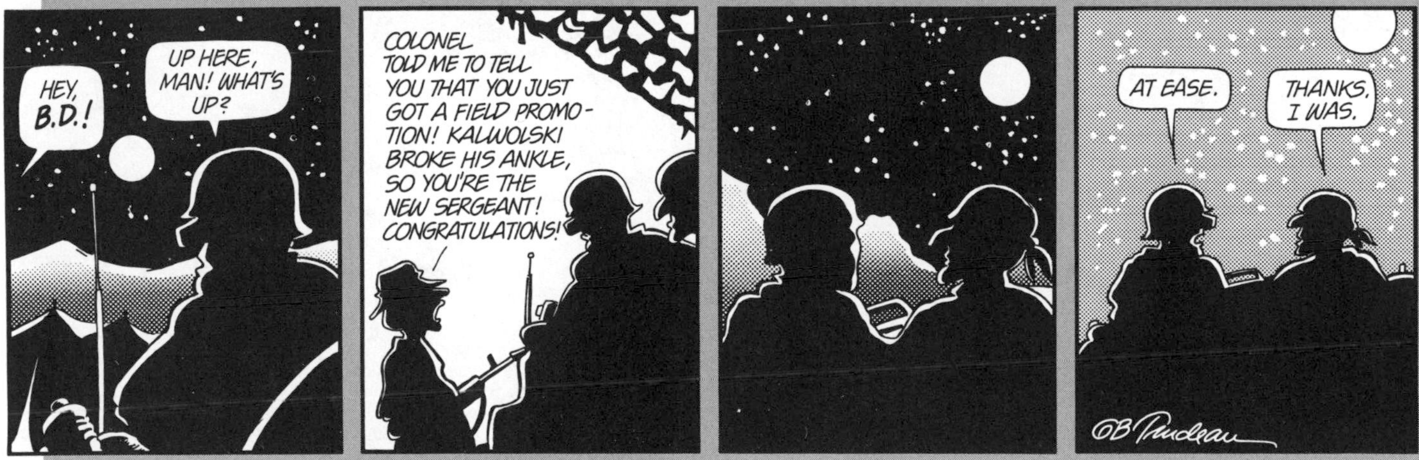
HEY, B.D.!
UP HERE, MAN! WHAT'S UP?
COLONEL TOLD ME TO TELL YOU THAT YOU JUST GOT A FIELD PROMOTION! KALWOLSKI BROKE HIS ANKLE, SO YOU'RE THE NEW SERGEANT! CONGRATULATIONS!
AT EASE.
THANKS, I WAS.

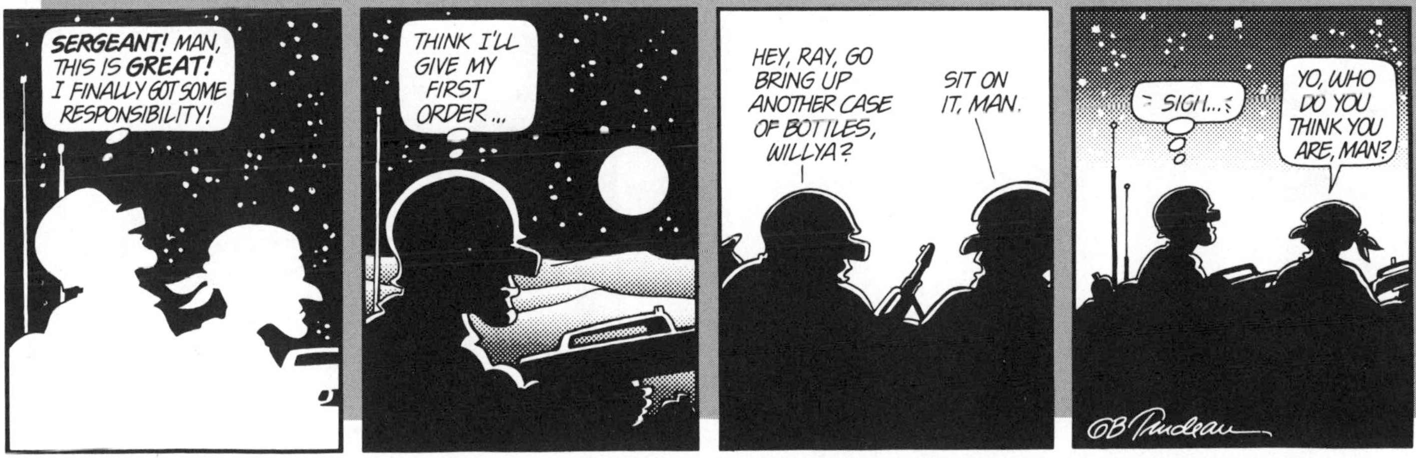
SERGEANT! MAN, THIS IS GREAT! I FINALLY GOT SOME RESPONSIBILITY!
THINK I'LL GIVE MY FIRST ORDER...
HEY, RAY, GO BRING UP ANOTHER CASE OF BOTTLES, WILLYA?
SIT ON IT, MAN.
SIGH...
YO, WHO DO YOU THINK YOU ARE, MAN?

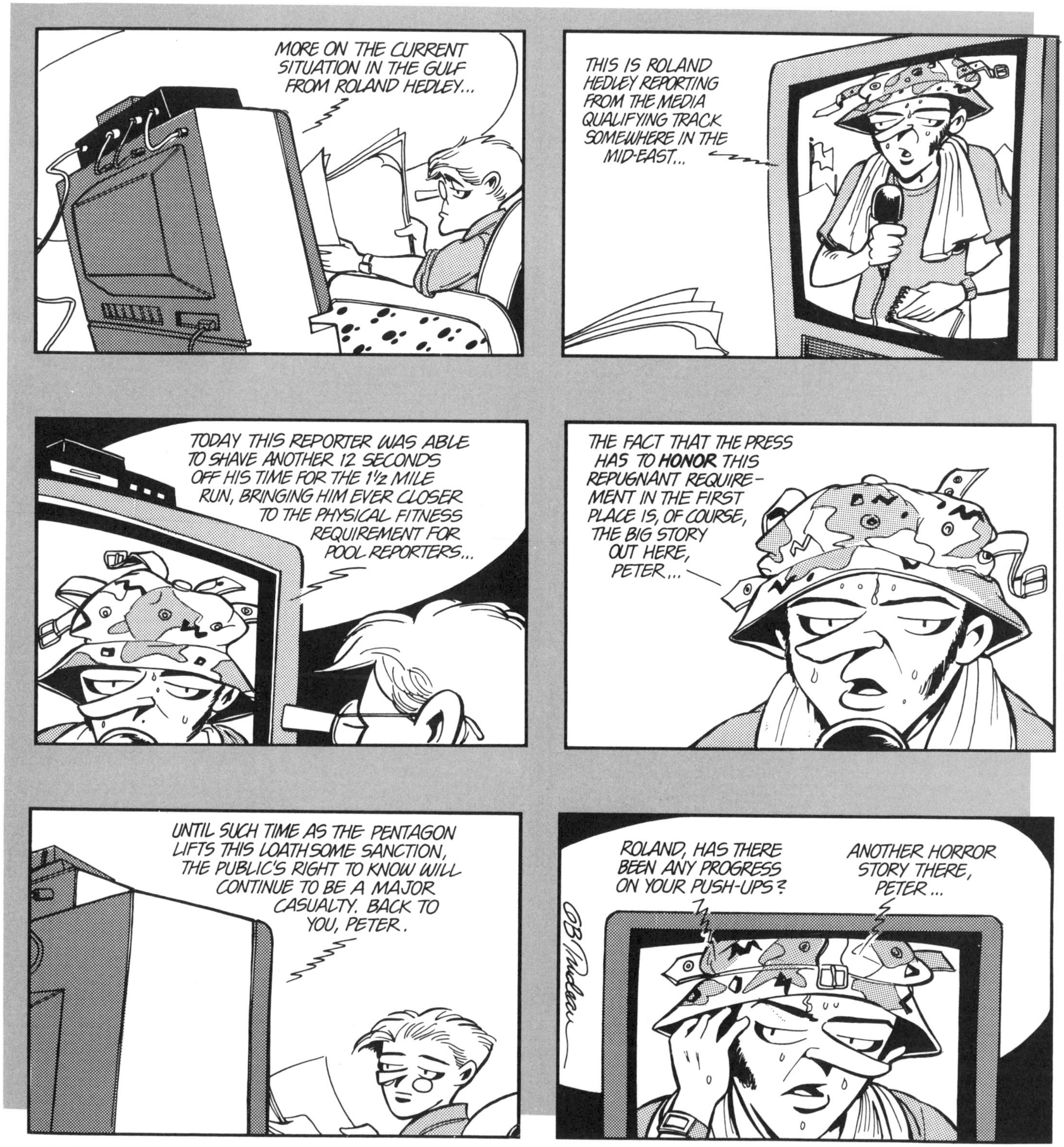

MORE ON THE CURRENT SITUATION IN THE GULF FROM ROLAND HEDLEY...
THIS IS ROLAND HEDLEY REPORTING FROM THE MEDIA QUALIFYING TRACK SOMEWHERE IN THE MID-EAST...
TODAY THIS REPORTER WAS ABLE TO SHAVE ANOTHER 12 SECONDS OFF HIS TIME FOR THE 1½ MILE RUN, BRINGING HIM EVER CLOSER TO THE PHYSICAL FITNESS REQUIREMENT FOR POOL REPORTERS...
THE FACT THAT THE PRESS HAS TO **HONOR** THIS REPUGNANT REQUIREMENT IN THE FIRST PLACE IS, OF COURSE, THE BIG STORY OUT HERE, PETER...
UNTIL SUCH TIME AS THE PENTAGON LIFTS THIS LOATHSOME SANCTION, THE PUBLIC'S RIGHT TO KNOW WILL CONTINUE TO BE A MAJOR CASUALTY. BACK TO YOU, PETER.
ROLAND, HAS THERE BEEN ANY PROGRESS ON YOUR PUSH-UPS?
ANOTHER HORROR STORY THERE, PETER...
GB Trudeau

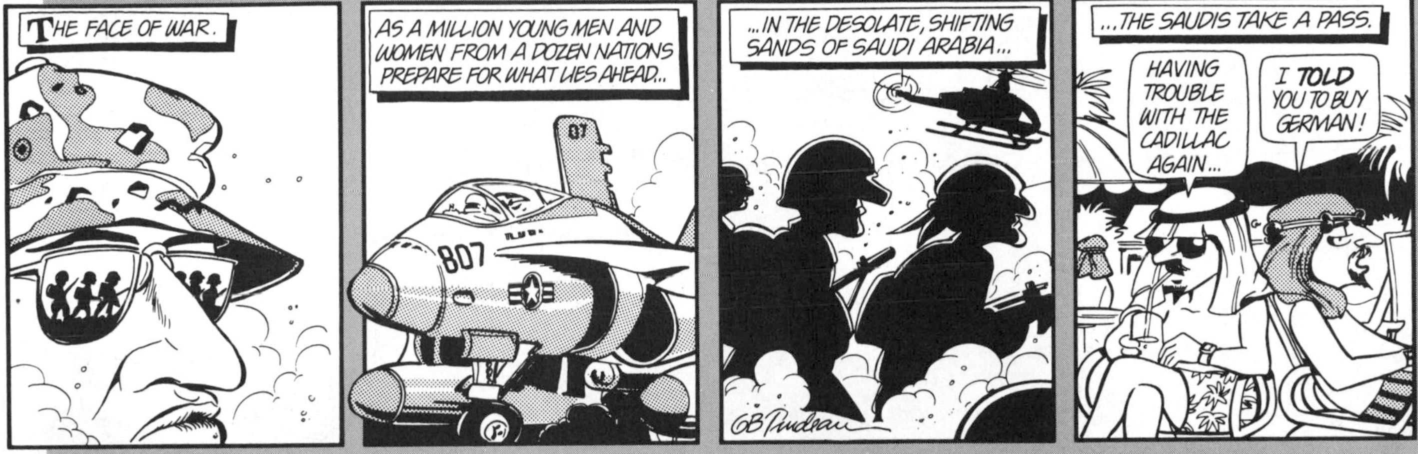
THE FACE OF WAR.
AS A MILLION YOUNG MEN AND WOMEN FROM A DOZEN NATIONS PREPARE FOR WHAT LIES AHEAD...
807
...IN THE DESOLATE, SHIFTING SANDS OF SAUDI ARABIA...
GB Trudeau
...THE SAUDIS TAKE A PASS.
HAVING TROUBLE WITH THE CADILLAC AGAIN...
I TOLD YOU TO BUY GERMAN!

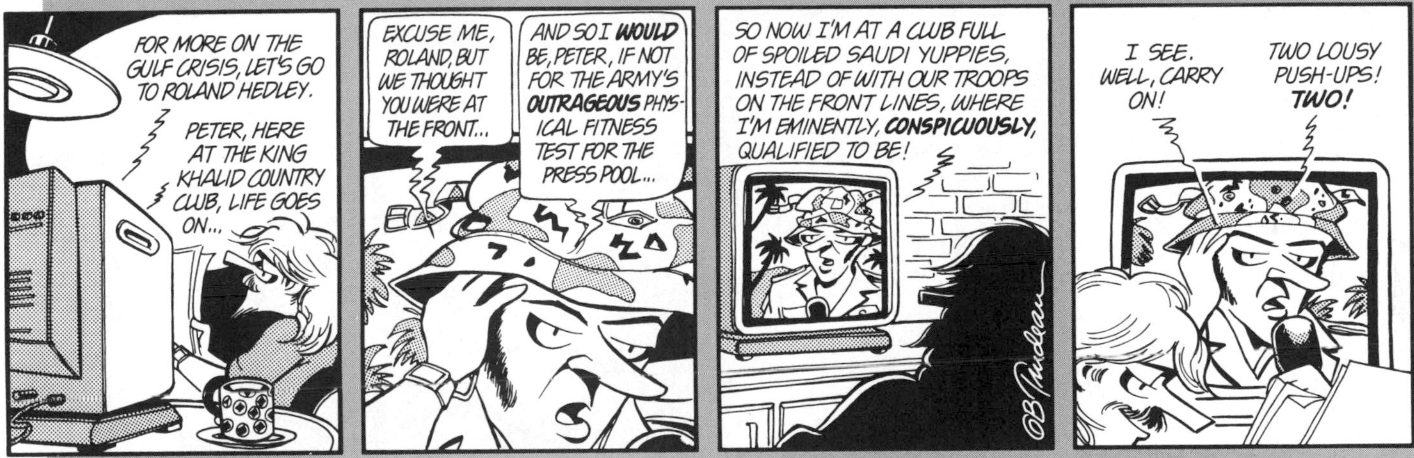
FOR MORE ON THE GULF CRISIS, LET'S GO TO ROLAND HEDLEY.
PETER, HERE AT THE KING KHALID COUNTRY CLUB, LIFE GOES ON...
EXCUSE ME, ROLAND, BUT WE THOUGHT YOU WERE AT THE FRONT...
AND SO I WOULD BE, PETER, IF NOT FOR THE ARMY'S OUTRAGEOUS PHYSICAL FITNESS TEST FOR THE PRESS POOL...
SO NOW I'M AT A CLUB FULL OF SPOILED SAUDI YUPPIES, INSTEAD OF WITH OUR TROOPS ON THE FRONT LINES, WHERE I'M EMINENTLY, CONSPICUOUSLY, QUALIFIED TO BE!
GB Trudeau
I SEE. WELL, CARRY ON!
TWO LOUSY PUSH-UPS! TWO!

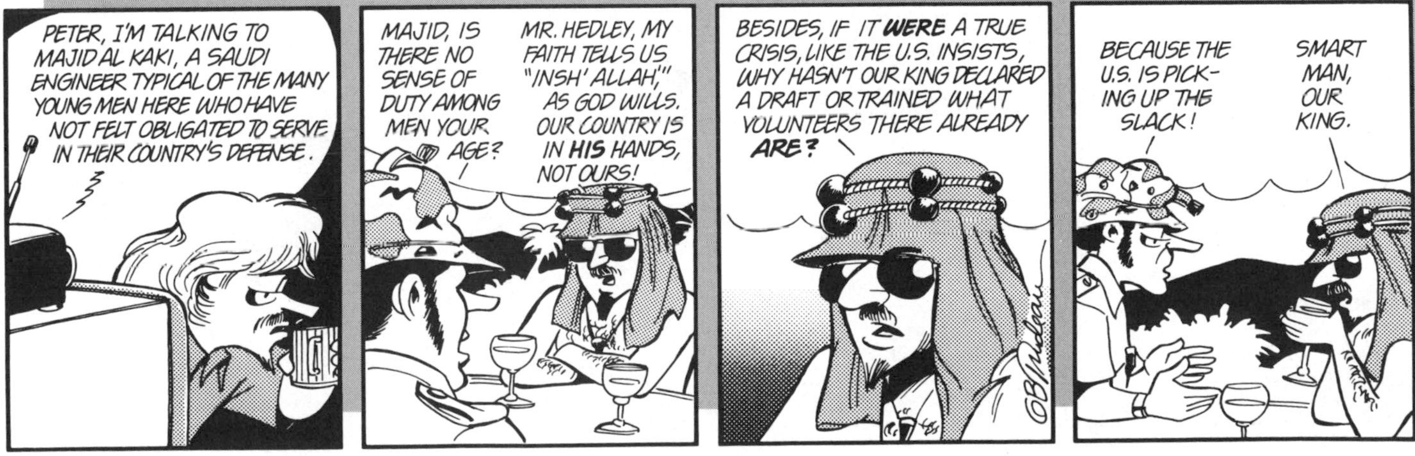
PETER, I'M TALKING TO MAJID AL KAKI, A SAUDI ENGINEER TYPICAL OF THE MANY YOUNG MEN HERE WHO HAVE NOT FELT OBLIGATED TO SERVE IN THEIR COUNTRY'S DEFENSE.
MAJID, IS THERE NO SENSE OF DUTY AMONG MEN YOUR AGE?
MR. HEDLEY, MY FAITH TELLS US "INSH' ALLAH," AS GOD WILLS. OUR COUNTRY IS IN HIS HANDS, NOT OURS!
BESIDES, IF IT WERE A TRUE CRISIS, LIKE THE U.S. INSISTS, WHY HASN'T OUR KING DECLARED A DRAFT OR TRAINED WHAT VOLUNTEERS THERE ALREADY ARE?
GB Trudeau
BECAUSE THE U.S. IS PICKING UP THE SLACK!
SMART MAN, OUR KING.

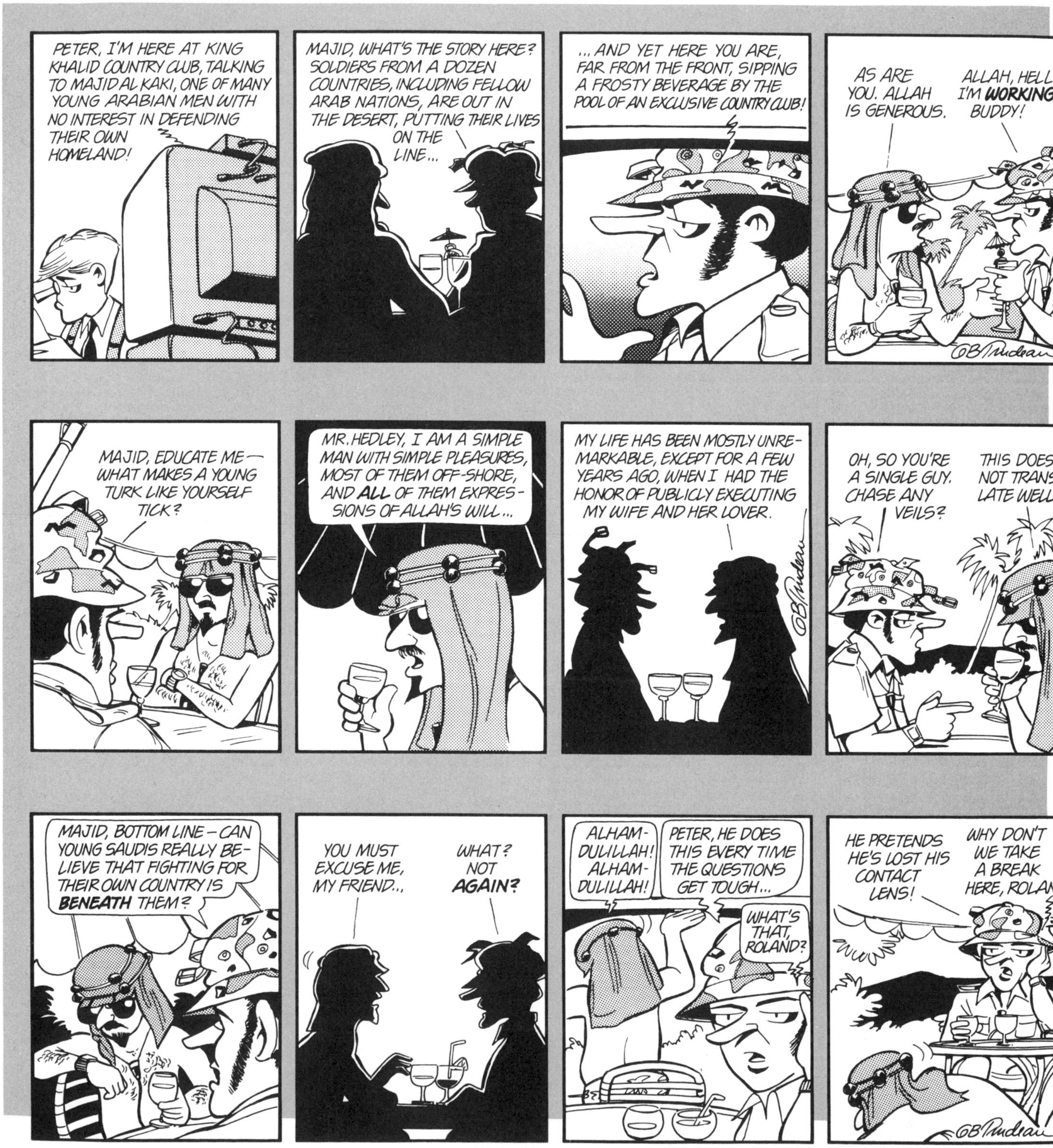
PETER, I'M HERE AT KING KHALID COUNTRY CLUB, TALKING TO MAJID AL KAKI, ONE OF MANY YOUNG ARABIAN MEN WITH NO INTEREST IN DEFENDING THEIR OWN HOMELAND!
MAJID, WHAT'S THE STORY HERE? SOLDIERS FROM A DOZEN COUNTRIES, INCLUDING FELLOW ARAB NATIONS, ARE OUT IN THE DESERT, PUTTING THEIR LIVES ON THE LINE...
... AND YET HERE YOU ARE, FAR FROM THE FRONT, SIPPING A FROSTY BEVERAGE BY THE POOL OF AN EXCLUSIVE COUNTRY CLUB!
AS ARE YOU. ALLAH IS GENEROUS.
ALLAH, HELL. I'M **WORKING,** BUDDY!
MAJID, EDUCATE ME— WHAT MAKES A YOUNG TURK LIKE YOURSELF TICK?
MR. HEDLEY, I AM A SIMPLE MAN WITH SIMPLE PLEASURES, MOST OF THEM OFF-SHORE, AND **ALL** OF THEM EXPRESSIONS OF ALLAH'S WILL...
MY LIFE HAS BEEN MOSTLY UNREMARKABLE, EXCEPT FOR A FEW YEARS AGO, WHEN I HAD THE HONOR OF PUBLICLY EXECUTING MY WIFE AND HER LOVER.
OH, SO YOU'RE A SINGLE GUY. CHASE ANY VEILS?
THIS DOES NOT TRANSLATE WELL.
MAJID, BOTTOM LINE — CAN YOUNG SAUDIS REALLY BELIEVE THAT FIGHTING FOR THEIR OWN COUNTRY IS **BENEATH** THEM?
YOU MUST EXCUSE ME, MY FRIEND...
WHAT? NOT **AGAIN?**
ALHAMDULILLAH! ALHAMDULILLAH!
PETER, HE DOES THIS EVERY TIME THE QUESTIONS GET TOUGH...
WHAT'S THAT, ROLAND?
HE PRETENDS HE'S LOST HIS CONTACT LENS!
WHY DON'T WE TAKE A BREAK HERE, ROLAND?

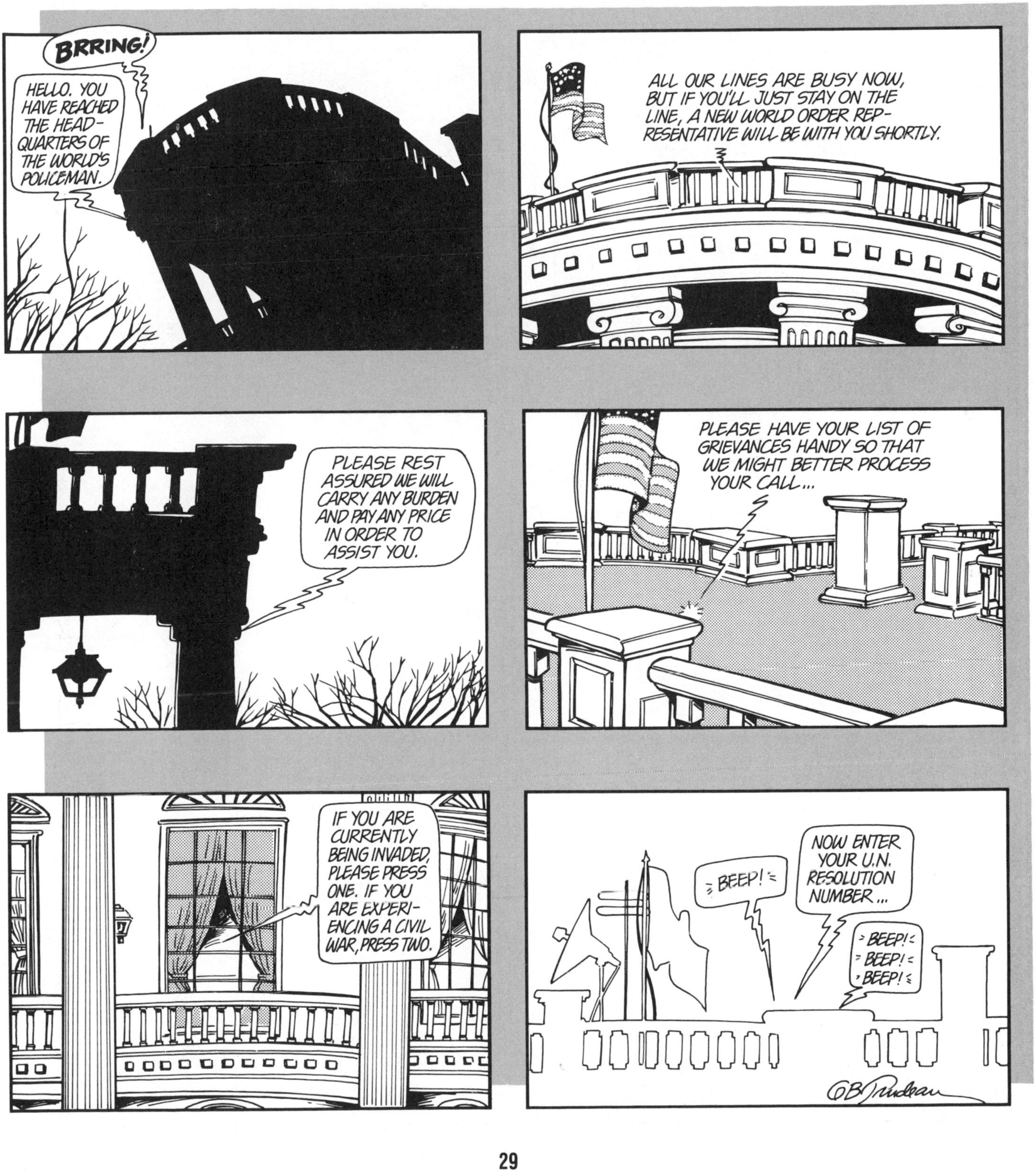
BRRING!
HELLO. YOU HAVE REACHED THE HEAD-QUARTERS OF THE WORLD'S POLICEMAN.
ALL OUR LINES ARE BUSY NOW, BUT IF YOU'LL JUST STAY ON THE LINE, A NEW WORLD ORDER REP-RESENTATIVE WILL BE WITH YOU SHORTLY.
PLEASE REST ASSURED WE WILL CARRY ANY BURDEN AND PAY ANY PRICE IN ORDER TO ASSIST YOU.
PLEASE HAVE YOUR LIST OF GRIEVANCES HANDY SO THAT WE MIGHT BETTER PROCESS YOUR CALL...
IF YOU ARE CURRENTLY BEING INVADED, PLEASE PRESS ONE. IF YOU ARE EXPERI-ENCING A CIVIL WAR, PRESS TWO.
BEEP!
NOW ENTER YOUR U.N. RESOLUTION NUMBER...
BEEP! BEEP! BEEP!

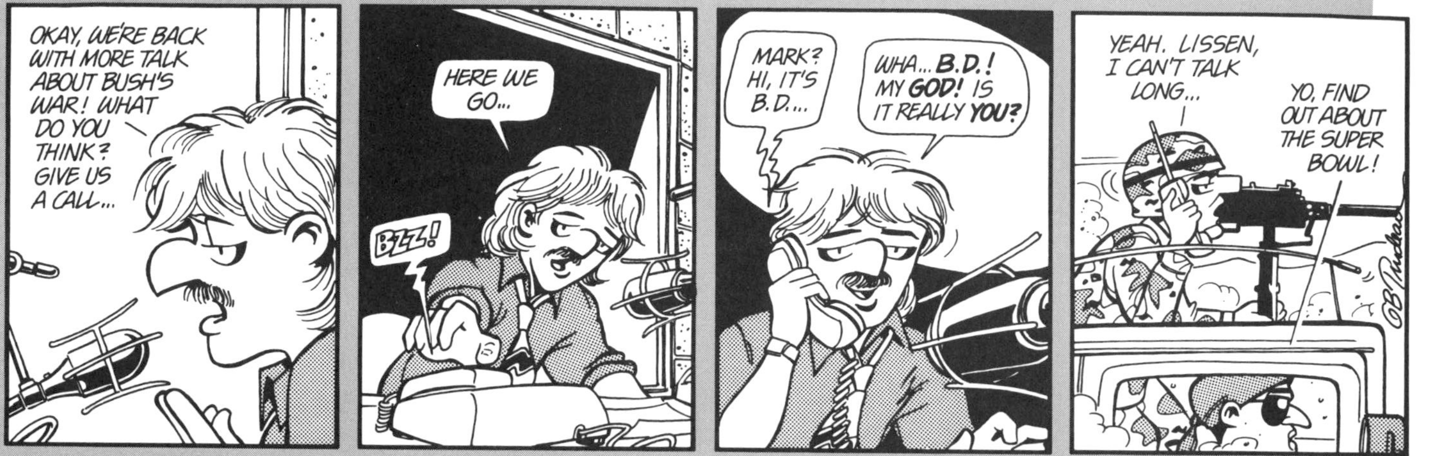
OKAY, WE'RE BACK WITH MORE TALK ABOUT BUSH'S WAR! WHAT DO YOU THINK? GIVE US A CALL...
HERE WE GO...
BZZ!
MARK? HI, IT'S B.D....
WHA... B.D.! MY GOD! IS IT REALLY YOU?
YEAH. LISSEN, I CAN'T TALK LONG...
YO, FIND OUT ABOUT THE SUPER BOWL!

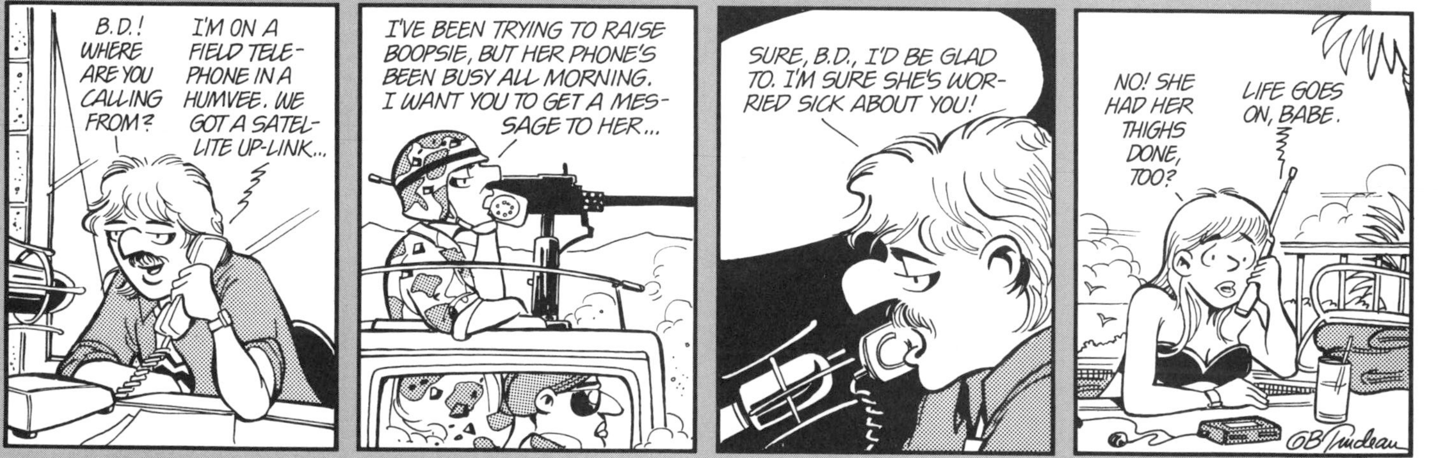
B.D.! WHERE ARE YOU CALLING FROM?
I'M ON A FIELD TELEPHONE IN A HUMVEE. WE GOT A SATELLITE UP-LINK...
I'VE BEEN TRYING TO RAISE BOOPSIE, BUT HER PHONE'S BEEN BUSY ALL MORNING. I WANT YOU TO GET A MESSAGE TO HER...
SURE, B.D., I'D BE GLAD TO. I'M SURE SHE'S WORRIED SICK ABOUT YOU!
NO! SHE HAD HER THIGHS DONE, TOO?
LIFE GOES ON, BABE.

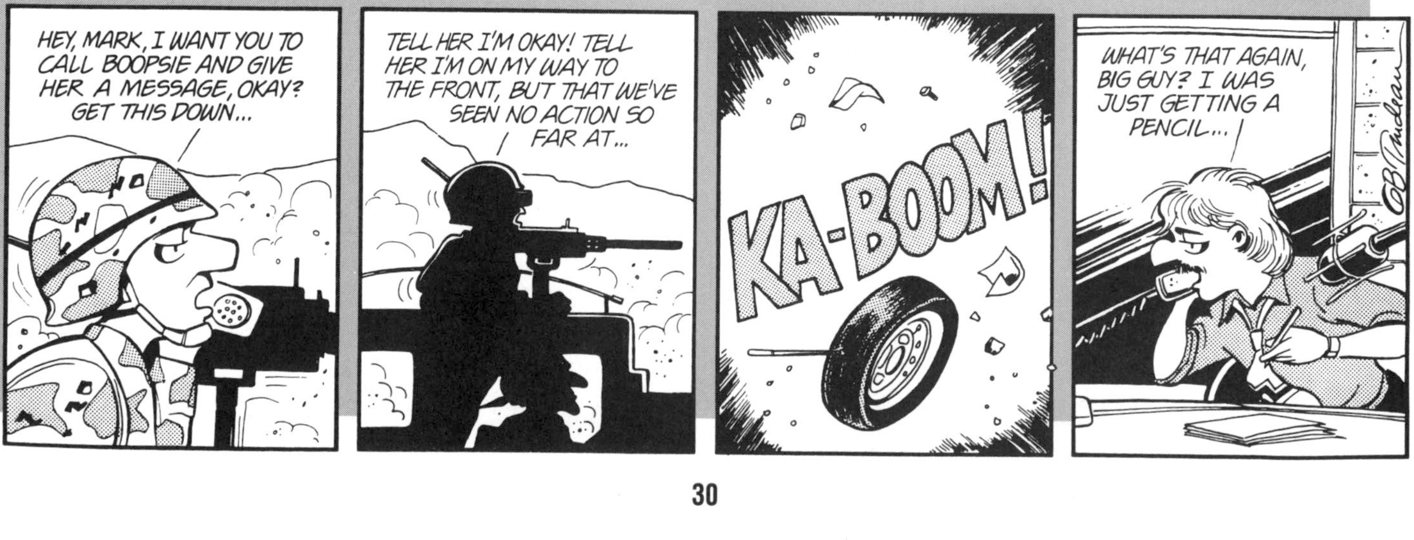
HEY, MARK, I WANT YOU TO CALL BOOPSIE AND GIVE HER A MESSAGE, OKAY? GET THIS DOWN...
TELL HER I'M OKAY! TELL HER I'M ON MY WAY TO THE FRONT, BUT THAT WE'VE SEEN NO ACTION SO FAR AT...
KA-BOOM!
WHAT'S THAT AGAIN, BIG GUY? I WAS JUST GETTING A PENCIL...

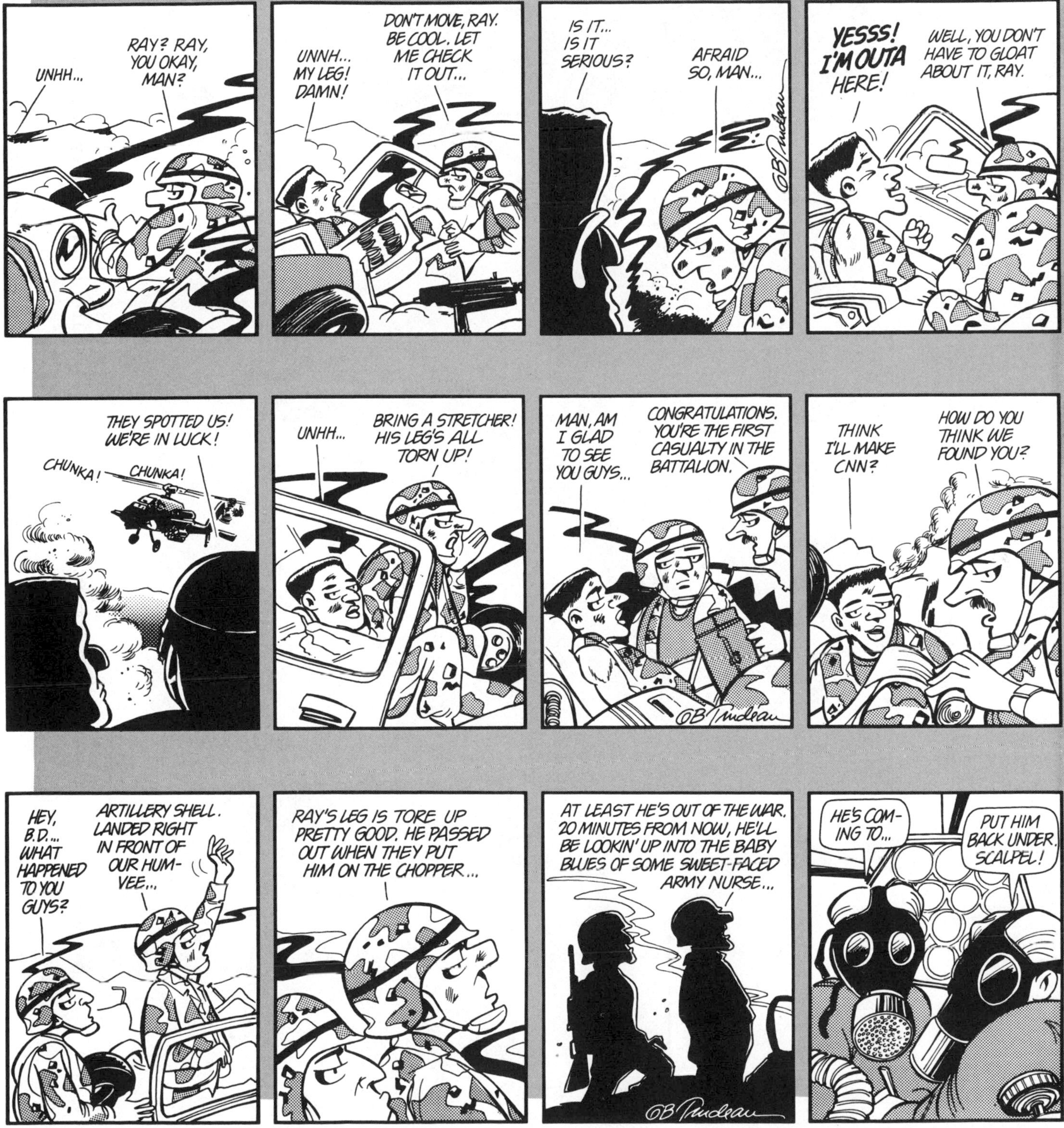
UNHH...
RAY? RAY, YOU OKAY, MAN?
UNNH... MY LEG! DAMN!
DON'T MOVE, RAY. BE COOL. LET ME CHECK IT OUT...
IS IT... IS IT SERIOUS?
AFRAID SO, MAN...
YESSS! I'M OUTA HERE!
WELL, YOU DON'T HAVE TO GLOAT ABOUT IT, RAY.
THEY SPOTTED US! WE'RE IN LUCK!
CHUNKA! CHUNKA!
UNHH...
BRING A STRETCHER! HIS LEG'S ALL TORN UP!
MAN, AM I GLAD TO SEE YOU GUYS...
CONGRATULATIONS. YOU'RE THE FIRST CASUALTY IN THE BATTALION.
THINK I'LL MAKE CNN?
HOW DO YOU THINK WE FOUND YOU?
HEY, B.D.... WHAT HAPPENED TO YOU GUYS?
ARTILLERY SHELL. LANDED RIGHT IN FRONT OF OUR HUMVEE...
RAY'S LEG IS TORE UP PRETTY GOOD. HE PASSED OUT WHEN THEY PUT HIM ON THE CHOPPER...
AT LEAST HE'S OUT OF THE WAR. 20 MINUTES FROM NOW, HE'LL BE LOOKIN' UP INTO THE BABY BLUES OF SOME SWEET-FACED ARMY NURSE...
HE'S COMING TO...
PUT HIM BACK UNDER. SCALPEL!

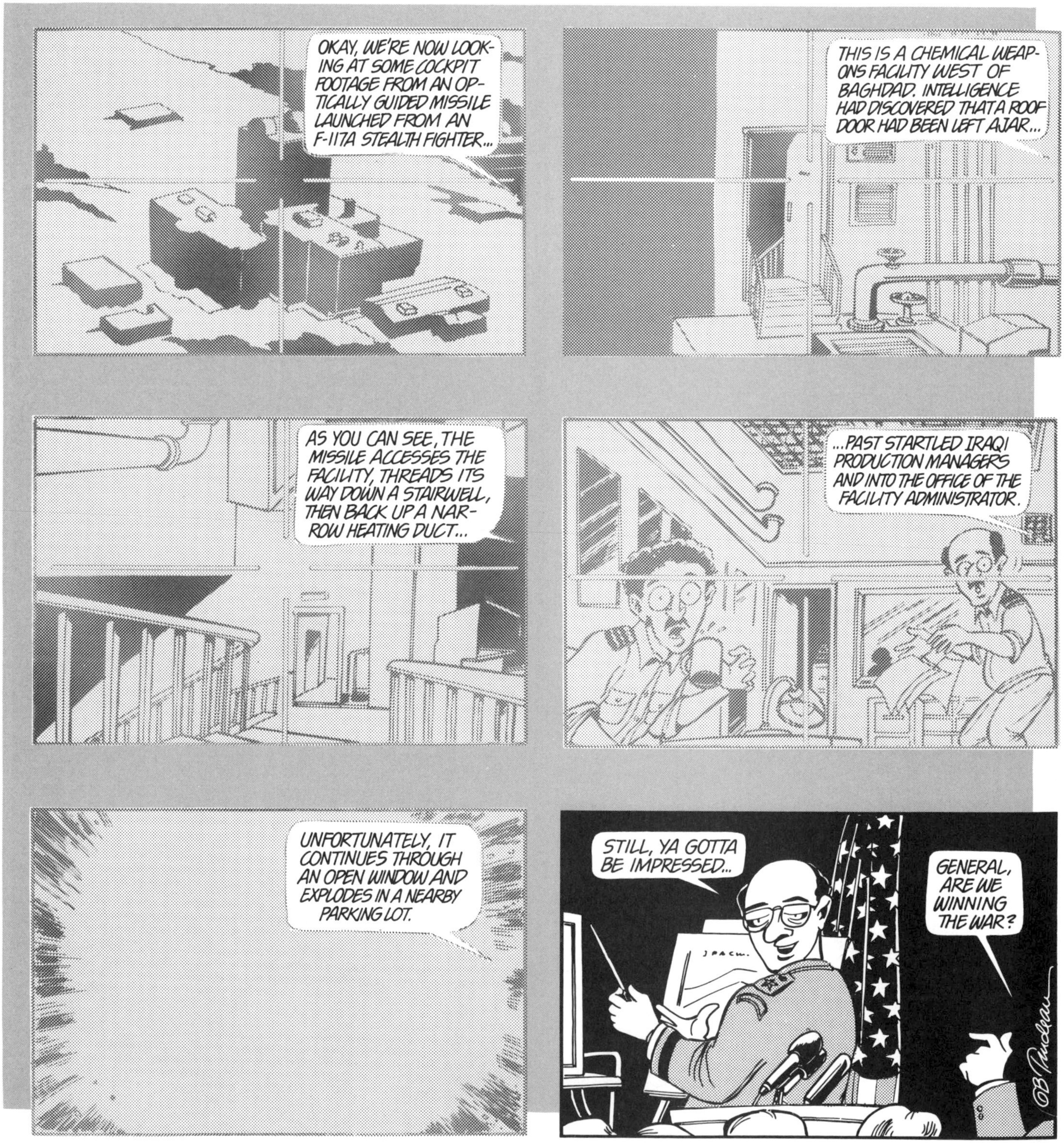
OKAY, WE'RE NOW LOOKING AT SOME COCKPIT FOOTAGE FROM AN OPTICALLY GUIDED MISSILE LAUNCHED FROM AN F-117A STEALTH FIGHTER...
THIS IS A CHEMICAL WEAPONS FACILITY WEST OF BAGHDAD. INTELLIGENCE HAD DISCOVERED THAT A ROOF DOOR HAD BEEN LEFT AJAR...
AS YOU CAN SEE, THE MISSILE ACCESSES THE FACILITY, THREADS ITS WAY DOWN A STAIRWELL, THEN BACK UP A NARROW HEATING DUCT...
...PAST STARTLED IRAQI PRODUCTION MANAGERS AND INTO THE OFFICE OF THE FACILITY ADMINISTRATOR.
UNFORTUNATELY, IT CONTINUES THROUGH AN OPEN WINDOW AND EXPLODES IN A NEARBY PARKING LOT.
STILL, YA GOTTA BE IMPRESSED...
GENERAL, ARE WE WINNING THE WAR?
©B Trudeau

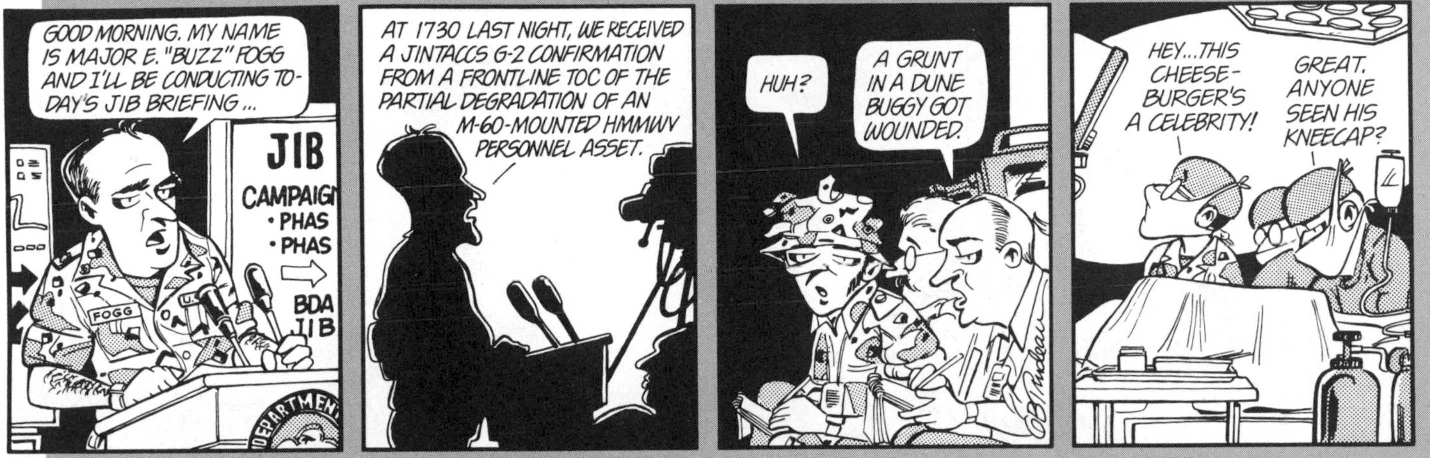
GOOD MORNING. MY NAME IS MAJOR E. "BUZZ" FOGG AND I'LL BE CONDUCTING TO-DAY'S JIB BRIEFING...
JIB
CAMPAIGN
• PHAS
• PHAS
BDA
JIB
FOGG
DEPARTMENT
AT 1730 LAST NIGHT, WE RECEIVED A JINTACCS G-2 CONFIRMATION FROM A FRONTLINE TOC OF THE PARTIAL DEGRADATION OF AN M-60-MOUNTED HMMWV PERSONNEL ASSET.
HUH?
A GRUNT IN A DUNE BUGGY GOT WOUNDED.
HEY...THIS CHEESE-BURGER'S A CELEBRITY!
GREAT. ANYONE SEEN HIS KNEECAP?

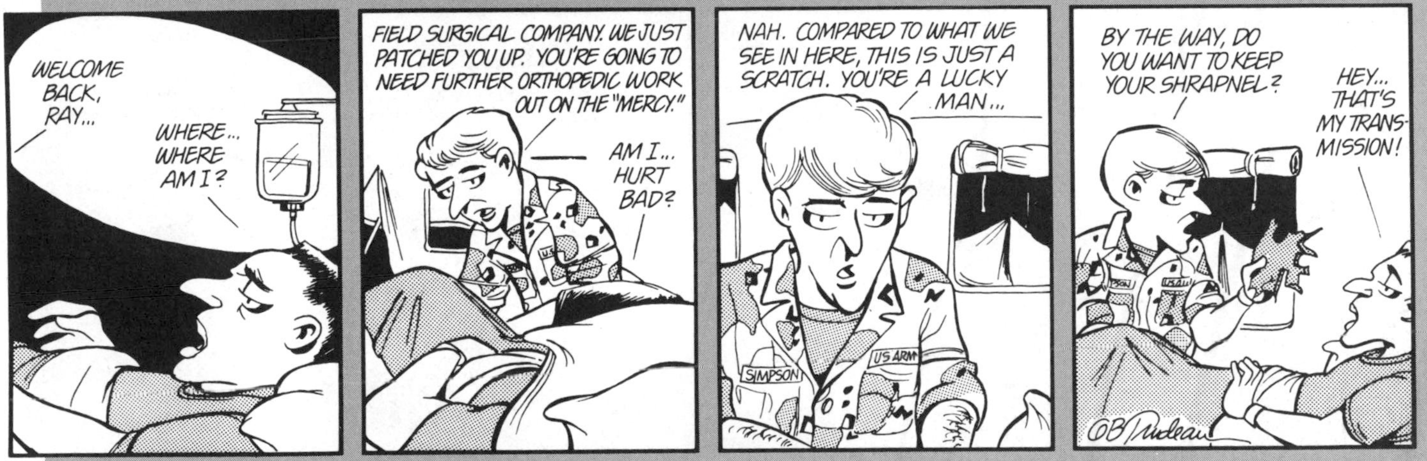
WELCOME BACK, RAY...
WHERE... WHERE AM I?
FIELD SURGICAL COMPANY. WE JUST PATCHED YOU UP. YOU'RE GOING TO NEED FURTHER ORTHOPEDIC WORK OUT ON THE "MERCY."
AM I... HURT BAD?
NAH. COMPARED TO WHAT WE SEE IN HERE, THIS IS JUST A SCRATCH. YOU'RE A LUCKY MAN...
SIMPSON
U.S. ARMY
BY THE WAY, DO YOU WANT TO KEEP YOUR SHRAPNEL?
HEY... THAT'S MY TRANS-MISSION!

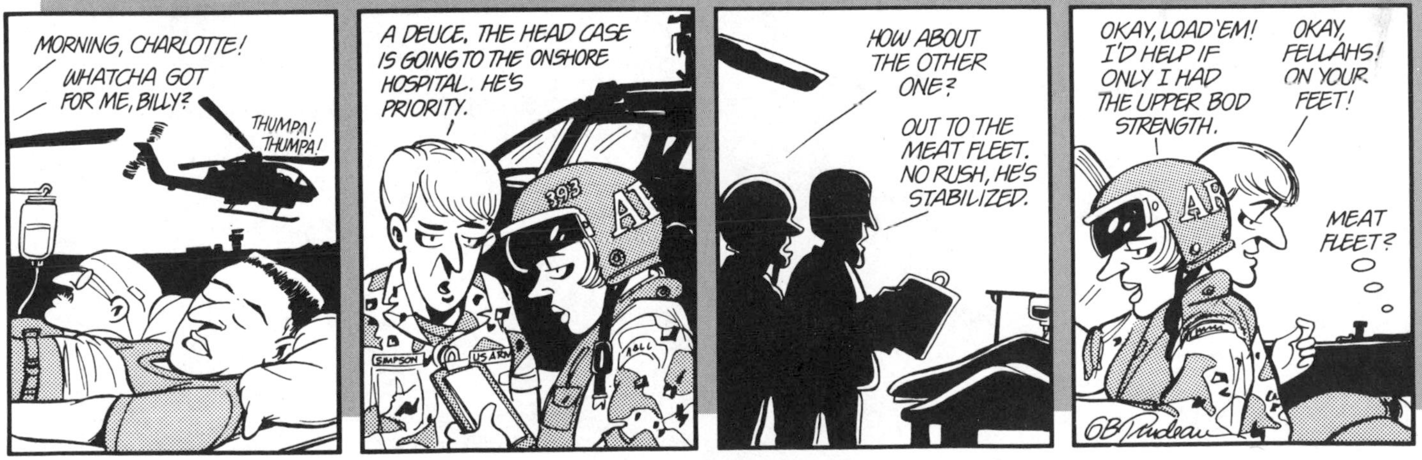
MORNING, CHARLOTTE!
WHATCHA GOT FOR ME, BILLY?
THUMPA! THUMPA!
A DEUCE. THE HEAD CASE IS GOING TO THE ONSHORE HOSPITAL. HE'S PRIORITY.
SIMPSON
U.S. ARMY
HOW ABOUT THE OTHER ONE?
OUT TO THE MEAT FLEET. NO RUSH, HE'S STABILIZED.
OKAY, LOAD 'EM! I'D HELP IF ONLY I HAD THE UPPER BOD STRENGTH.
OKAY, FELLAHS! ON YOUR FEET!
MEAT FLEET?

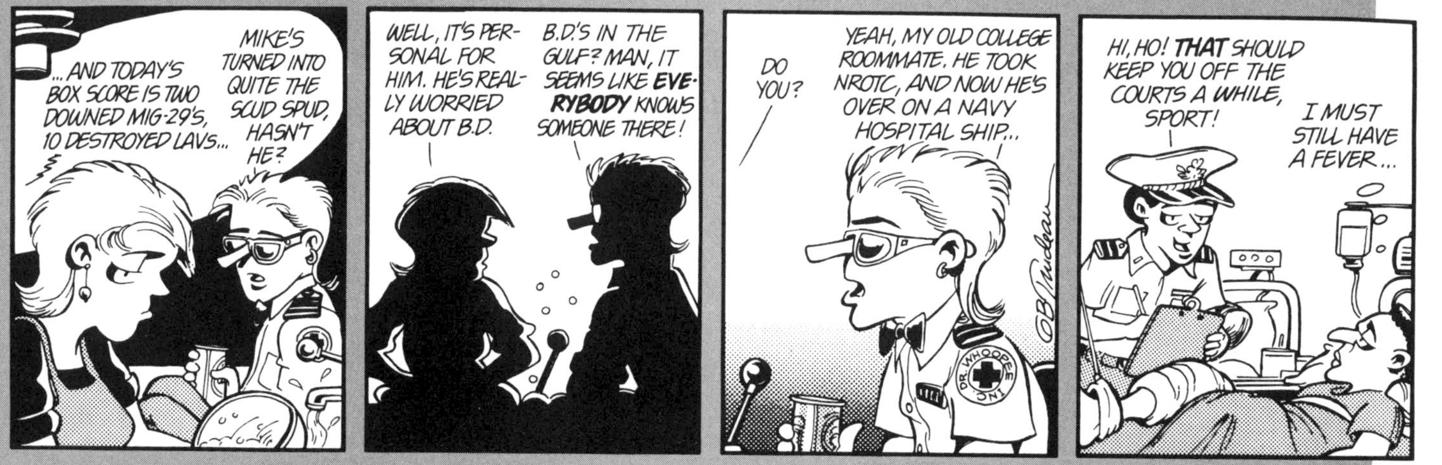
...AND TODAY'S BOX SCORE IS TWO DOWNED MIG-29'S, 10 DESTROYED LAVS...
MIKE'S TURNED INTO QUITE THE SCUD SPUD, HASN'T HE?
WELL, IT'S PERSONAL FOR HIM. HE'S REALLY WORRIED ABOUT B.D.
B.D.'S IN THE GULF? MAN, IT SEEMS LIKE **EVERYBODY** KNOWS SOMEONE THERE!
DO YOU?
YEAH, MY OLD COLLEGE ROOMMATE. HE TOOK NROTC, AND NOW HE'S OVER ON A NAVY HOSPITAL SHIP...
DR. WHOOPEE INC
HI, HO! **THAT** SHOULD KEEP YOU OFF THE COURTS A WHILE, SPORT!
I MUST STILL HAVE A FEVER...

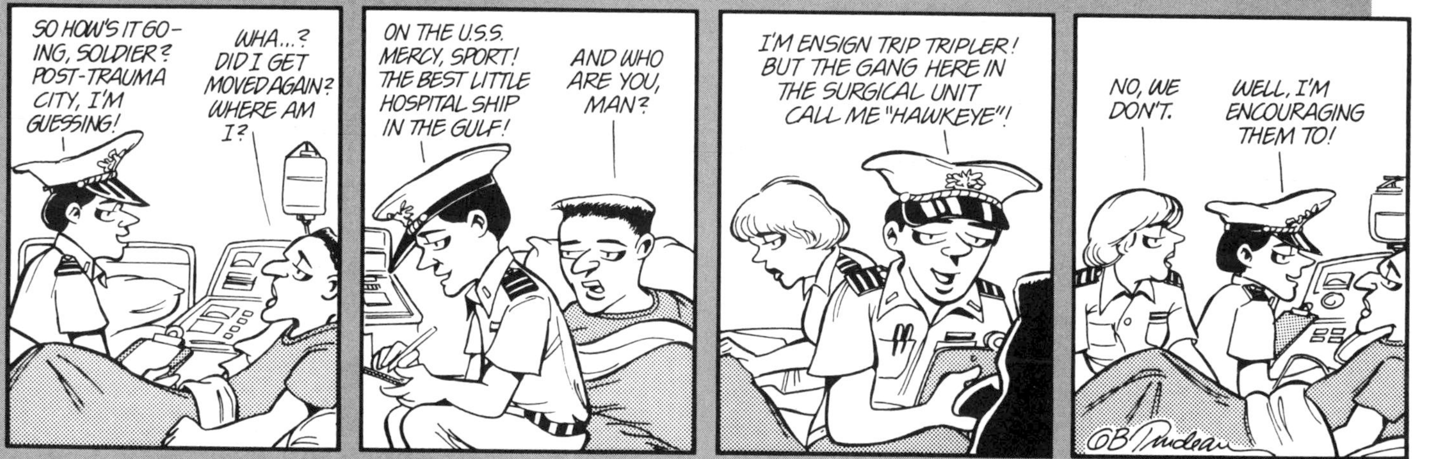
SO HOW'S IT GOING, SOLDIER? POST-TRAUMA CITY, I'M GUESSING!
WHA...? DID I GET MOVED AGAIN? WHERE AM I?
ON THE U.S.S. MERCY, SPORT! THE BEST LITTLE HOSPITAL SHIP IN THE GULF!
AND WHO ARE YOU, MAN?
I'M ENSIGN TRIP TRIPLER! BUT THE GANG HERE IN THE SURGICAL UNIT CALL ME "HAWKEYE"!
NO, WE DON'T.
WELL, I'M ENCOURAGING THEM TO!

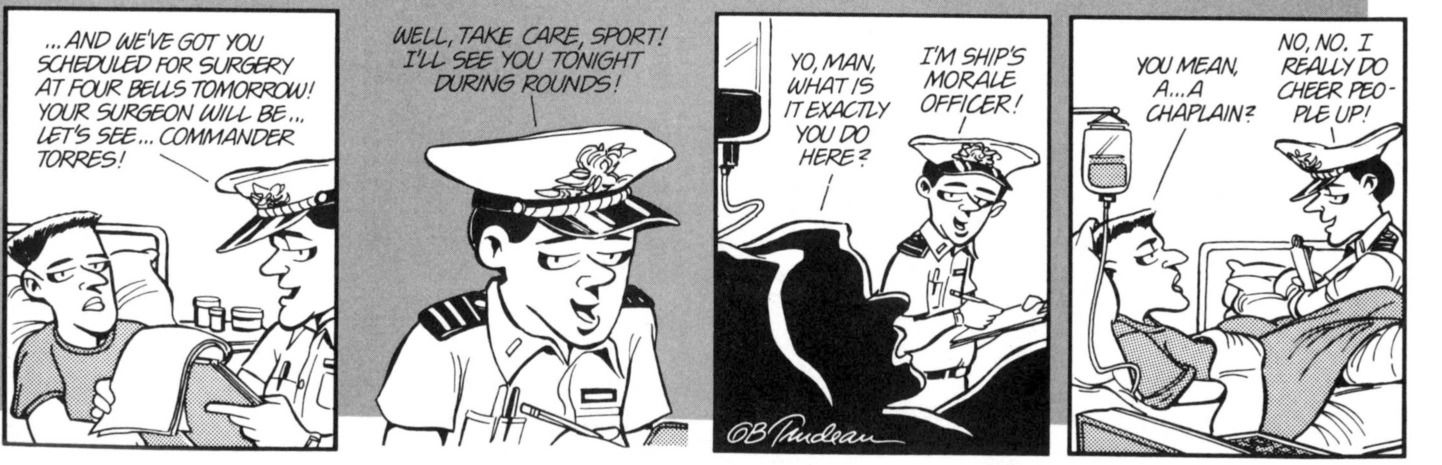
...AND WE'VE GOT YOU SCHEDULED FOR SURGERY AT FOUR BELLS TOMORROW! YOUR SURGEON WILL BE... LET'S SEE... COMMANDER TORRES!
WELL, TAKE CARE, SPORT! I'LL SEE YOU TONIGHT DURING ROUNDS!
YO, MAN, WHAT IS IT EXACTLY YOU DO HERE?
I'M SHIP'S MORALE OFFICER!
YOU MEAN, A...A CHAPLAIN?
NO, NO. I REALLY DO CHEER PEOPLE UP!

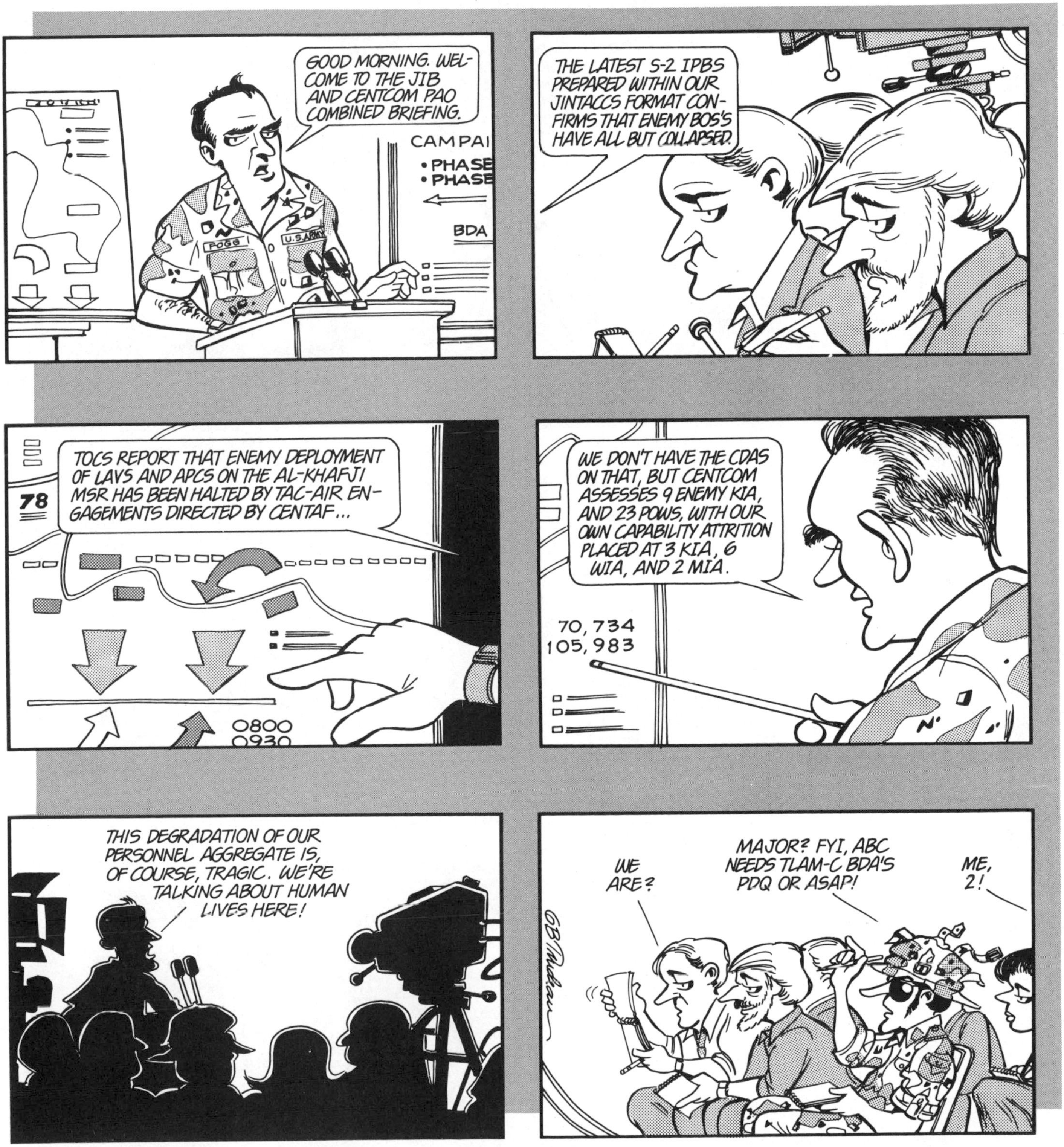
GOOD MORNING. WELCOME TO THE JIB AND CENTCOM PAO COMBINED BRIEFING.
CAMPAI
•PHASE
•PHASE
BDA
FOGG
U.S. ARMY
THE LATEST S-2 IPBS PREPARED WITHIN OUR JINTACCS FORMAT CONFIRMS THAT ENEMY BOS'S HAVE ALL BUT COLLAPSED.
TOCS REPORT THAT ENEMY DEPLOYMENT OF LAVS AND APCS ON THE AL-KHAFJI MSR HAS BEEN HALTED BY TAC-AIR ENGAGEMENTS DIRECTED BY CENTAF...
78
0800
0930
WE DON'T HAVE THE CDAS ON THAT, BUT CENTCOM ASSESSES 9 ENEMY KIA, AND 23 POWS, WITH OUR OWN CAPABILITY ATTRITION PLACED AT 3 KIA, 6 WIA, AND 2 MIA.
70,734
105,983
THIS DEGRADATION OF OUR PERSONNEL AGGREGATE IS, OF COURSE, TRAGIC. WE'RE TALKING ABOUT HUMAN LIVES HERE!
WE ARE?
MAJOR? FYI, ABC NEEDS TLAM-C BDA'S PDQ OR ASAP!
ME, 2!
GBTrudeau

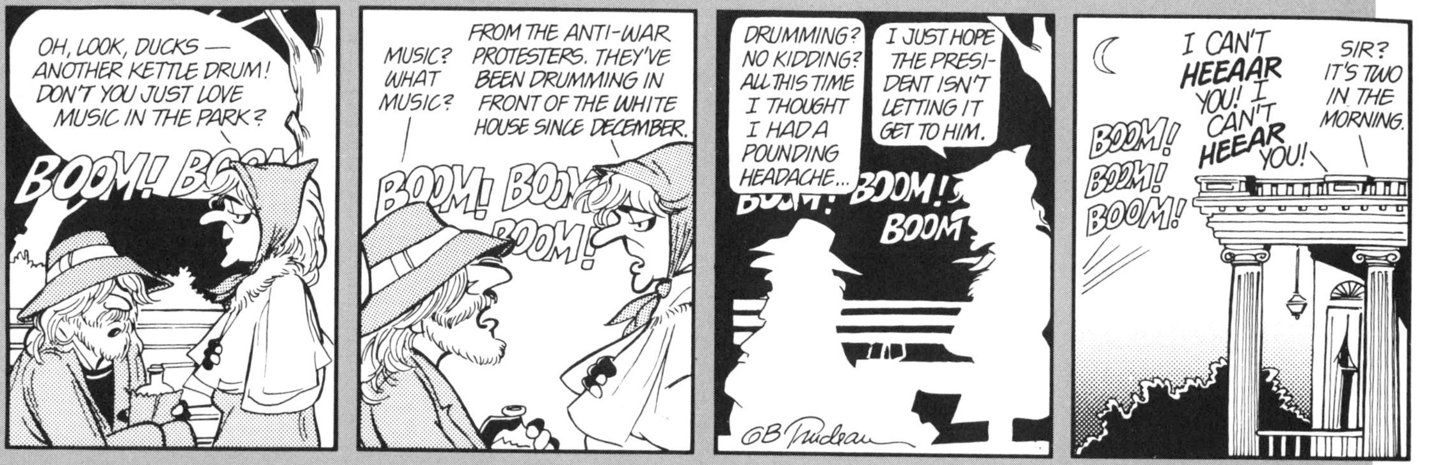
OH, LOOK, DUCKS — ANOTHER KETTLE DRUM! DON'T YOU JUST LOVE MUSIC IN THE PARK?
BOOM!
MUSIC? WHAT MUSIC?
FROM THE ANTI-WAR PROTESTERS. THEY'VE BEEN DRUMMING IN FRONT OF THE WHITE HOUSE SINCE DECEMBER.
BOOM! BOOM!
DRUMMING? NO KIDDING? ALL THIS TIME I THOUGHT I HAD A POUNDING HEADACHE...
I JUST HOPE THE PRESIDENT ISN'T LETTING IT GET TO HIM.
BOOM! BOOM
BOOM! BOOM! BOOM!
I CAN'T HEEAAR YOU! I CAN'T HEEAR YOU!
SIR? IT'S TWO IN THE MORNING.

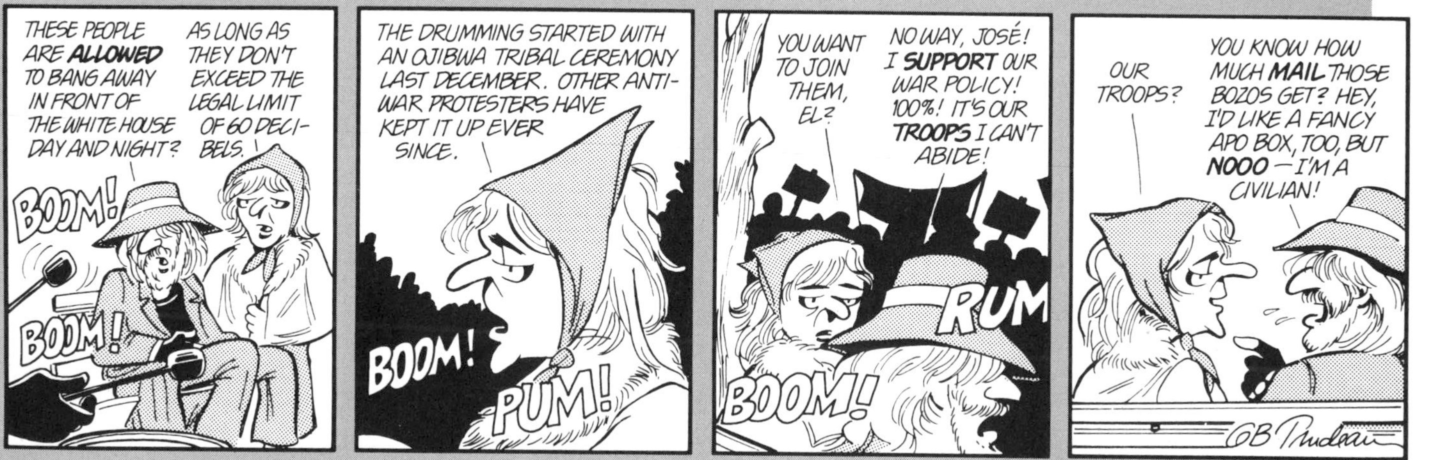
THESE PEOPLE ARE ALLOWED TO BANG AWAY IN FRONT OF THE WHITE HOUSE DAY AND NIGHT?
AS LONG AS THEY DON'T EXCEED THE LEGAL LIMIT OF 60 DECIBELS.
BOOM! BOOM!
THE DRUMMING STARTED WITH AN OJIBWA TRIBAL CEREMONY LAST DECEMBER. OTHER ANTI-WAR PROTESTERS HAVE KEPT IT UP EVER SINCE.
BOOM! PUM!
YOU WANT TO JOIN THEM, EL?
NO WAY, JOSÉ! I SUPPORT OUR WAR POLICY! 100%! IT'S OUR TROOPS I CAN'T ABIDE!
RUM BOOM!
OUR TROOPS?
YOU KNOW HOW MUCH MAIL THOSE BOZOS GET? HEY, I'D LIKE A FANCY APO BOX, TOO, BUT NOOO — I'M A CIVILIAN!

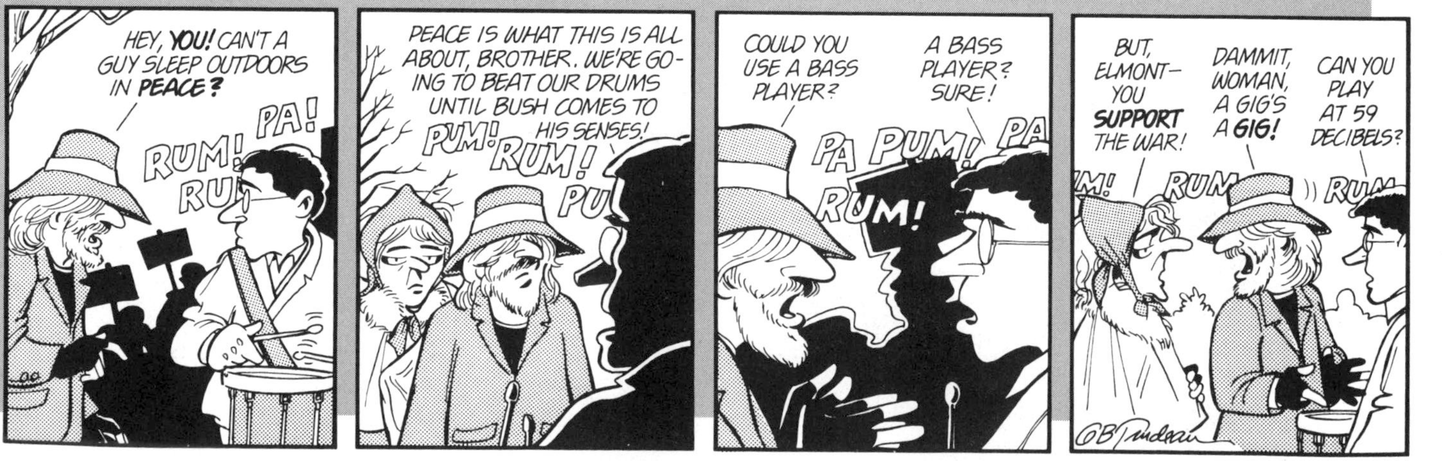
HEY, YOU! CAN'T A GUY SLEEP OUTDOORS IN PEACE?
PA! RUM!
PEACE IS WHAT THIS IS ALL ABOUT, BROTHER. WE'RE GOING TO BEAT OUR DRUMS UNTIL BUSH COMES TO HIS SENSES!
PUM! RUM!
COULD YOU USE A BASS PLAYER?
A BASS PLAYER? SURE!
PA PUM! RUM!
BUT, ELMONT — YOU SUPPORT THE WAR!
DAMMIT, WOMAN, A GIG'S A GIG!
CAN YOU PLAY AT 59 DECIBELS?
RUM

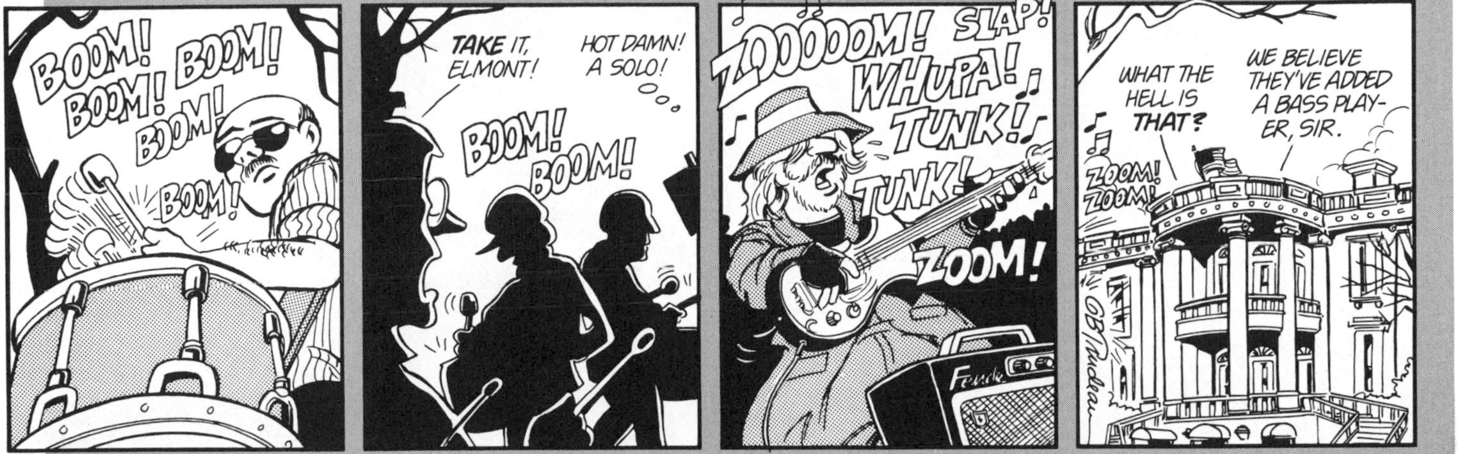
BOOM! BOOM! BOOM! BOOM!
BOOM!
TAKE IT, ELMONT!
HOT DAMN! A SOLO!
BOOM! BOOM!
ZOOOOOM! SLAP! WHUPA! TUNK! TUNK!
ZOOM!
Fender
WHAT THE HELL IS THAT?
WE BELIEVE THEY'VE ADDED A BASS PLAYER, SIR.
ZOOM! ZOOM!
GB Trudeau

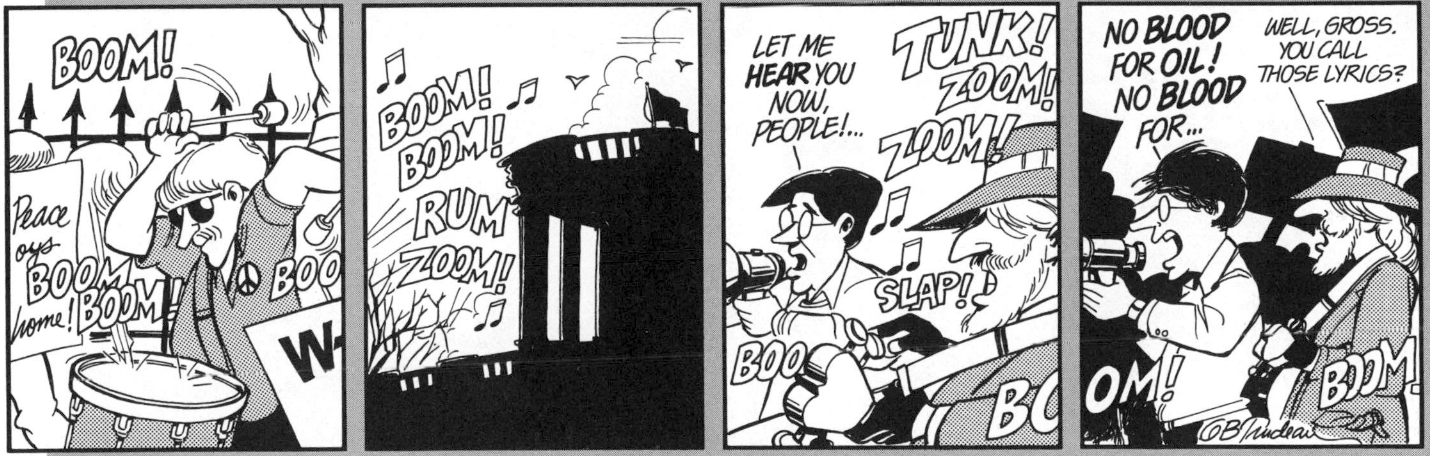
BOOM!
Peace
home!
BOOM BOOM!
BOO
BOOM! BOOM!
RUM
ZOOM!
LET ME HEAR YOU NOW, PEOPLE!...
TUNK! ZOOM! ZOOM!
SLAP!
BOO
BO
NO BLOOD FOR OIL! NO BLOOD FOR...
WELL, GROSS. YOU CALL THOSE LYRICS?
OM!
BOOM
GB Trudeau

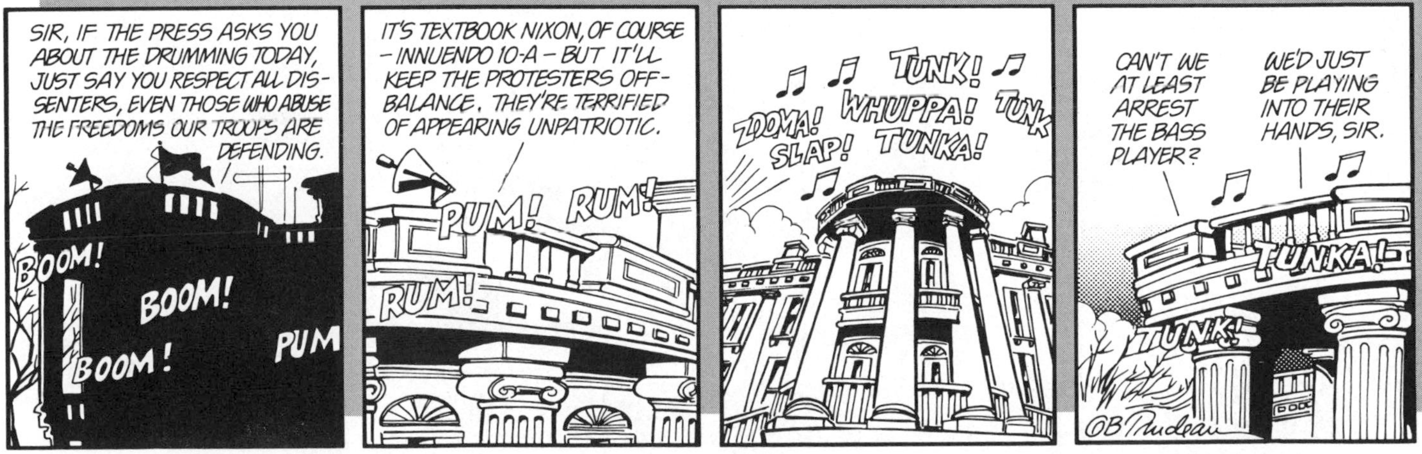
SIR, IF THE PRESS ASKS YOU ABOUT THE DRUMMING TODAY, JUST SAY YOU RESPECT ALL DISSENTERS, EVEN THOSE WHO ABUSE THE FREEDOMS OUR TROOPS ARE DEFENDING.
BOOM!
BOOM!
BOOM!
PUM
IT'S TEXTBOOK NIXON, OF COURSE - INNUENDO 10-A - BUT IT'LL KEEP THE PROTESTERS OFF-BALANCE. THEY'RE TERRIFIED OF APPEARING UNPATRIOTIC.
PUM! RUM!
RUM!
TUNK!
ZOOMA! WHUPPA! TUNK
SLAP! TUNKA!
CAN'T WE AT LEAST ARREST THE BASS PLAYER?
WE'D JUST BE PLAYING INTO THEIR HANDS, SIR.
TUNKA!
TUNK!
GB Trudeau

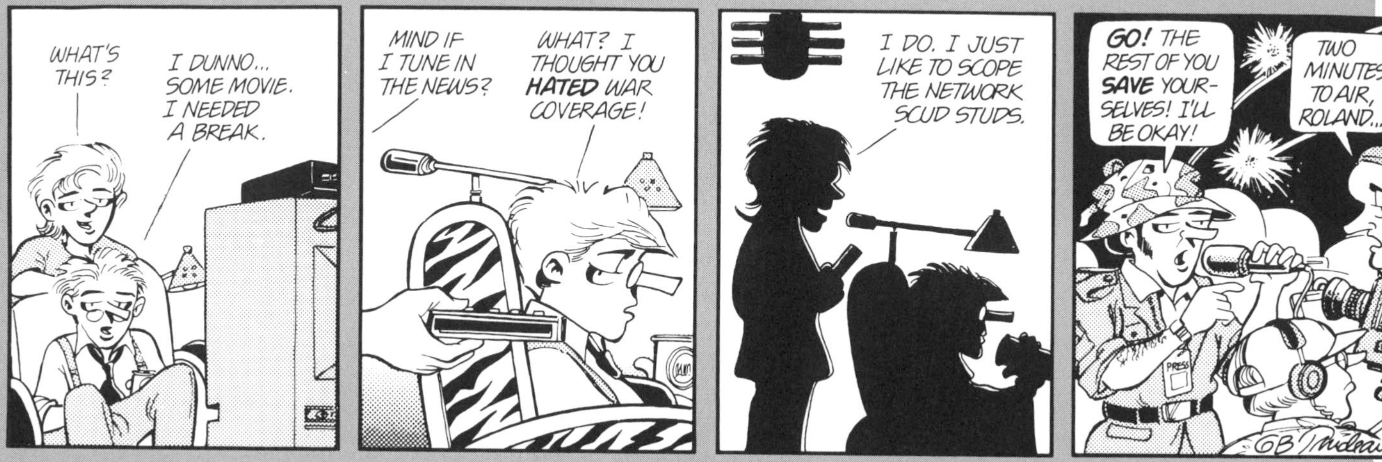
WHAT'S THIS?
I DUNNO... SOME MOVIE. I NEEDED A BREAK.
MIND IF I TUNE IN THE NEWS?
WHAT? I THOUGHT YOU **HATED** WAR COVERAGE!
I DO. I JUST LIKE TO SCOPE THE NETWORK SCUD STUDS.
GO! THE REST OF YOU **SAVE** YOURSELVES! I'LL BE OKAY!
TWO MINUTES TO AIR, ROLAND...
PRESS
GB Trudeau

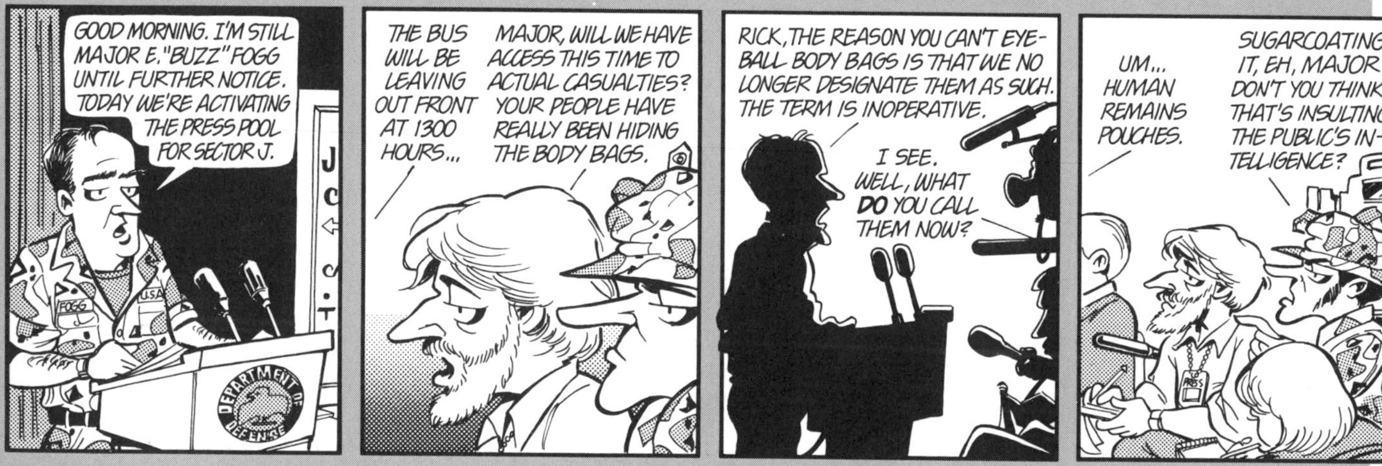
GOOD MORNING. I'M STILL MAJOR E. "BUZZ" FOGG UNTIL FURTHER NOTICE. TODAY WE'RE ACTIVATING THE PRESS POOL FOR SECTOR J.
FOGG
U.S.A.
DEPARTMENT OF DEFENSE
THE BUS WILL BE LEAVING OUT FRONT AT 1300 HOURS...
MAJOR, WILL WE HAVE ACCESS THIS TIME TO ACTUAL CASUALTIES? YOUR PEOPLE HAVE REALLY BEEN HIDING THE BODY BAGS.
RICK, THE REASON YOU CAN'T EYEBALL BODY BAGS IS THAT WE NO LONGER DESIGNATE THEM AS SUCH. THE TERM IS INOPERATIVE.
I SEE. WELL, WHAT **DO** YOU CALL THEM NOW?
UM... HUMAN REMAINS POUCHES.
SUGARCOATING IT, EH, MAJOR? DON'T YOU THINK THAT'S INSULTING THE PUBLIC'S INTELLIGENCE?
PRESS
GB Trudeau

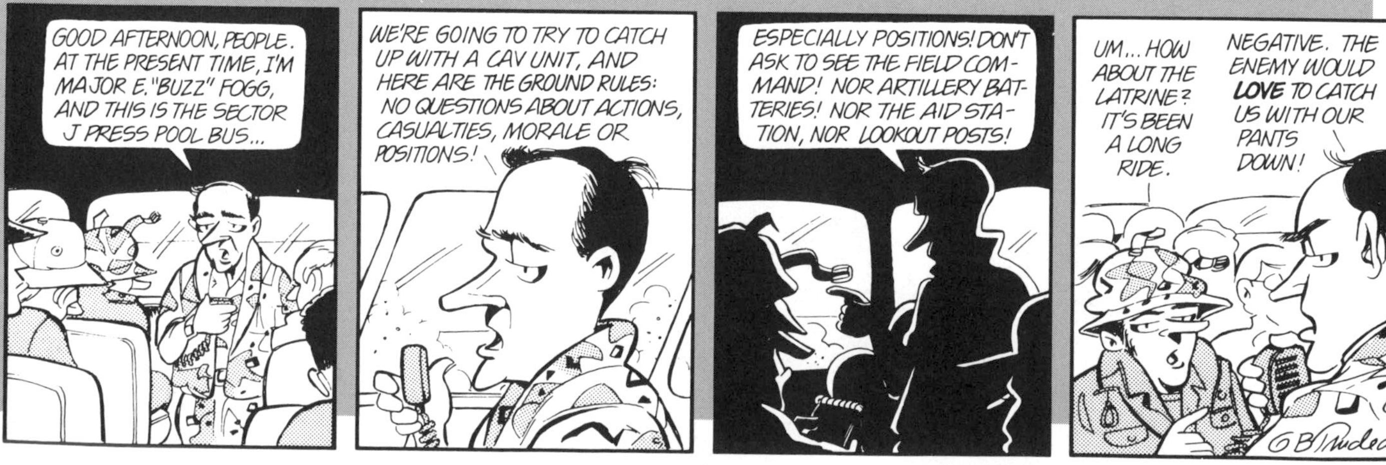
GOOD AFTERNOON, PEOPLE. AT THE PRESENT TIME, I'M MAJOR E. "BUZZ" FOGG, AND THIS IS THE SECTOR J PRESS POOL BUS...
WE'RE GOING TO TRY TO CATCH UP WITH A CAV UNIT, AND HERE ARE THE GROUND RULES: NO QUESTIONS ABOUT ACTIONS, CASUALTIES, MORALE OR POSITIONS!
ESPECIALLY POSITIONS! DON'T ASK TO SEE THE FIELD COMMAND! NOR ARTILLERY BATTERIES! NOR THE AID STATION, NOR LOOKOUT POSTS!
UM... HOW ABOUT THE LATRINE? IT'S BEEN A LONG RIDE.
NEGATIVE. THE ENEMY WOULD **LOVE** TO CATCH US WITH OUR PANTS DOWN!
GB Trudeau

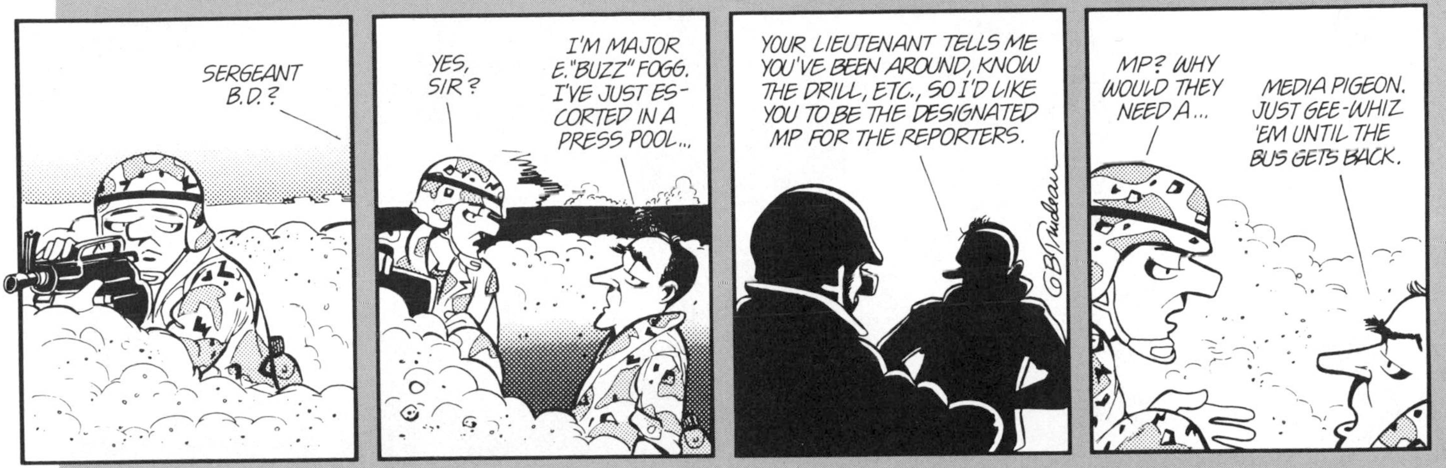
SERGEANT B.D.?
YES, SIR?
I'M MAJOR E. "BUZZ" FOGG. I'VE JUST ESCORTED IN A PRESS POOL...
YOUR LIEUTENANT TELLS ME YOU'VE BEEN AROUND, KNOW THE DRILL, ETC., SO I'D LIKE YOU TO BE THE DESIGNATED MP FOR THE REPORTERS.
MP? WHY WOULD THEY NEED A...
MEDIA PIGEON. JUST GEE-WHIZ 'EM UNTIL THE BUS GETS BACK.

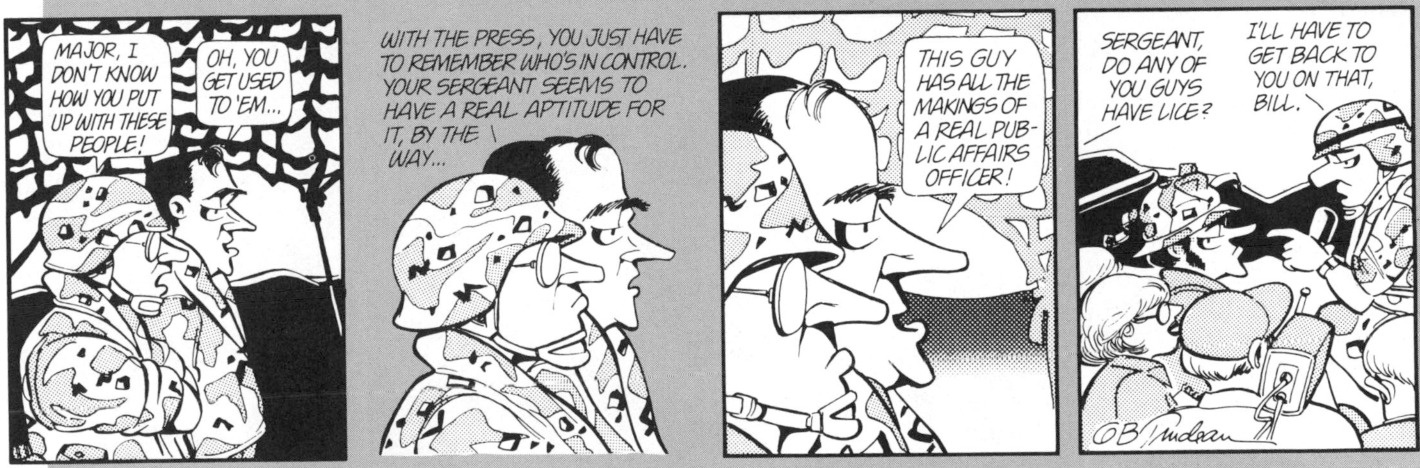
MAJOR, I DON'T KNOW HOW YOU PUT UP WITH THESE PEOPLE!
OH, YOU GET USED TO 'EM...
WITH THE PRESS, YOU JUST HAVE TO REMEMBER WHO'S IN CONTROL. YOUR SERGEANT SEEMS TO HAVE A REAL APTITUDE FOR IT, BY THE WAY...
THIS GUY HAS ALL THE MAKINGS OF A REAL PUBLIC AFFAIRS OFFICER!
SERGEANT, DO ANY OF YOU GUYS HAVE LICE?
I'LL HAVE TO GET BACK TO YOU ON THAT, BILL.

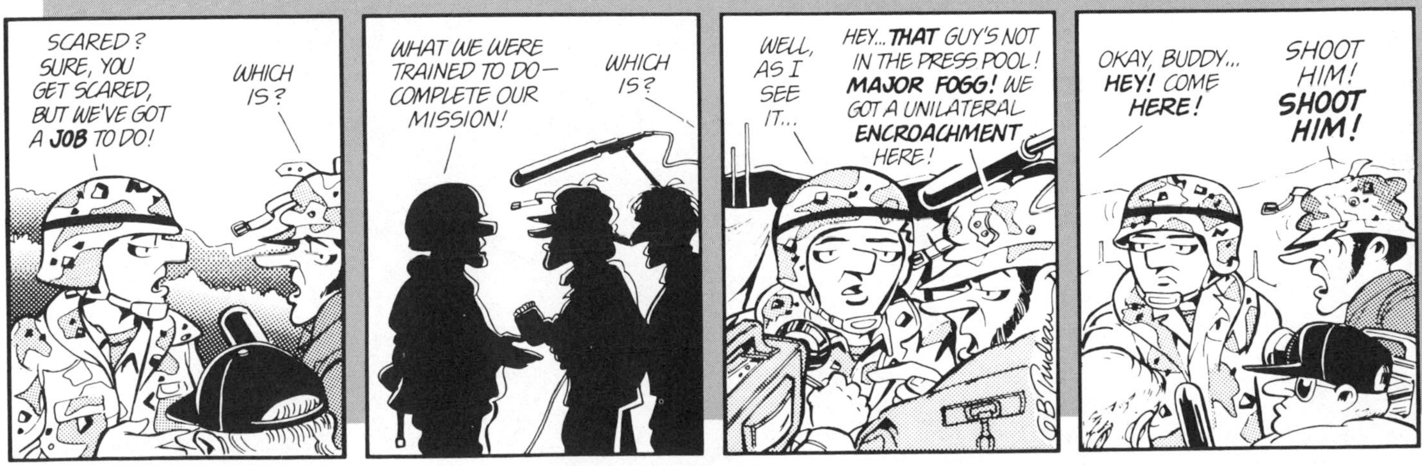
SCARED? SURE, YOU GET SCARED, BUT WE'VE GOT A **JOB** TO DO!
WHICH IS?
WHAT WE WERE TRAINED TO DO— COMPLETE OUR MISSION!
WHICH IS?
WELL, AS I SEE IT...
HEY... **THAT** GUY'S NOT IN THE PRESS POOL! **MAJOR FOGG!** WE GOT A UNILATERAL **ENCROACHMENT** HERE!
OKAY, BUDDY... **HEY!** COME **HERE!**
SHOOT HIM! **SHOOT HIM!**

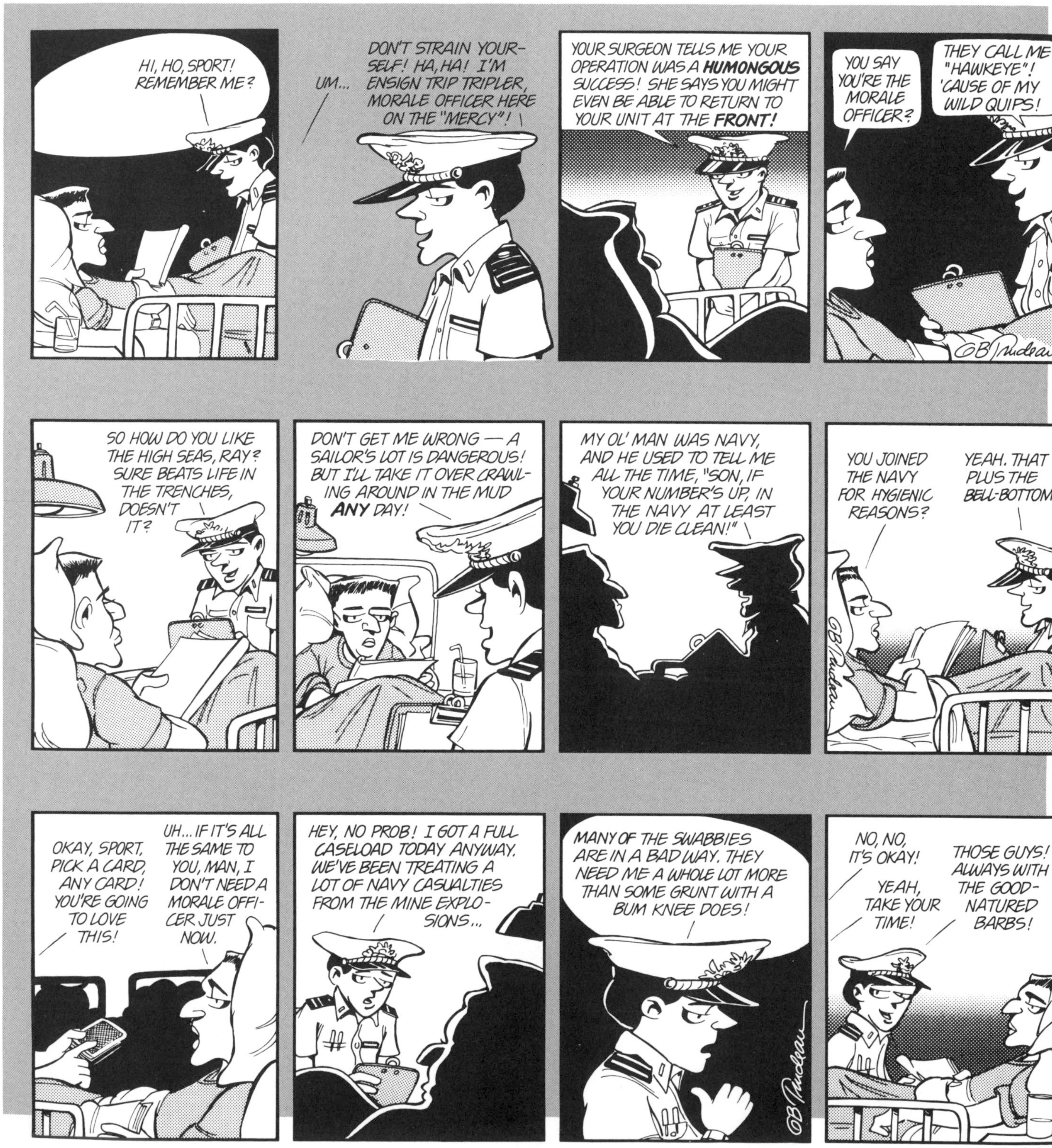
HI, HO, SPORT! REMEMBER ME?
UM...
DON'T STRAIN YOURSELF! HA, HA! I'M ENSIGN TRIP TRIPLER, MORALE OFFICER HERE ON THE "MERCY"!
YOUR SURGEON TELLS ME YOUR OPERATION WAS A **HUMONGOUS** SUCCESS! SHE SAYS YOU MIGHT EVEN BE ABLE TO RETURN TO YOUR UNIT AT THE **FRONT!**
YOU SAY YOU'RE THE MORALE OFFICER?
THEY CALL ME "HAWKEYE"! 'CAUSE OF MY WILD QUIPS!
SO HOW DO YOU LIKE THE HIGH SEAS, RAY? SURE BEATS LIFE IN THE TRENCHES, DOESN'T IT?
DON'T GET ME WRONG — A SAILOR'S LOT IS DANGEROUS! BUT I'LL TAKE IT OVER CRAWLING AROUND IN THE MUD **ANY** DAY!
MY OL' MAN WAS NAVY, AND HE USED TO TELL ME ALL THE TIME, "SON, IF YOUR NUMBER'S UP, IN THE NAVY AT LEAST YOU DIE CLEAN!"
YOU JOINED THE NAVY FOR HYGIENIC REASONS?
YEAH. THAT PLUS THE BELL-BOTTOMS.
OKAY, SPORT, PICK A CARD, ANY CARD! YOU'RE GOING TO LOVE THIS!
UH... IF IT'S ALL THE SAME TO YOU, MAN, I DON'T NEED A MORALE OFFICER JUST NOW.
HEY, NO PROB! I GOT A FULL CASELOAD TODAY ANYWAY. WE'VE BEEN TREATING A LOT OF NAVY CASUALTIES FROM THE MINE EXPLOSIONS...
MANY OF THE SWABBIES ARE IN A BAD WAY. THEY NEED ME A WHOLE LOT MORE THAN SOME GRUNT WITH A BUM KNEE DOES!
NO, NO, IT'S OKAY!
YEAH, TAKE YOUR TIME!
THOSE GUYS! ALWAYS WITH THE GOOD-NATURED BARBS!

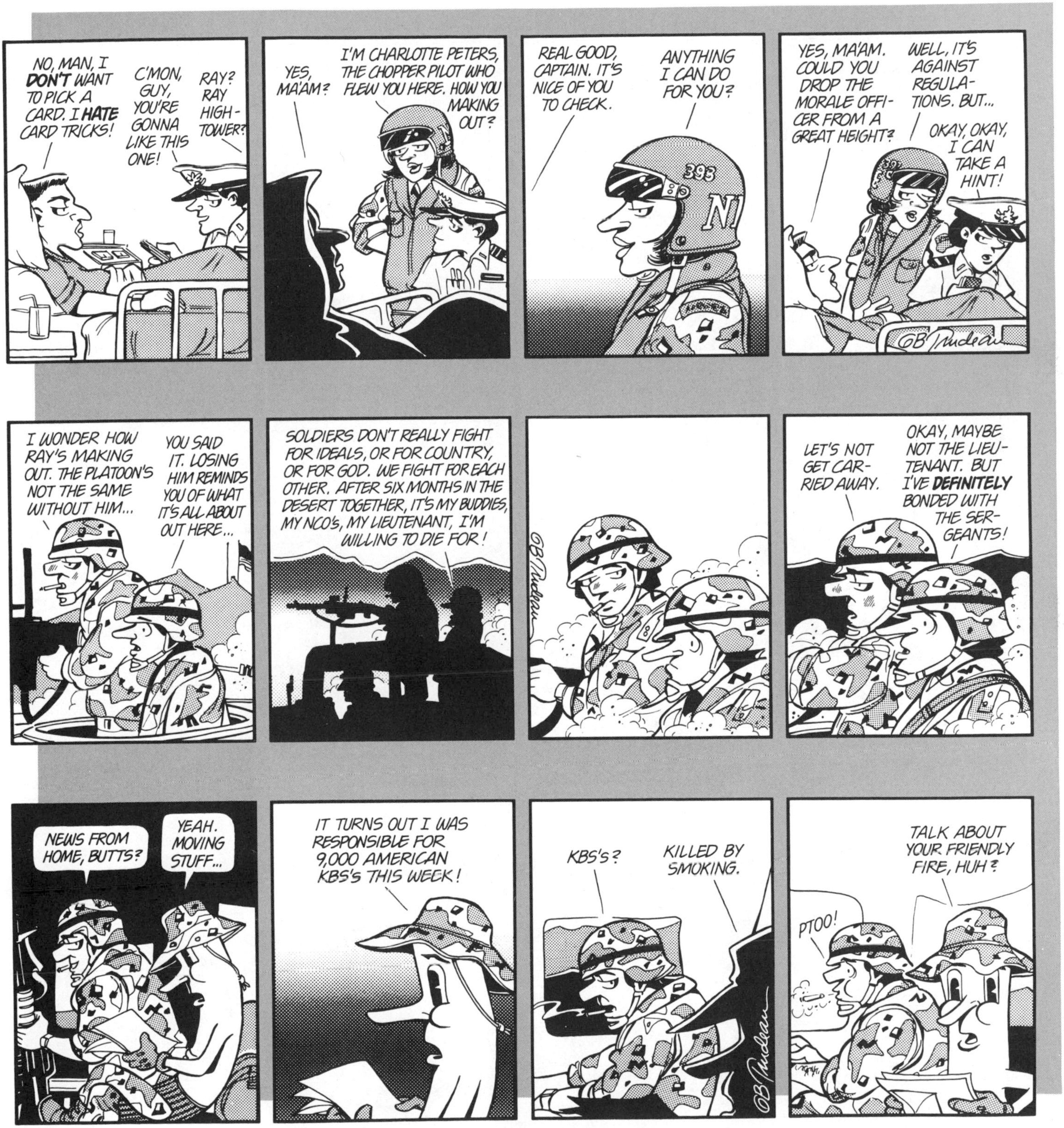
NO, MAN, I **DON'T** WANT TO PICK A CARD. I **HATE** CARD TRICKS!
C'MON, GUY, YOU'RE GONNA LIKE THIS ONE!
RAY? RAY HIGH-TOWER?
YES, MA'AM?
I'M CHARLOTTE PETERS, THE CHOPPER PILOT WHO FLEW YOU HERE. HOW YOU MAKING OUT?
REAL GOOD, CAPTAIN. IT'S NICE OF YOU TO CHECK.
ANYTHING I CAN DO FOR YOU?
YES, MA'AM. COULD YOU DROP THE MORALE OFFI-CER FROM A GREAT HEIGHT?
WELL, IT'S AGAINST REGULA-TIONS. BUT...
OKAY, OKAY, I CAN TAKE A HINT!
I WONDER HOW RAY'S MAKING OUT. THE PLATOON'S NOT THE SAME WITHOUT HIM...
YOU SAID IT. LOSING HIM REMINDS YOU OF WHAT IT'S ALL ABOUT OUT HERE...
SOLDIERS DON'T REALLY FIGHT FOR IDEALS, OR FOR COUNTRY, OR FOR GOD. WE FIGHT FOR EACH OTHER. AFTER SIX MONTHS IN THE DESERT TOGETHER, IT'S MY BUDDIES, MY NCO'S, MY LIEUTENANT, I'M WILLING TO DIE FOR!
LET'S NOT GET CAR-RIED AWAY.
OKAY, MAYBE NOT THE LIEU-TENANT. BUT I'VE **DEFINITELY** BONDED WITH THE SER-GEANTS!
NEWS FROM HOME, BUTTS?
YEAH. MOVING STUFF...
IT TURNS OUT I WAS RESPONSIBLE FOR 9,000 AMERICAN KBS'S THIS WEEK!
KBS'S?
KILLED BY SMOKING.
PTOO!
TALK ABOUT YOUR FRIENDLY FIRE, HUH?

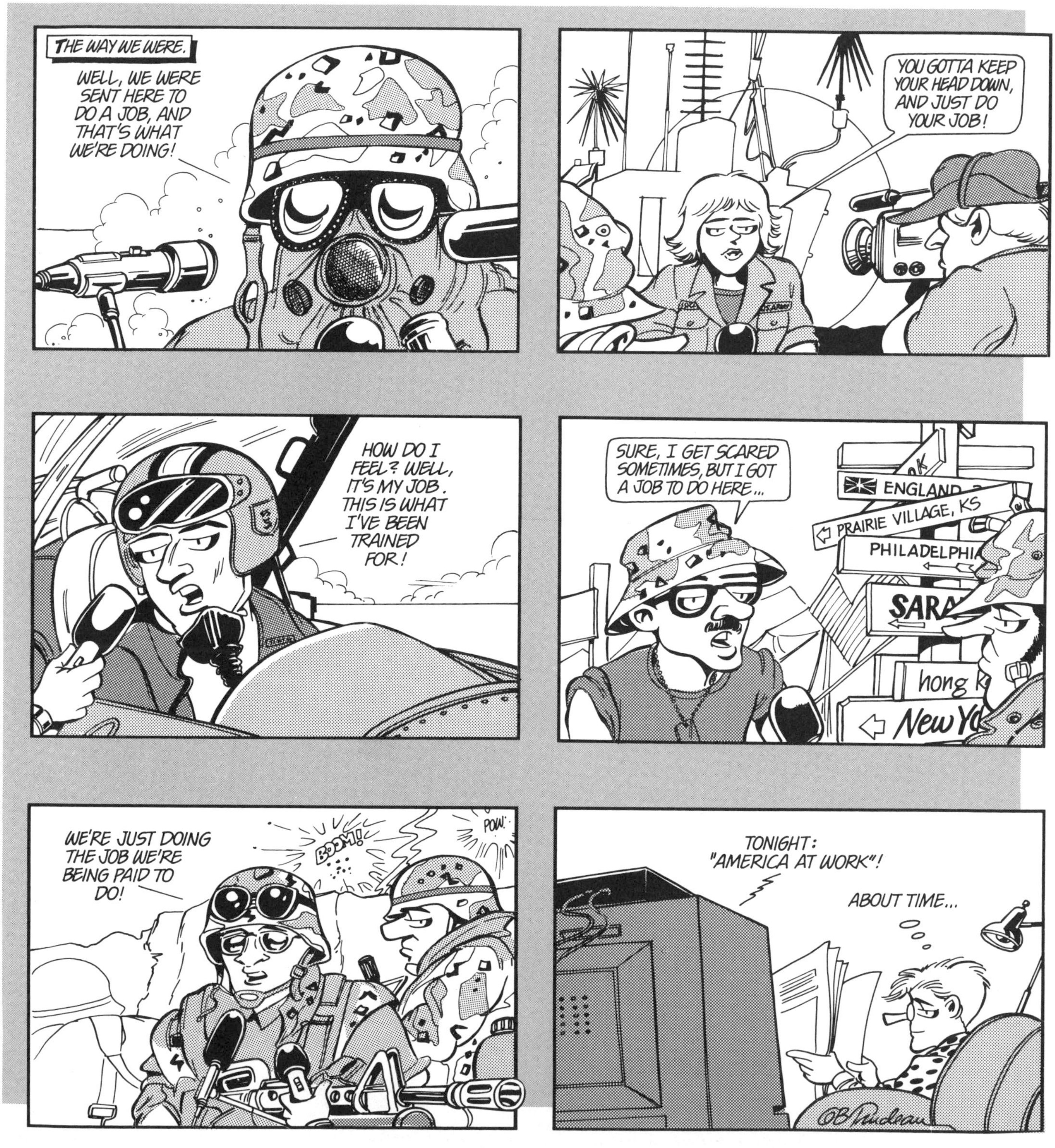
THE WAY WE WERE.
WELL, WE WERE SENT HERE TO DO A JOB, AND THAT'S WHAT WE'RE DOING!
YOU GOTTA KEEP YOUR HEAD DOWN, AND JUST DO YOUR JOB!
HOW DO I FEEL? WELL, IT'S MY JOB. THIS IS WHAT I'VE BEEN TRAINED FOR!
SURE, I GET SCARED SOMETIMES, BUT I GOT A JOB TO DO HERE...
ENGLAND
PRAIRIE VILLAGE, KS
PHILADELPHIA
hong
WE'RE JUST DOING THE JOB WE'RE BEING PAID TO DO!
BOOM!
POW!
TONIGHT: "AMERICA AT WORK"!
ABOUT TIME...
GBTrudeau

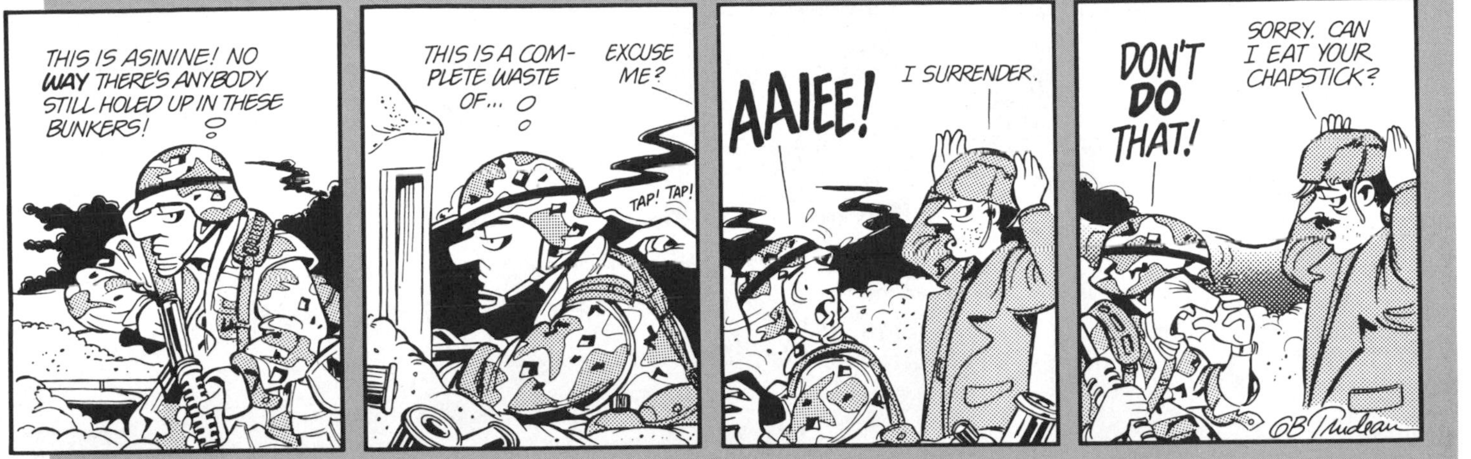
THIS IS ASININE! NO WAY THERE'S ANYBODY STILL HOLED UP IN THESE BUNKERS!
THIS IS A COMPLETE WASTE OF...
EXCUSE ME?
TAP! TAP!
AAIEE!
I SURRENDER.
DON'T DO THAT!
SORRY. CAN I EAT YOUR CHAPSTICK?
©B Trudeau

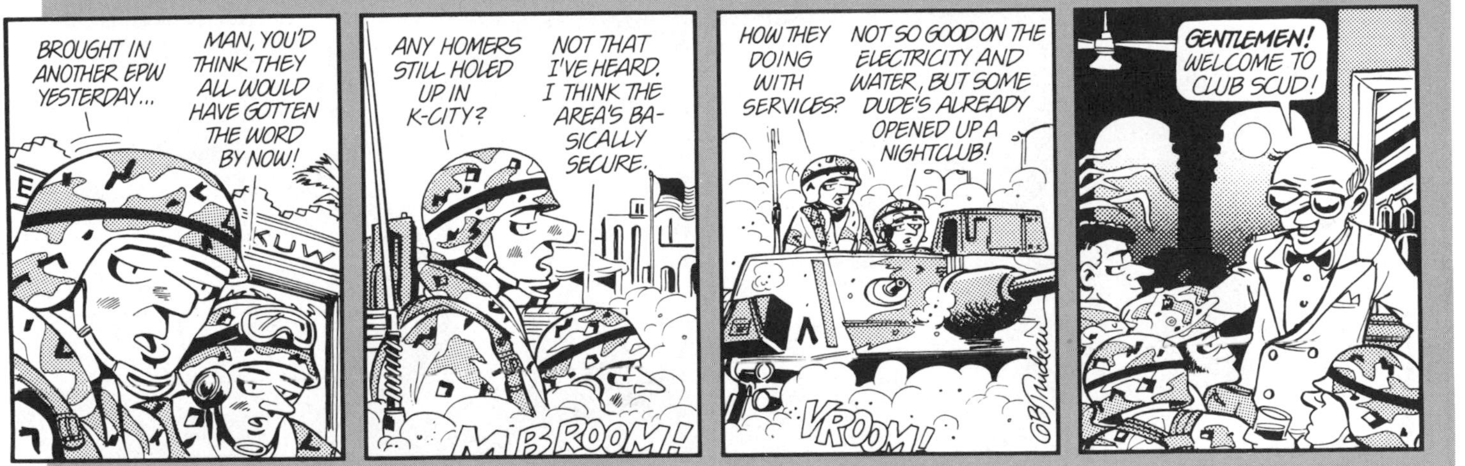
BROUGHT IN ANOTHER EPW YESTERDAY...
MAN, YOU'D THINK THEY ALL WOULD HAVE GOTTEN THE WORD BY NOW!
KUW
ANY HOMERS STILL HOLED UP IN K-CITY?
NOT THAT I'VE HEARD. I THINK THE AREA'S BASICALLY SECURE.
MBROOM!
HOW THEY DOING WITH SERVICES?
NOT SO GOOD ON THE ELECTRICITY AND WATER, BUT SOME DUDE'S ALREADY OPENED UP A NIGHTCLUB!
VROOM!
©B Trudeau
GENTLEMEN! WELCOME TO CLUB SCUD!

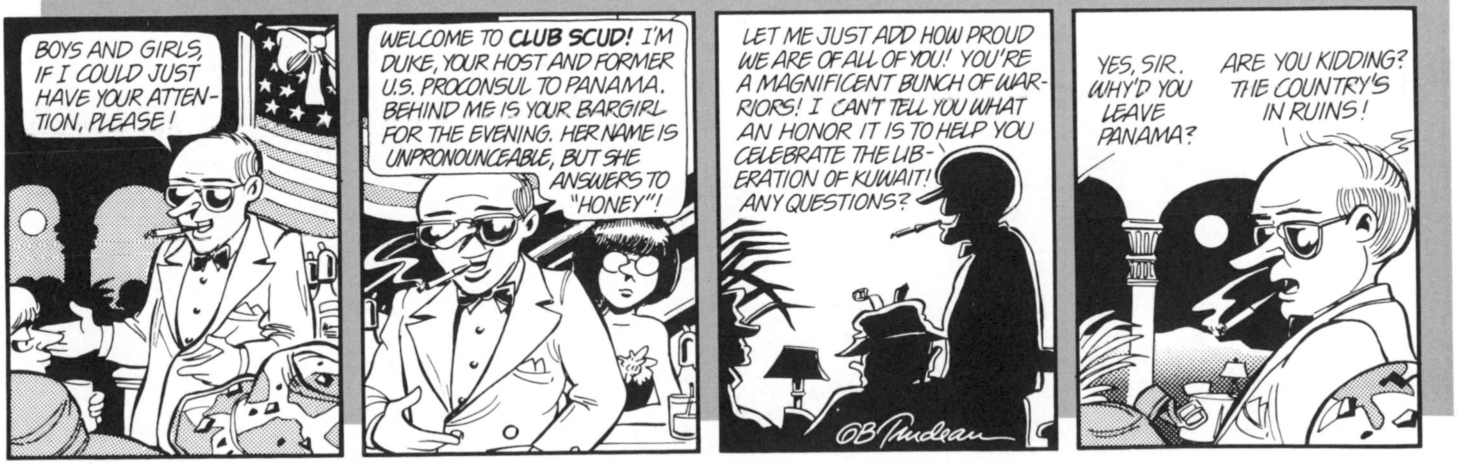
BOYS AND GIRLS, IF I COULD JUST HAVE YOUR ATTENTION, PLEASE!
WELCOME TO CLUB SCUD! I'M DUKE, YOUR HOST AND FORMER U.S. PROCONSUL TO PANAMA. BEHIND ME IS YOUR BARGIRL FOR THE EVENING. HER NAME IS UNPRONOUNCEABLE, BUT SHE ANSWERS TO "HONEY"!
LET ME JUST ADD HOW PROUD WE ARE OF ALL OF YOU! YOU'RE A MAGNIFICENT BUNCH OF WARRIORS! I CAN'T TELL YOU WHAT AN HONOR IT IS TO HELP YOU CELEBRATE THE LIBERATION OF KUWAIT! ANY QUESTIONS?
©B Trudeau
YES, SIR. WHY'D YOU LEAVE PANAMA?
ARE YOU KIDDING? THE COUNTRY'S IN RUINS!

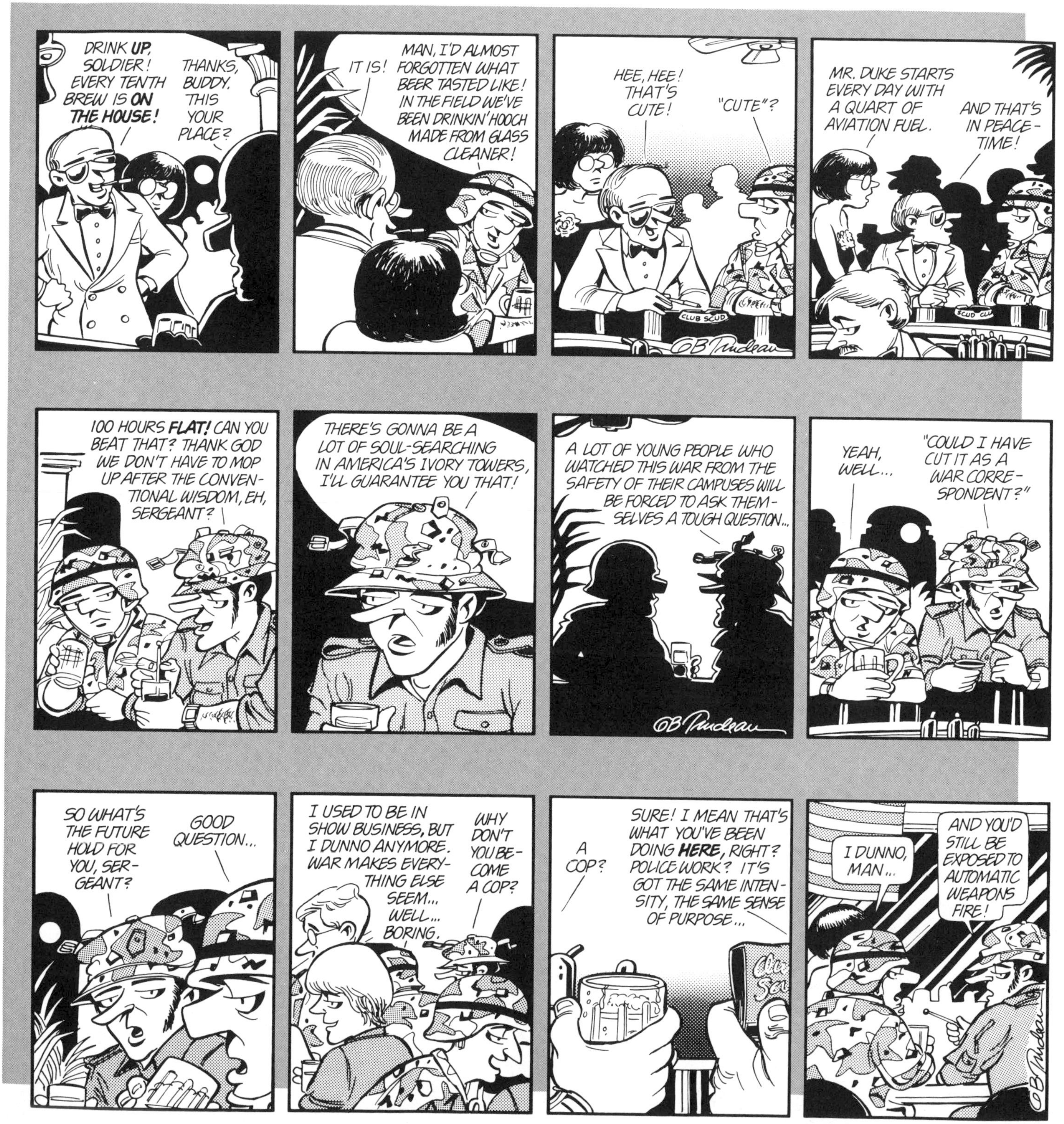
DRINK UP, SOLDIER! EVERY TENTH BREW IS ON THE HOUSE!
THANKS, BUDDY. THIS YOUR PLACE?
IT IS!
MAN, I'D ALMOST FORGOTTEN WHAT BEER TASTED LIKE! IN THE FIELD WE'VE BEEN DRINKIN' HOOCH MADE FROM GLASS CLEANER!
HEE, HEE! THAT'S CUTE!
"CUTE"?
CLUB SCUD
MR. DUKE STARTS EVERY DAY WITH A QUART OF AVIATION FUEL.
AND THAT'S IN PEACE-TIME!
SCUD
100 HOURS FLAT! CAN YOU BEAT THAT? THANK GOD WE DON'T HAVE TO MOP UP AFTER THE CONVENTIONAL WISDOM, EH, SERGEANT?
THERE'S GONNA BE A LOT OF SOUL-SEARCHING IN AMERICA'S IVORY TOWERS, I'LL GUARANTEE YOU THAT!
A LOT OF YOUNG PEOPLE WHO WATCHED THIS WAR FROM THE SAFETY OF THEIR CAMPUSES WILL BE FORCED TO ASK THEMSELVES A TOUGH QUESTION...
YEAH, WELL...
"COULD I HAVE CUT IT AS A WAR CORRESPONDENT?"
SO WHAT'S THE FUTURE HOLD FOR YOU, SERGEANT?
GOOD QUESTION...
I USED TO BE IN SHOW BUSINESS, BUT I DUNNO ANYMORE. WAR MAKES EVERYTHING ELSE SEEM... WELL... BORING.
WHY DON'T YOU BECOME A COP?
A COP?
SURE! I MEAN THAT'S WHAT YOU'VE BEEN DOING HERE, RIGHT? POLICE WORK? IT'S GOT THE SAME INTENSITY, THE SAME SENSE OF PURPOSE...
I DUNNO, MAN...
AND YOU'D STILL BE EXPOSED TO AUTOMATIC WEAPONS FIRE!

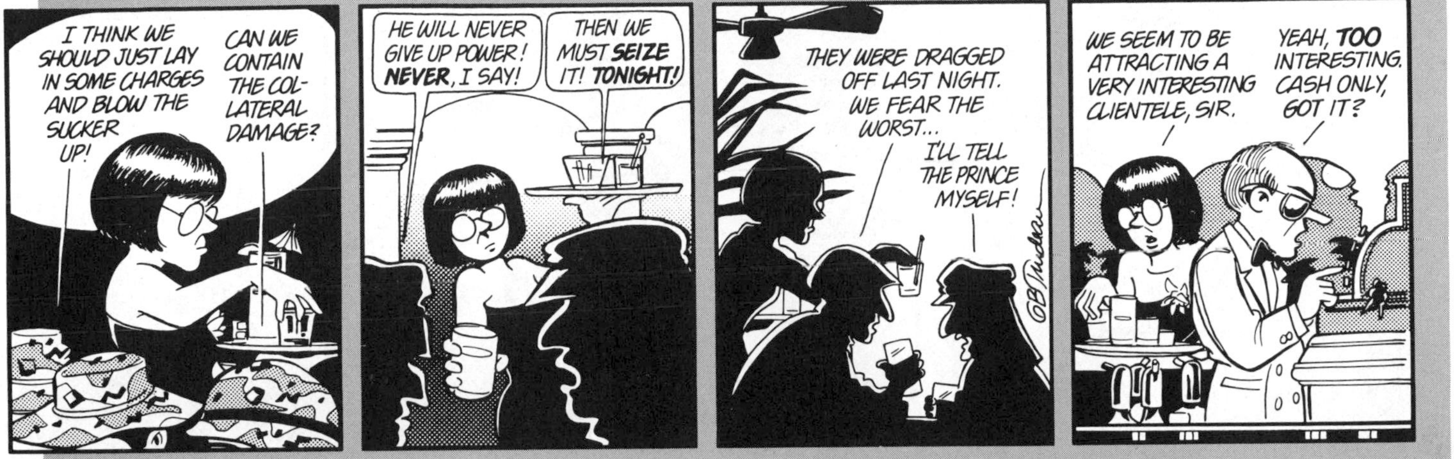
I THINK WE SHOULD JUST LAY IN SOME CHARGES AND BLOW THE SUCKER UP!
CAN WE CONTAIN THE COLLATERAL DAMAGE?
HE WILL NEVER GIVE UP POWER! NEVER, I SAY!
THEN WE MUST SEIZE IT! TONIGHT!
THEY WERE DRAGGED OFF LAST NIGHT. WE FEAR THE WORST...
I'LL TELL THE PRINCE MYSELF!
WE SEEM TO BE ATTRACTING A VERY INTERESTING CLIENTELE, SIR.
YEAH, TOO INTERESTING. CASH ONLY, GOT IT?
GB Trudeau

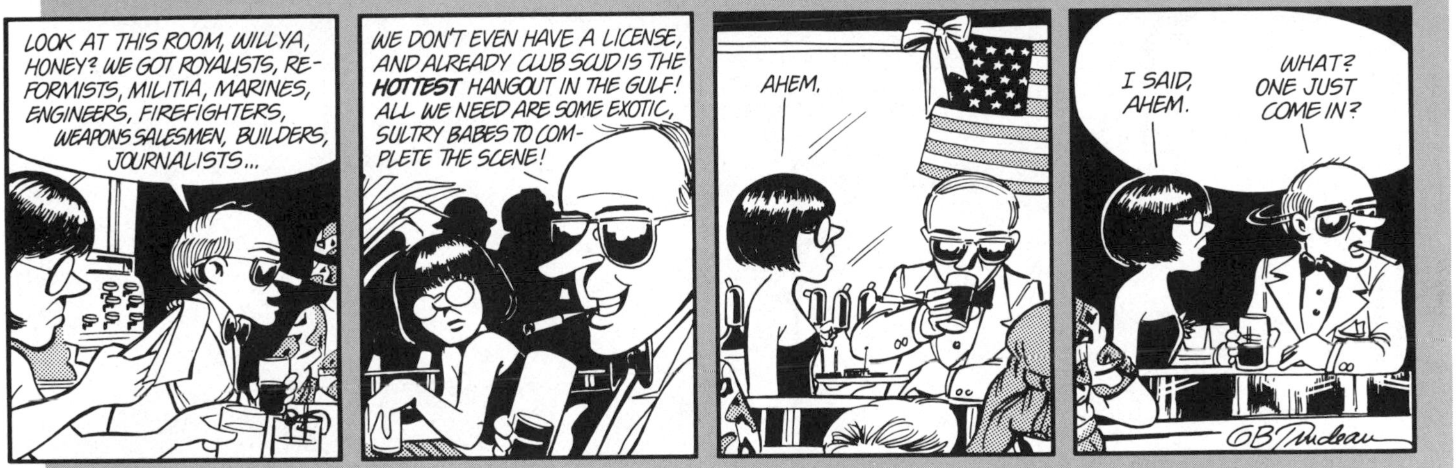
LOOK AT THIS ROOM, WILLYA, HONEY? WE GOT ROYALISTS, REFORMISTS, MILITIA, MARINES, ENGINEERS, FIREFIGHTERS, WEAPONS SALESMEN, BUILDERS, JOURNALISTS...
WE DON'T EVEN HAVE A LICENSE, AND ALREADY CLUB SCUD IS THE HOTTEST HANGOUT IN THE GULF! ALL WE NEED ARE SOME EXOTIC, SULTRY BABES TO COMPLETE THE SCENE!
AHEM.
I SAID, AHEM.
WHAT? ONE JUST COME IN?
GB Trudeau

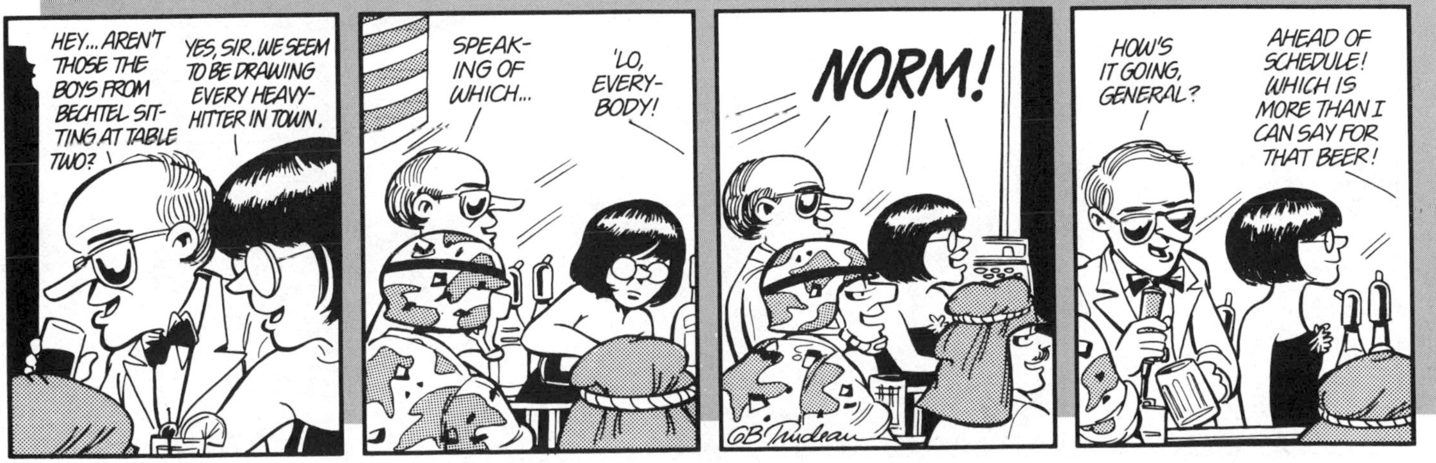
HEY... AREN'T THOSE THE BOYS FROM BECHTEL SITTING AT TABLE TWO?
YES, SIR. WE SEEM TO BE DRAWING EVERY HEAVY-HITTER IN TOWN.
SPEAKING OF WHICH...
'LO, EVERYBODY!
NORM!
GB Trudeau
HOW'S IT GOING, GENERAL?
AHEAD OF SCHEDULE! WHICH IS MORE THAN I CAN SAY FOR THAT BEER!

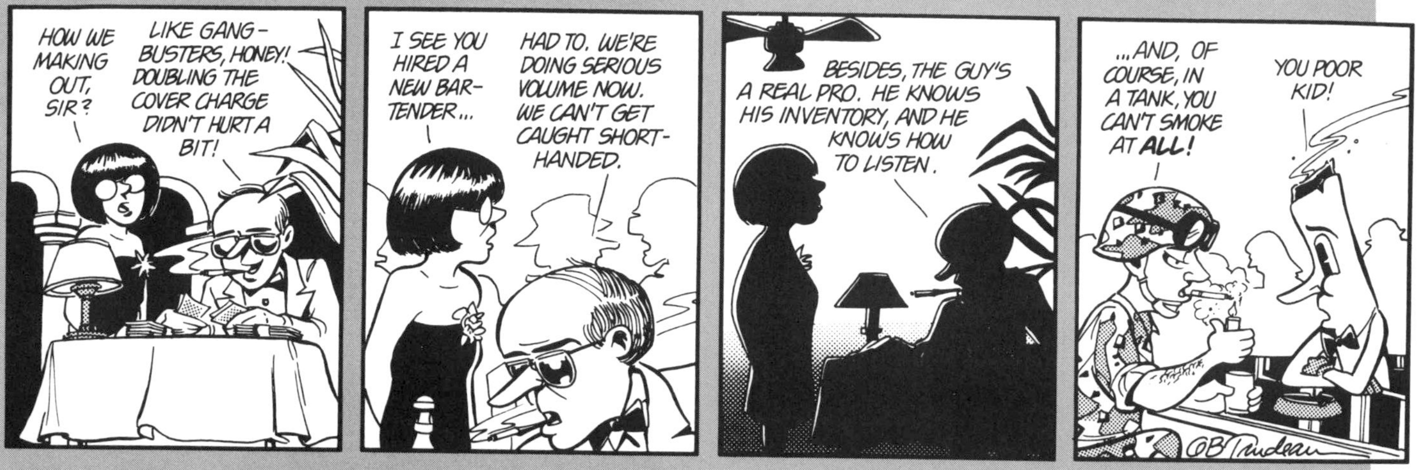
HOW WE MAKING OUT, SIR?
LIKE GANG-BUSTERS, HONEY! DOUBLING THE COVER CHARGE DIDN'T HURT A BIT!
I SEE YOU HIRED A NEW BAR-TENDER...
HAD TO. WE'RE DOING SERIOUS VOLUME NOW. WE CAN'T GET CAUGHT SHORT-HANDED.
BESIDES, THE GUY'S A REAL PRO. HE KNOWS HIS INVENTORY, AND HE KNOWS HOW TO LISTEN.
...AND, OF COURSE, IN A TANK, YOU CAN'T SMOKE AT **ALL!**
YOU POOR KID!

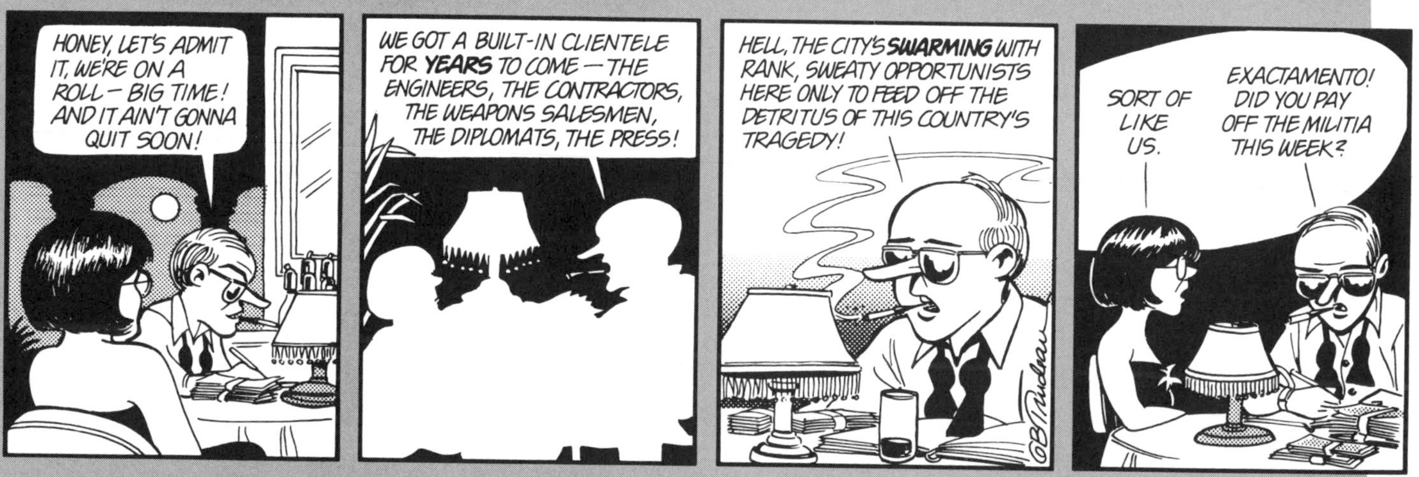
HONEY, LET'S ADMIT IT, WE'RE ON A ROLL – BIG TIME! AND IT AIN'T GONNA QUIT SOON!
WE GOT A BUILT-IN CLIENTELE FOR **YEARS** TO COME — THE ENGINEERS, THE CONTRACTORS, THE WEAPONS SALESMEN, THE DIPLOMATS, THE PRESS!
HELL, THE CITY'S **SWARMING** WITH RANK, SWEATY OPPORTUNISTS HERE ONLY TO FEED OFF THE DETRITUS OF THIS COUNTRY'S TRAGEDY!
SORT OF LIKE US.
EXACTAMENTO! DID YOU PAY OFF THE MILITIA THIS WEEK?

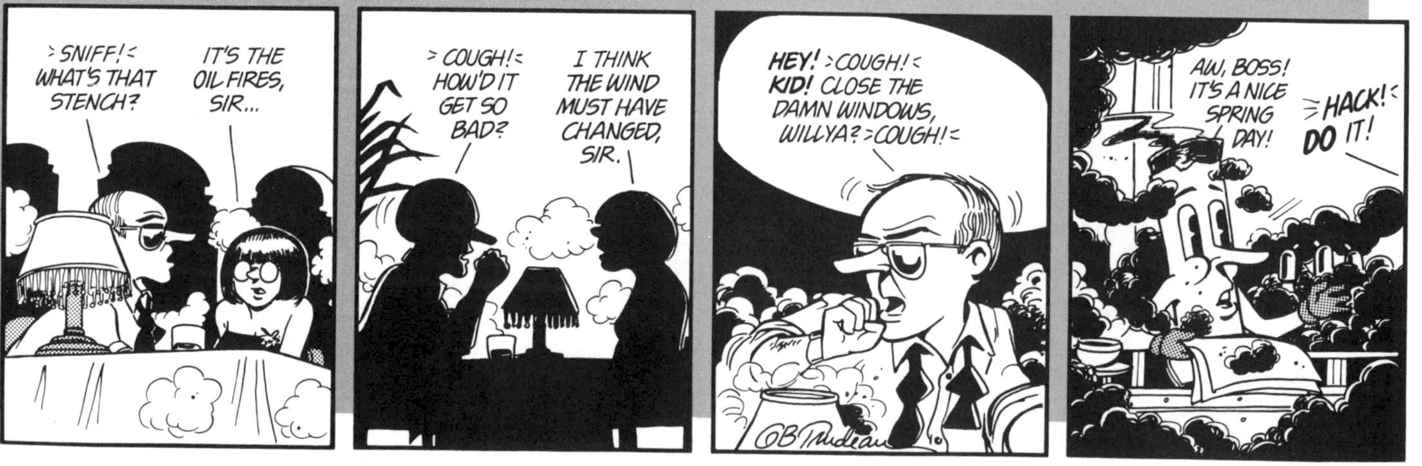
>SNIFF!< WHAT'S THAT STENCH?
IT'S THE OIL FIRES, SIR...
>COUGH!< HOW'D IT GET SO BAD?
I THINK THE WIND MUST HAVE CHANGED, SIR.
HEY! >COUGH!< **KID!** CLOSE THE DAMN WINDOWS, WILLYA? >COUGH!<
AW, BOSS! IT'S A NICE SPRING DAY!
>**HACK!**< **DO** IT!

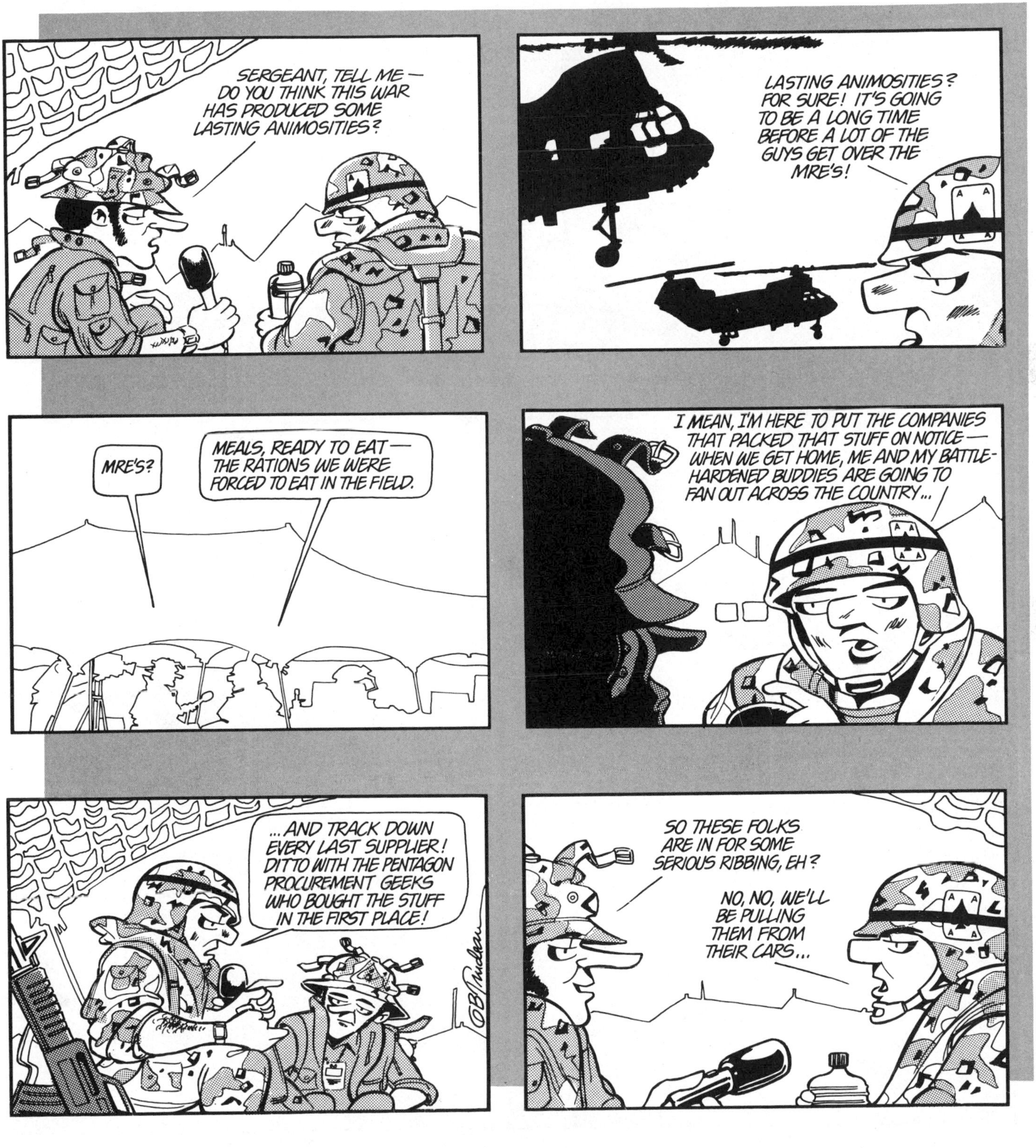
SERGEANT, TELL ME — DO YOU THINK THIS WAR HAS PRODUCED SOME LASTING ANIMOSITIES?
LASTING ANIMOSITIES? FOR SURE! IT'S GOING TO BE A LONG TIME BEFORE A LOT OF THE GUYS GET OVER THE MRE'S!
MRE'S?
MEALS, READY TO EAT — THE RATIONS WE WERE FORCED TO EAT IN THE FIELD.
I MEAN, I'M HERE TO PUT THE COMPANIES THAT PACKED THAT STUFF ON NOTICE — WHEN WE GET HOME, ME AND MY BATTLE-HARDENED BUDDIES ARE GOING TO FAN OUT ACROSS THE COUNTRY...
...AND TRACK DOWN EVERY LAST SUPPLIER! DITTO WITH THE PENTAGON PROCUREMENT GEEKS WHO BOUGHT THE STUFF IN THE FIRST PLACE!
SO THESE FOLKS ARE IN FOR SOME SERIOUS RIBBING, EH?
NO, NO, WE'LL BE PULLING THEM FROM THEIR CARS...

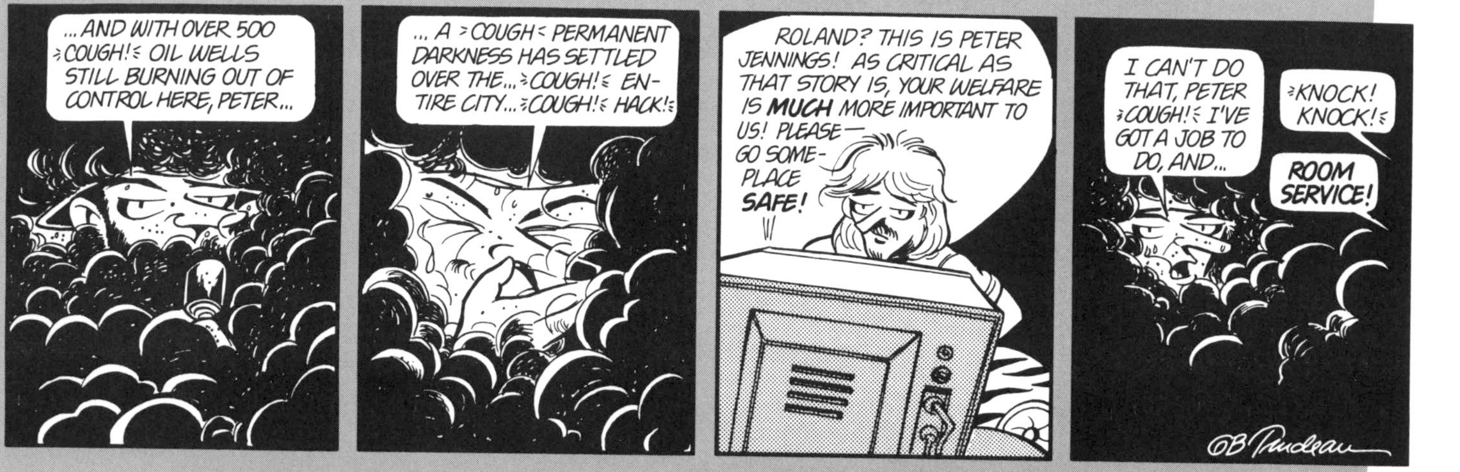
...AND WITH OVER 500 ≷COUGH!≷ OIL WELLS STILL BURNING OUT OF CONTROL HERE, PETER...
... A ≷COUGH≷ PERMANENT DARKNESS HAS SETTLED OVER THE... ≷COUGH!≷ ENTIRE CITY... ≷COUGH!≷ HACK!≷
ROLAND? THIS IS PETER JENNINGS! AS CRITICAL AS THAT STORY IS, YOUR WELFARE IS **MUCH** MORE IMPORTANT TO US! PLEASE— GO SOME-PLACE **SAFE**!
I CAN'T DO THAT, PETER ≷COUGH!≷ I'VE GOT A JOB TO DO, AND...
≷KNOCK! KNOCK!≷
ROOM SERVICE!
©B Trudeau

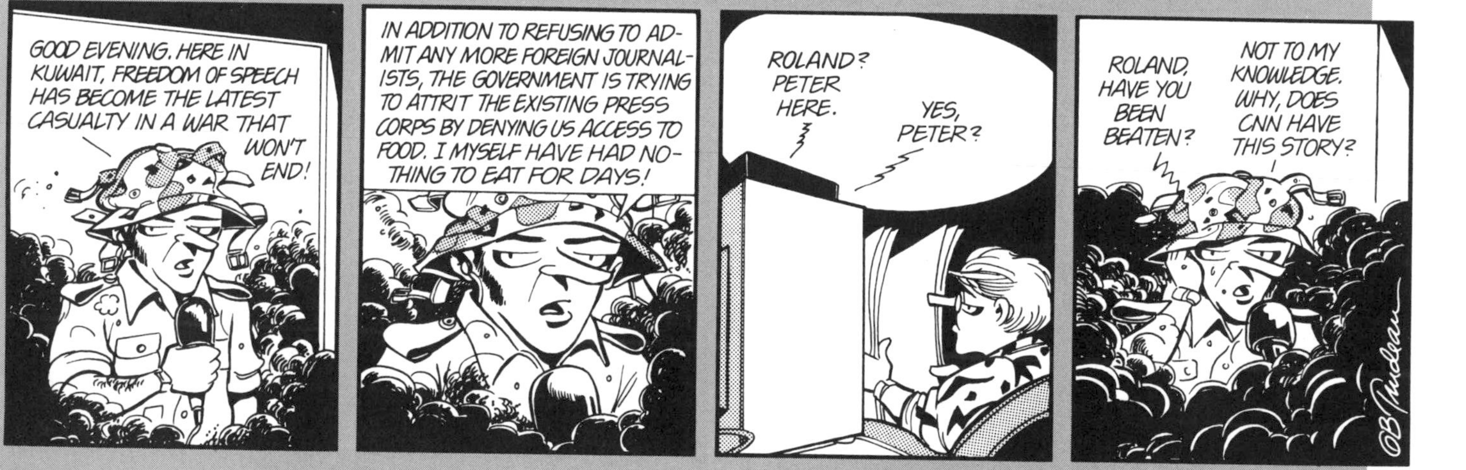
GOOD EVENING. HERE IN KUWAIT, FREEDOM OF SPEECH HAS BECOME THE LATEST CASUALTY IN A WAR THAT WON'T END!
IN ADDITION TO REFUSING TO ADMIT ANY MORE FOREIGN JOURNALISTS, THE GOVERNMENT IS TRYING TO ATTRIT THE EXISTING PRESS CORPS BY DENYING US ACCESS TO FOOD. I MYSELF HAVE HAD NOTHING TO EAT FOR DAYS!
ROLAND? PETER HERE.
YES, PETER?
ROLAND, HAVE YOU BEEN BEATEN?
NOT TO MY KNOWLEDGE. WHY, DOES CNN HAVE THIS STORY?
©B Trudeau

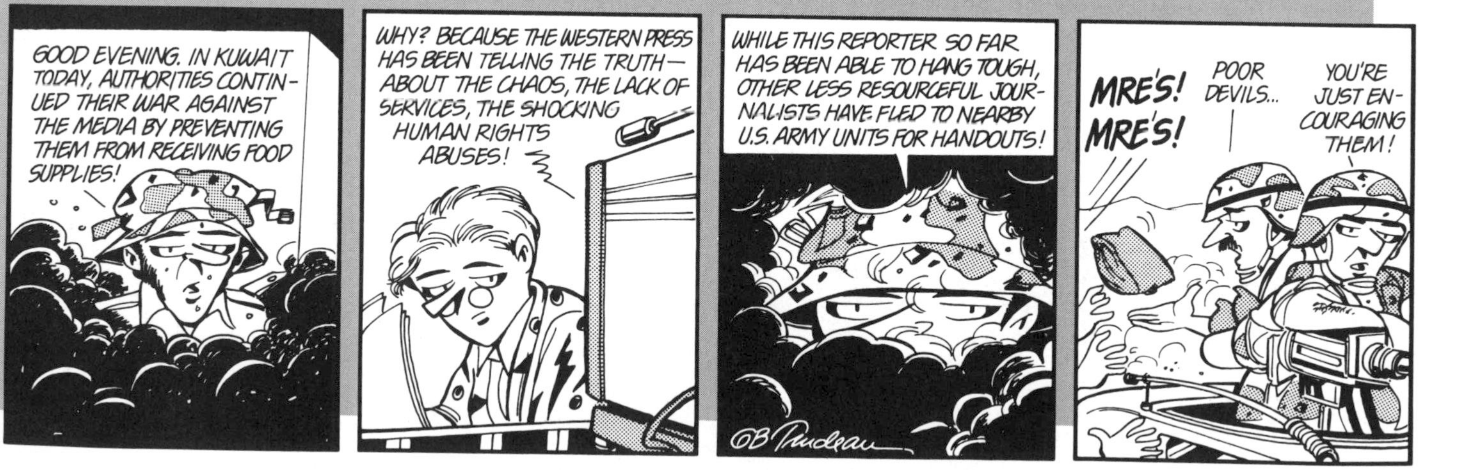
GOOD EVENING. IN KUWAIT TODAY, AUTHORITIES CONTINUED THEIR WAR AGAINST THE MEDIA BY PREVENTING THEM FROM RECEIVING FOOD SUPPLIES!
WHY? BECAUSE THE WESTERN PRESS HAS BEEN TELLING THE TRUTH— ABOUT THE CHAOS, THE LACK OF SERVICES, THE SHOCKING HUMAN RIGHTS ABUSES!
WHILE THIS REPORTER SO FAR HAS BEEN ABLE TO HANG TOUGH, OTHER LESS RESOURCEFUL JOURNALISTS HAVE FLED TO NEARBY U.S. ARMY UNITS FOR HANDOUTS!
©B Trudeau
MRE'S! MRE'S!
POOR DEVILS...
YOU'RE JUST ENCOURAGING THEM!

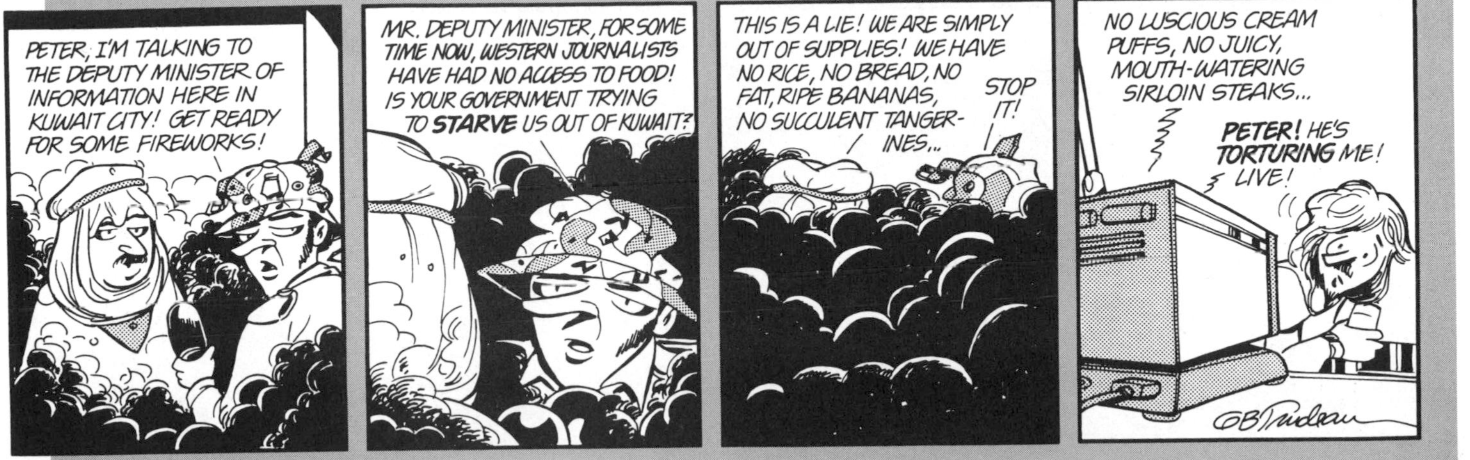
PETER, I'M TALKING TO THE DEPUTY MINISTER OF INFORMATION HERE IN KUWAIT CITY! GET READY FOR SOME FIREWORKS!
MR. DEPUTY MINISTER, FOR SOME TIME NOW, WESTERN JOURNALISTS HAVE HAD NO ACCESS TO FOOD! IS YOUR GOVERNMENT TRYING TO STARVE US OUT OF KUWAIT?
THIS IS A LIE! WE ARE SIMPLY OUT OF SUPPLIES! WE HAVE NO RICE, NO BREAD, NO FAT, RIPE BANANAS, NO SUCCULENT TANGER- INES...
STOP IT!
NO LUSCIOUS CREAM PUFFS, NO JUICY, MOUTH-WATERING SIRLOIN STEAKS...
PETER! HE'S TORTURING ME! LIVE!

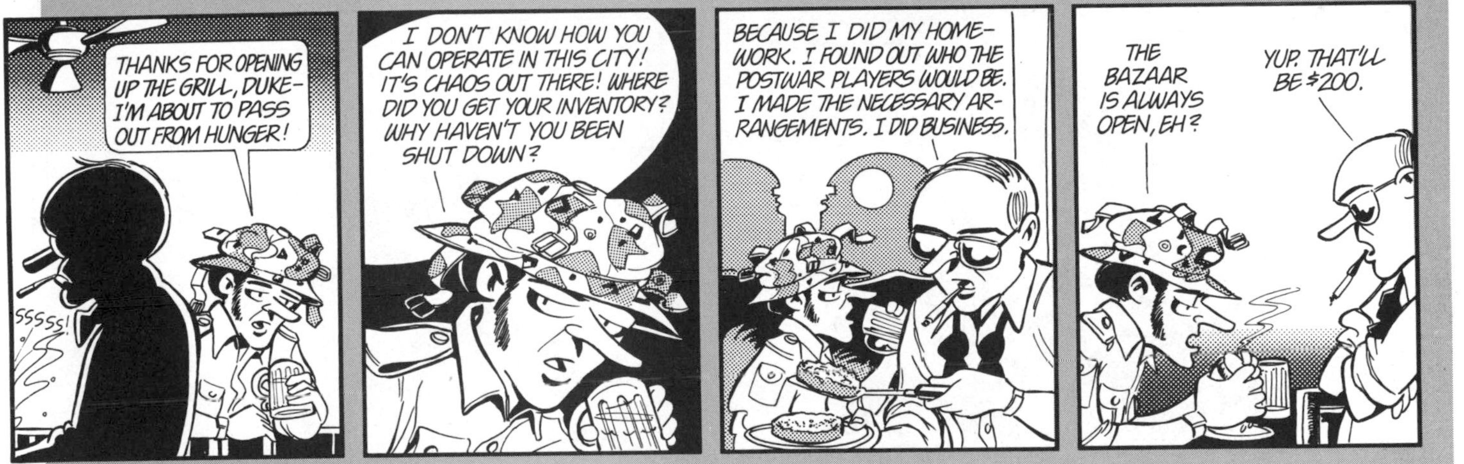
THANKS FOR OPENING UP THE GRILL, DUKE— I'M ABOUT TO PASS OUT FROM HUNGER!
SSSSS!
I DON'T KNOW HOW YOU CAN OPERATE IN THIS CITY! IT'S CHAOS OUT THERE! WHERE DID YOU GET YOUR INVENTORY? WHY HAVEN'T YOU BEEN SHUT DOWN?
BECAUSE I DID MY HOME-WORK. I FOUND OUT WHO THE POSTWAR PLAYERS WOULD BE. I MADE THE NECESSARY AR-RANGEMENTS. I DID BUSINESS.
THE BAZAAR IS ALWAYS OPEN, EH?
YUP. THAT'LL BE $200.

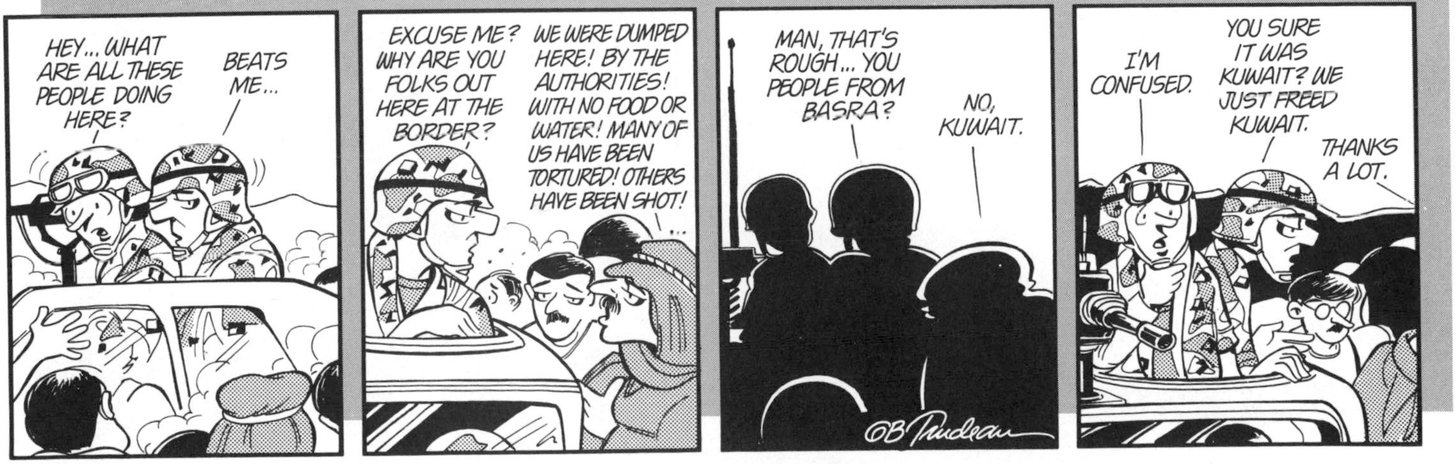
HEY... WHAT ARE ALL THESE PEOPLE DOING HERE?
BEATS ME...
EXCUSE ME? WHY ARE YOU FOLKS OUT HERE AT THE BORDER?
WE WERE DUMPED HERE! BY THE AUTHORITIES! WITH NO FOOD OR WATER! MANY OF US HAVE BEEN TORTURED! OTHERS HAVE BEEN SHOT!
MAN, THAT'S ROUGH... YOU PEOPLE FROM BASRA?
NO, KUWAIT.
I'M CONFUSED.
YOU SURE IT WAS KUWAIT? WE JUST FREED KUWAIT.
THANKS A LOT.

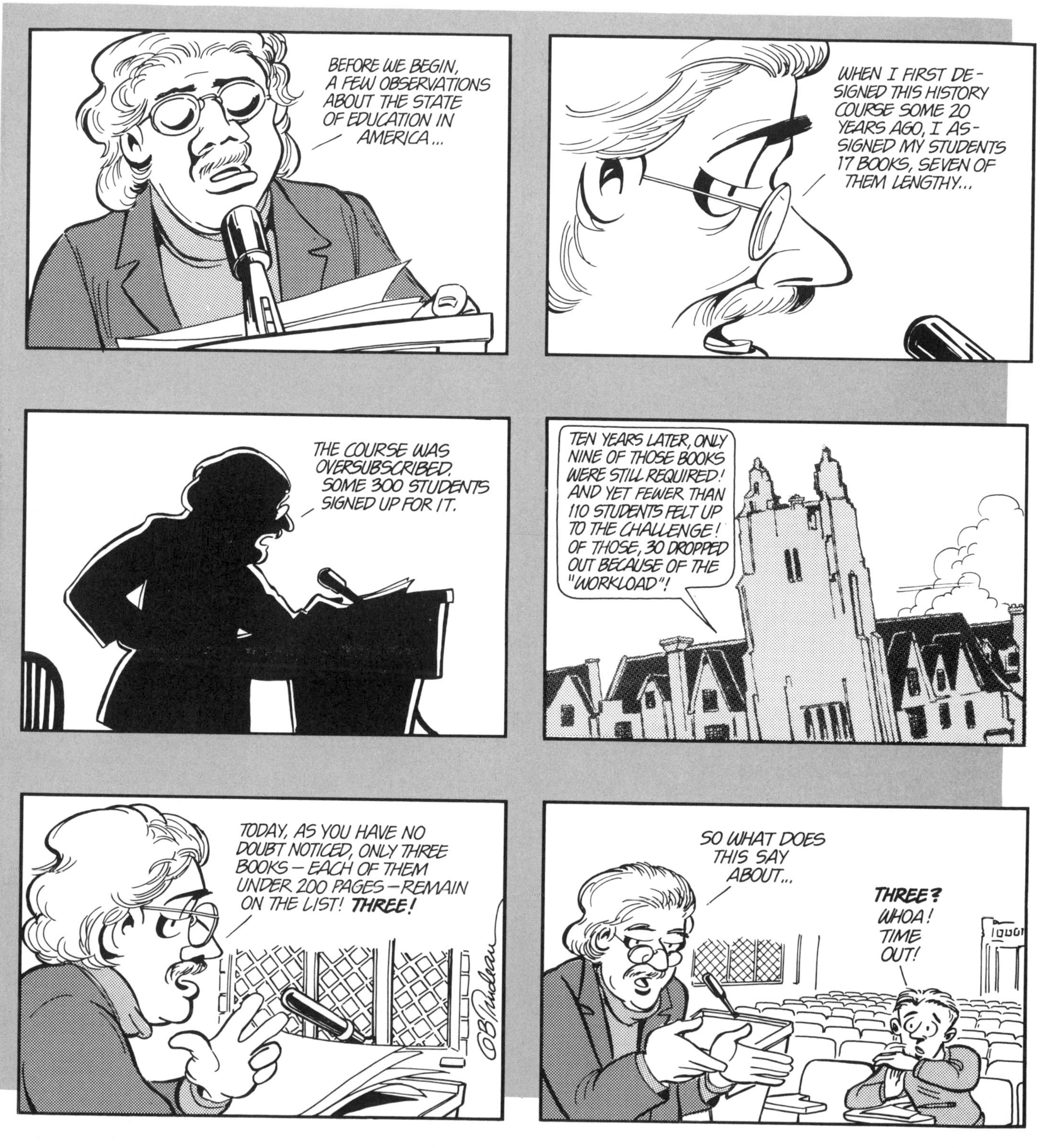
BEFORE WE BEGIN, A FEW OBSERVATIONS ABOUT THE STATE OF EDUCATION IN AMERICA...
WHEN I FIRST DE-SIGNED THIS HISTORY COURSE SOME 20 YEARS AGO, I AS-SIGNED MY STUDENTS 17 BOOKS, SEVEN OF THEM LENGTHY...
THE COURSE WAS OVERSUBSCRIBED. SOME 300 STUDENTS SIGNED UP FOR IT.
TEN YEARS LATER, ONLY NINE OF THOSE BOOKS WERE STILL REQUIRED! AND YET FEWER THAN 110 STUDENTS FELT UP TO THE CHALLENGE! OF THOSE, 30 DROPPED OUT BECAUSE OF THE "WORKLOAD"!
TODAY, AS YOU HAVE NO DOUBT NOTICED, ONLY THREE BOOKS—EACH OF THEM UNDER 200 PAGES—REMAIN ON THE LIST! **THREE!**
SO WHAT DOES THIS SAY ABOUT...
THREE? WHOA! TIME OUT!

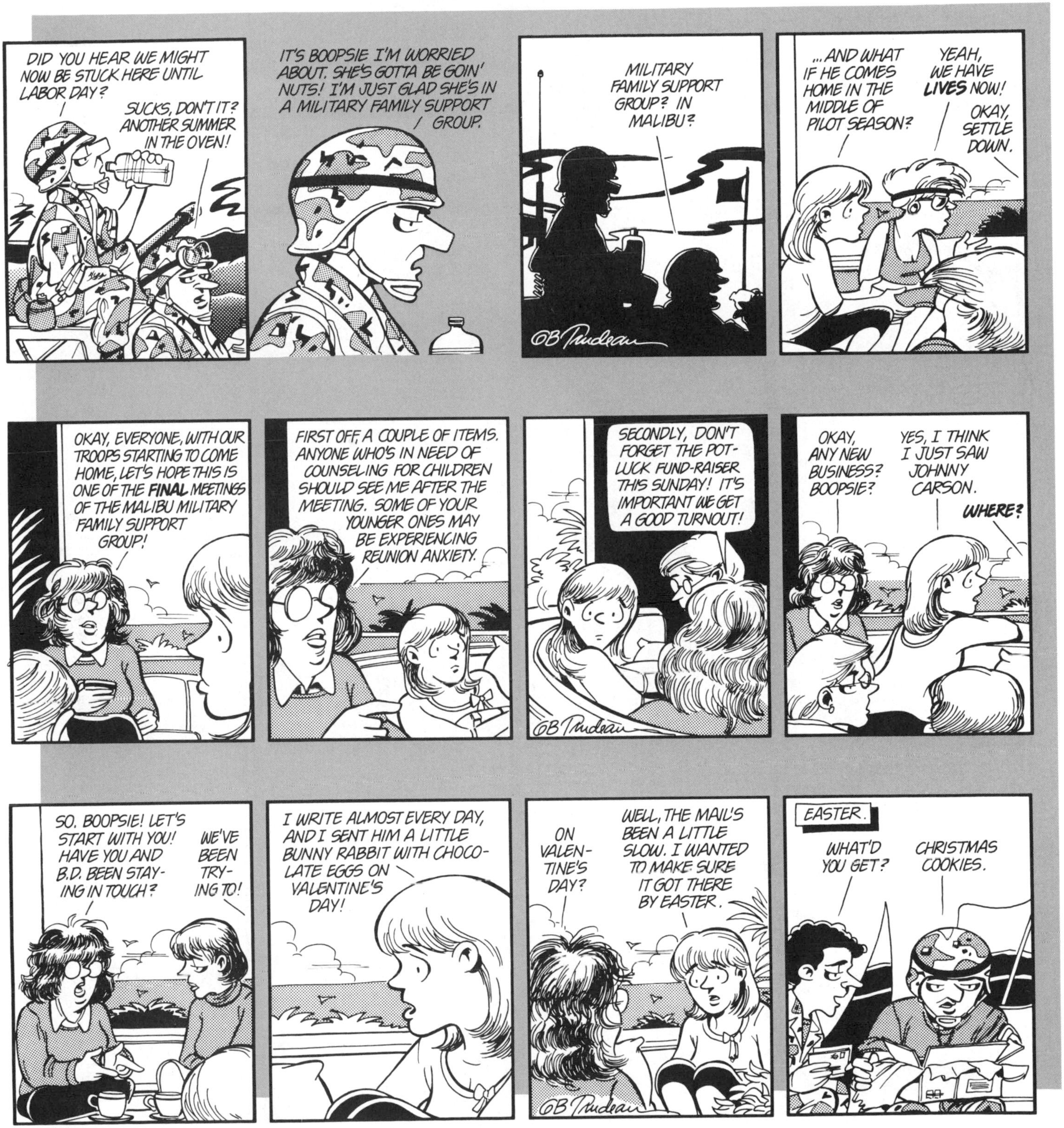
DID YOU HEAR WE MIGHT NOW BE STUCK HERE UNTIL LABOR DAY?
SUCKS, DON'T IT? ANOTHER SUMMER IN THE OVEN!
IT'S BOOPSIE I'M WORRIED ABOUT. SHE'S GOTTA BE GOIN' NUTS! I'M JUST GLAD SHE'S IN A MILITARY FAMILY SUPPORT GROUP.
MILITARY FAMILY SUPPORT GROUP? IN MALIBU?
©B Trudeau
...AND WHAT IF HE COMES HOME IN THE MIDDLE OF PILOT SEASON?
YEAH, WE HAVE LIVES NOW!
OKAY, SETTLE DOWN.
OKAY, EVERYONE, WITH OUR TROOPS STARTING TO COME HOME, LET'S HOPE THIS IS ONE OF THE FINAL MEETINGS OF THE MALIBU MILITARY FAMILY SUPPORT GROUP!
FIRST OFF, A COUPLE OF ITEMS. ANYONE WHO'S IN NEED OF COUNSELING FOR CHILDREN SHOULD SEE ME AFTER THE MEETING. SOME OF YOUR YOUNGER ONES MAY BE EXPERIENCING REUNION ANXIETY.
SECONDLY, DON'T FORGET THE POT-LUCK FUND-RAISER THIS SUNDAY! IT'S IMPORTANT WE GET A GOOD TURNOUT!
©B Trudeau
OKAY, ANY NEW BUSINESS? BOOPSIE?
YES, I THINK I JUST SAW JOHNNY CARSON.
WHERE?
SO. BOOPSIE! LET'S START WITH YOU! HAVE YOU AND B.D. BEEN STAY-ING IN TOUCH?
WE'VE BEEN TRY-ING TO!
I WRITE ALMOST EVERY DAY, AND I SENT HIM A LITTLE BUNNY RABBIT WITH CHOCO-LATE EGGS ON VALENTINE'S DAY!
ON VALEN-TINE'S DAY?
WELL, THE MAIL'S BEEN A LITTLE SLOW. I WANTED TO MAKE SURE IT GOT THERE BY EASTER.
©B Trudeau
EASTER.
WHAT'D YOU GET?
CHRISTMAS COOKIES.

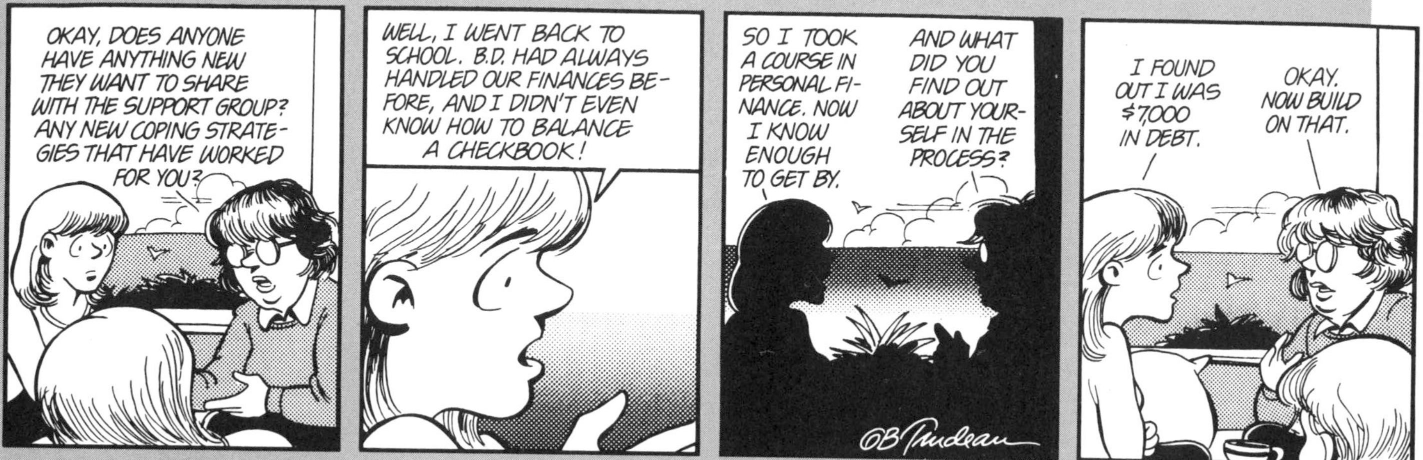
OKAY, DOES ANYONE HAVE ANYTHING NEW THEY WANT TO SHARE WITH THE SUPPORT GROUP? ANY NEW COPING STRATEGIES THAT HAVE WORKED FOR YOU?
WELL, I WENT BACK TO SCHOOL. B.D. HAD ALWAYS HANDLED OUR FINANCES BEFORE, AND I DIDN'T EVEN KNOW HOW TO BALANCE A CHECKBOOK!
SO I TOOK A COURSE IN PERSONAL FINANCE. NOW I KNOW ENOUGH TO GET BY.
AND WHAT DID YOU FIND OUT ABOUT YOURSELF IN THE PROCESS?
©B Trudeau
I FOUND OUT I WAS $7,000 IN DEBT.
OKAY. NOW BUILD ON THAT.

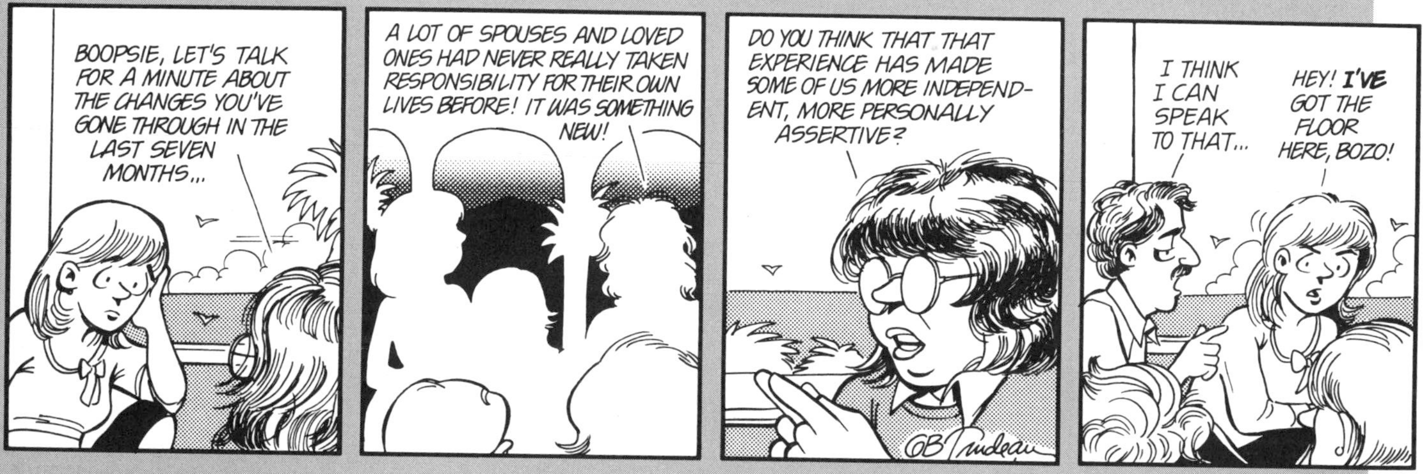
BOOPSIE, LET'S TALK FOR A MINUTE ABOUT THE CHANGES YOU'VE GONE THROUGH IN THE LAST SEVEN MONTHS...
A LOT OF SPOUSES AND LOVED ONES HAD NEVER REALLY TAKEN RESPONSIBILITY FOR THEIR OWN LIVES BEFORE! IT WAS SOMETHING NEW!
DO YOU THINK THAT THAT EXPERIENCE HAS MADE SOME OF US MORE INDEPENDENT, MORE PERSONALLY ASSERTIVE?
©B Trudeau
I THINK I CAN SPEAK TO THAT...
HEY! I'VE GOT THE FLOOR HERE, BOZO!

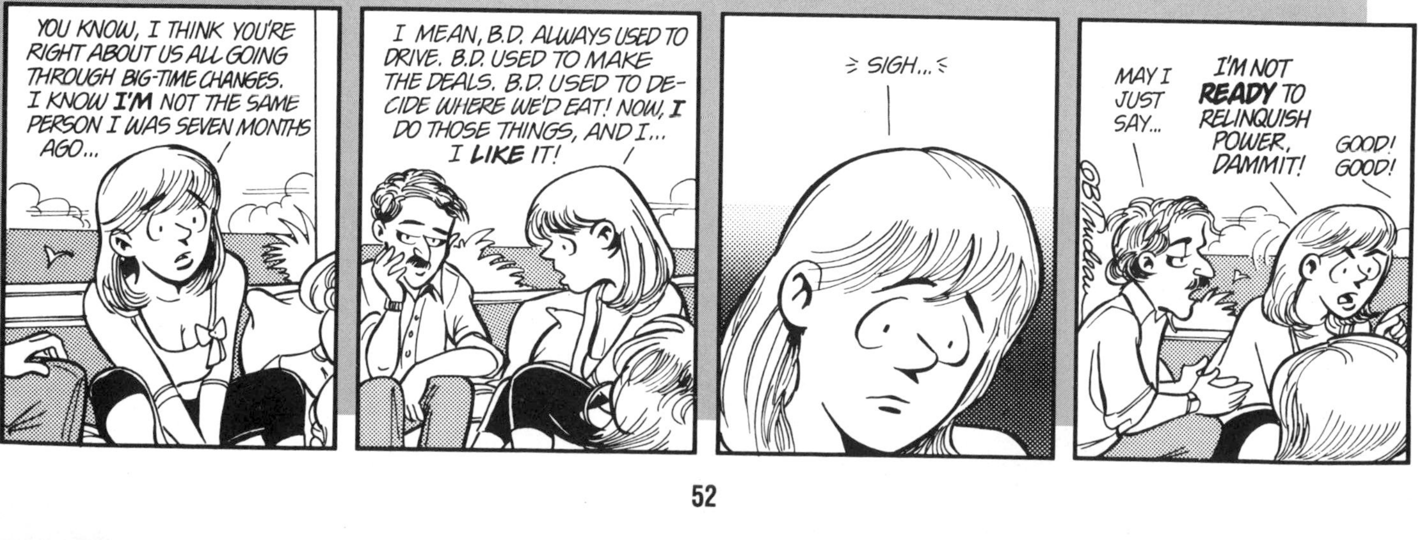
YOU KNOW, I THINK YOU'RE RIGHT ABOUT US ALL GOING THROUGH BIG-TIME CHANGES. I KNOW I'M NOT THE SAME PERSON I WAS SEVEN MONTHS AGO...
I MEAN, B.D. ALWAYS USED TO DRIVE. B.D. USED TO MAKE THE DEALS. B.D. USED TO DECIDE WHERE WE'D EAT! NOW, I DO THOSE THINGS, AND I... I LIKE IT!
SIGH...
©B Trudeau
MAY I JUST SAY...
I'M NOT READY TO RELINQUISH POWER, DAMMIT!
GOOD! GOOD!

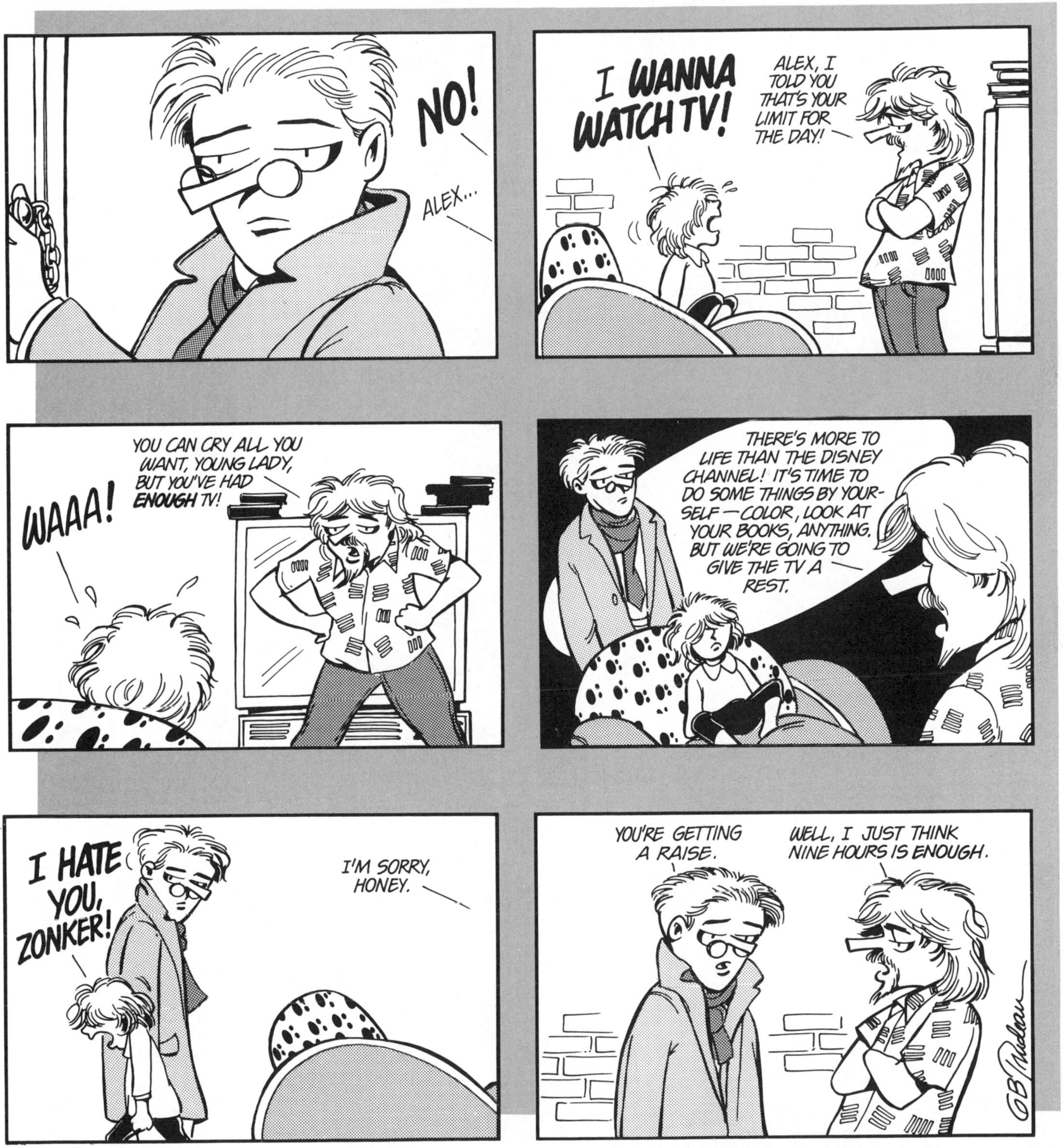
NO!
ALEX...
I WANNA WATCH TV!
ALEX, I TOLD YOU THAT'S YOUR LIMIT FOR THE DAY!
WAAA!
YOU CAN CRY ALL YOU WANT, YOUNG LADY, BUT YOU'VE HAD ENOUGH TV!
THERE'S MORE TO LIFE THAN THE DISNEY CHANNEL! IT'S TIME TO DO SOME THINGS BY YOURSELF — COLOR, LOOK AT YOUR BOOKS, ANYTHING. BUT WE'RE GOING TO GIVE THE TV A REST.
I HATE YOU, ZONKER!
I'M SORRY, HONEY.
YOU'RE GETTING A RAISE.
WELL, I JUST THINK NINE HOURS IS ENOUGH.
GB Trudeau

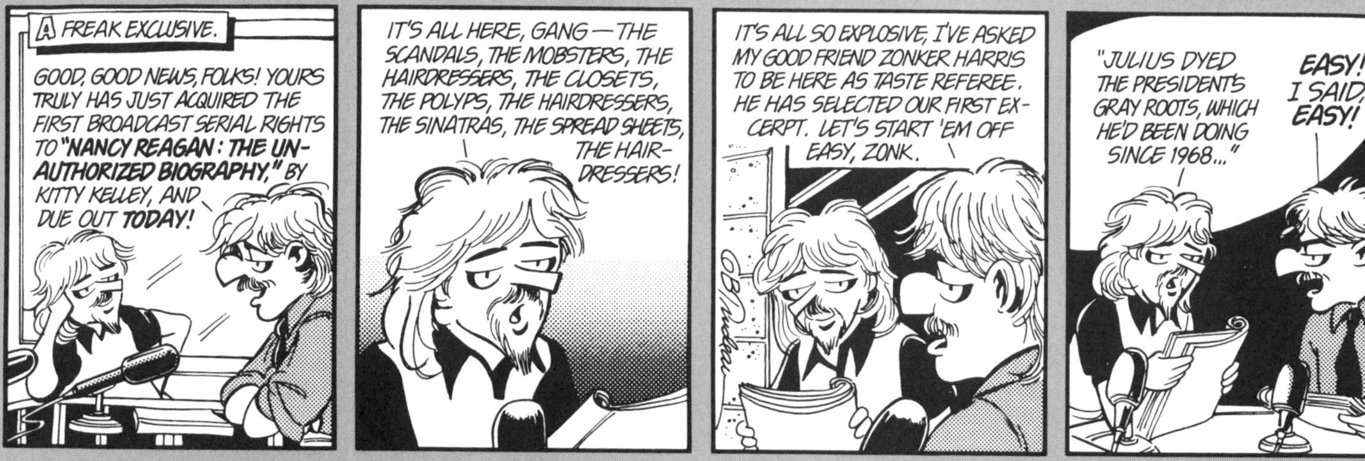
A FREAK EXCLUSIVE.
GOOD, GOOD NEWS, FOLKS! YOURS TRULY HAS JUST ACQUIRED THE FIRST BROADCAST SERIAL RIGHTS TO "NANCY REAGAN: THE UNAUTHORIZED BIOGRAPHY," BY KITTY KELLEY, AND DUE OUT TODAY!
IT'S ALL HERE, GANG — THE SCANDALS, THE MOBSTERS, THE HAIRDRESSERS, THE CLOSETS, THE POLYPS, THE HAIRDRESSERS, THE SINATRAS, THE SPREAD SHEETS, THE HAIRDRESSERS!
IT'S ALL SO EXPLOSIVE, I'VE ASKED MY GOOD FRIEND ZONKER HARRIS TO BE HERE AS TASTE REFEREE. HE HAS SELECTED OUR FIRST EXCERPT. LET'S START 'EM OFF EASY, ZONK.
"JULIUS DYED THE PRESIDENT'S GRAY ROOTS, WHICH HE'D BEEN DOING SINCE 1968..."
EASY! I SAID, EASY!

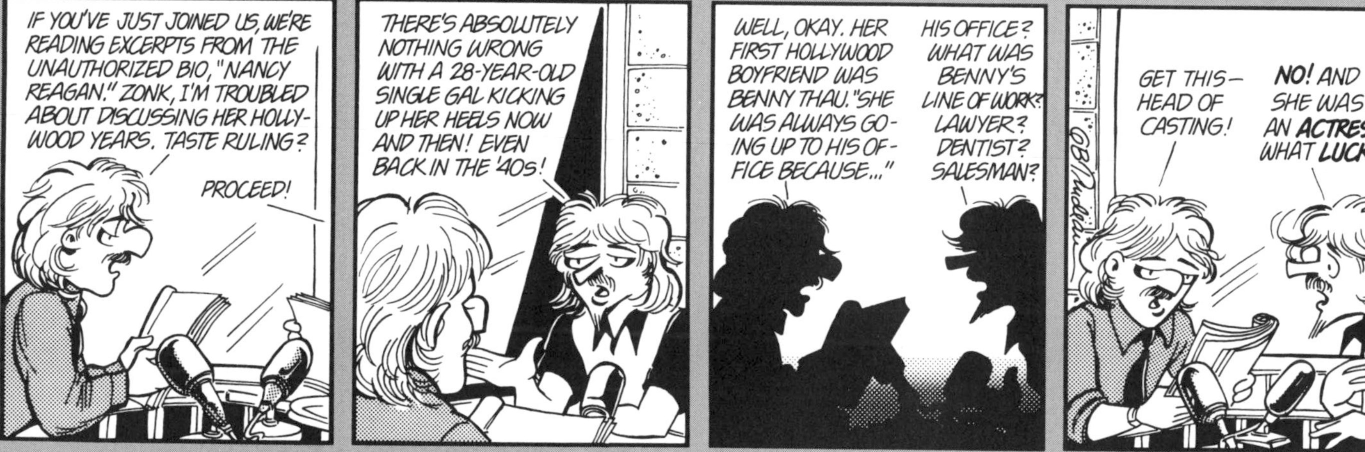
IF YOU'VE JUST JOINED US, WE'RE READING EXCERPTS FROM THE UNAUTHORIZED BIO, "NANCY REAGAN." ZONK, I'M TROUBLED ABOUT DISCUSSING HER HOLLYWOOD YEARS. TASTE RULING?
PROCEED!
THERE'S ABSOLUTELY NOTHING WRONG WITH A 28-YEAR-OLD SINGLE GAL KICKING UP HER HEELS NOW AND THEN! EVEN BACK IN THE '40s!
WELL, OKAY. HER FIRST HOLLYWOOD BOYFRIEND WAS BENNY THAU. "SHE WAS ALWAYS GOING UP TO HIS OFFICE BECAUSE..."
HIS OFFICE? WHAT WAS BENNY'S LINE OF WORK? LAWYER? DENTIST? SALESMAN?
GET THIS — HEAD OF CASTING!
NO! AND SHE WAS AN ACTRESS! WHAT LUCK!

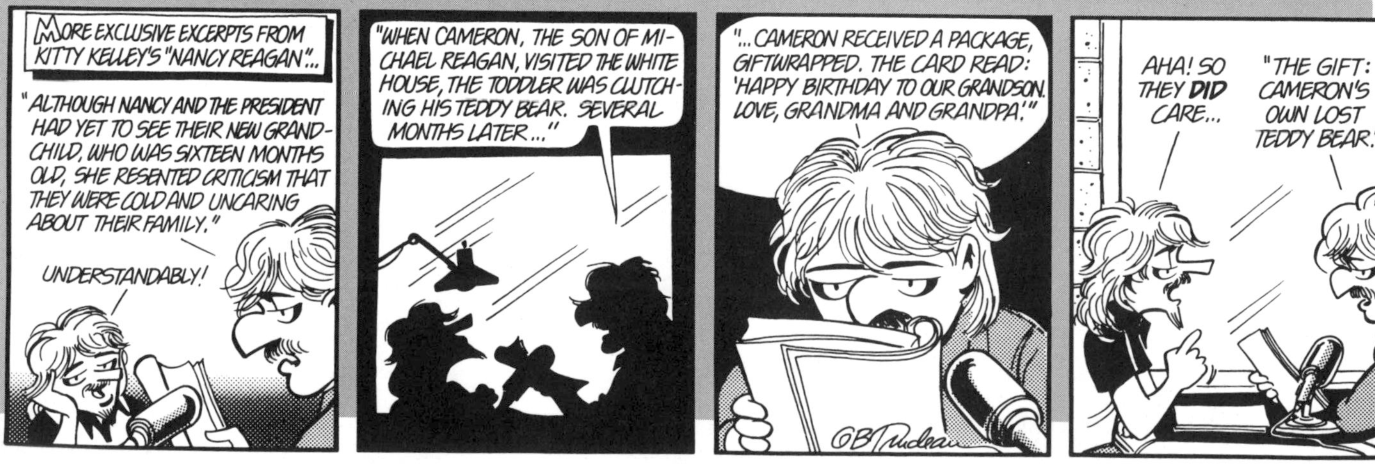
MORE EXCLUSIVE EXCERPTS FROM KITTY KELLEY'S "NANCY REAGAN"...
"ALTHOUGH NANCY AND THE PRESIDENT HAD YET TO SEE THEIR NEW GRANDCHILD, WHO WAS SIXTEEN MONTHS OLD, SHE RESENTED CRITICISM THAT THEY WERE COLD AND UNCARING ABOUT THEIR FAMILY."
UNDERSTANDABLY!
"WHEN CAMERON, THE SON OF MICHAEL REAGAN, VISITED THE WHITE HOUSE, THE TODDLER WAS CLUTCHING HIS TEDDY BEAR. SEVERAL MONTHS LATER..."
"...CAMERON RECEIVED A PACKAGE, GIFTWRAPPED. THE CARD READ: 'HAPPY BIRTHDAY TO OUR GRANDSON. LOVE, GRANDMA AND GRANDPA.'"
AHA! SO THEY DID CARE...
"THE GIFT: CAMERON'S OWN LOST TEDDY BEAR."

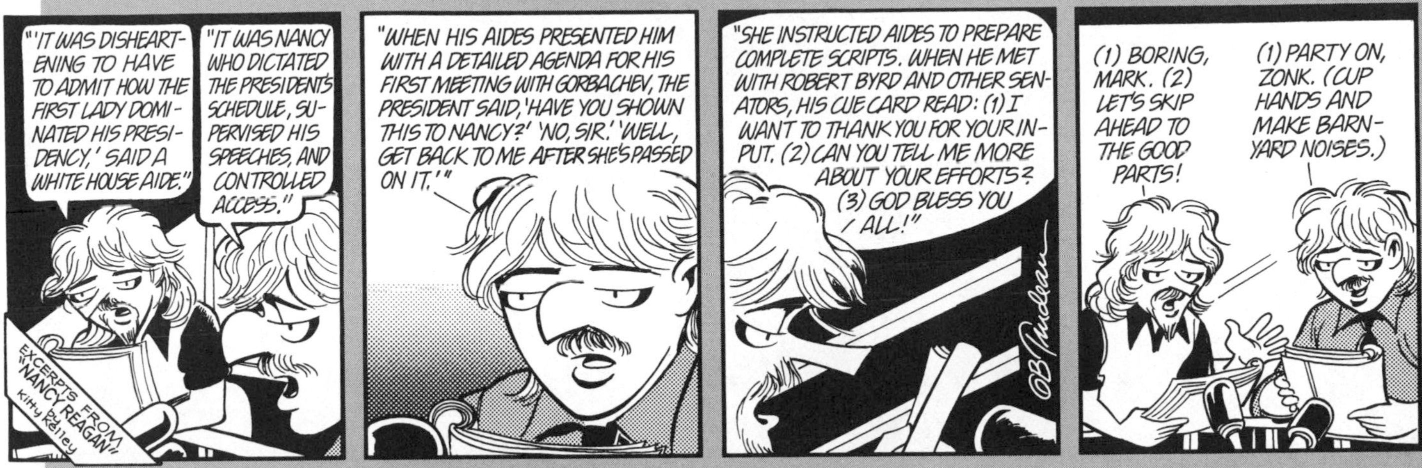
"'IT WAS DISHEARTENING TO HAVE TO ADMIT HOW THE FIRST LADY DOMINATED HIS PRESIDENCY,' SAID A WHITE HOUSE AIDE."
"IT WAS NANCY WHO DICTATED THE PRESIDENT'S SCHEDULE, SUPERVISED HIS SPEECHES, AND CONTROLLED ACCESS."
EXCERPTS FROM "NANCY REAGAN" By Kitty Kelley
"WHEN HIS AIDES PRESENTED HIM WITH A DETAILED AGENDA FOR HIS FIRST MEETING WITH GORBACHEV, THE PRESIDENT SAID, 'HAVE YOU SHOWN THIS TO NANCY?' 'NO, SIR.' 'WELL, GET BACK TO ME AFTER SHE'S PASSED ON IT.'"
"SHE INSTRUCTED AIDES TO PREPARE COMPLETE SCRIPTS. WHEN HE MET WITH ROBERT BYRD AND OTHER SENATORS, HIS CUE CARD READ: (1) I WANT TO THANK YOU FOR YOUR INPUT. (2) CAN YOU TELL ME MORE ABOUT YOUR EFFORTS? (3) GOD BLESS YOU ALL!"
(1) BORING, MARK. (2) LET'S SKIP AHEAD TO THE GOOD PARTS!
(1) PARTY ON, ZONK. (CUP HANDS AND MAKE BARNYARD NOISES.)

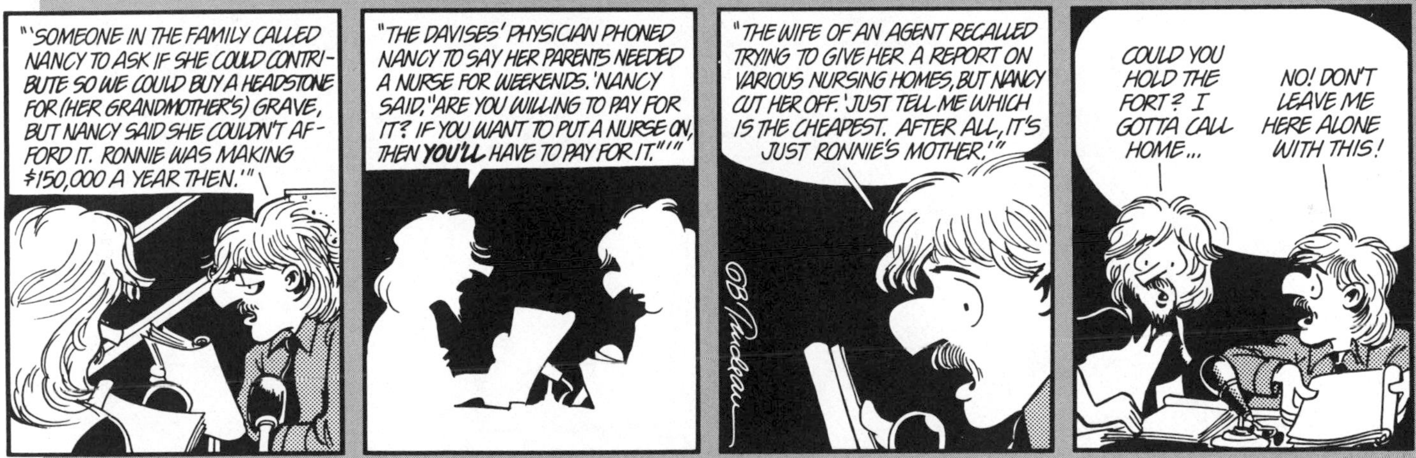
"'SOMEONE IN THE FAMILY CALLED NANCY TO ASK IF SHE COULD CONTRIBUTE SO WE COULD BUY A HEADSTONE FOR (HER GRANDMOTHER'S) GRAVE, BUT NANCY SAID SHE COULDN'T AFFORD IT. RONNIE WAS MAKING $150,000 A YEAR THEN.'"
"THE DAVISES' PHYSICIAN PHONED NANCY TO SAY HER PARENTS NEEDED A NURSE FOR WEEKENDS. 'NANCY SAID, "ARE YOU WILLING TO PAY FOR IT? IF YOU WANT TO PUT A NURSE ON, THEN YOU'LL HAVE TO PAY FOR IT."'"
"THE WIFE OF AN AGENT RECALLED TRYING TO GIVE HER A REPORT ON VARIOUS NURSING HOMES, BUT NANCY CUT HER OFF. 'JUST TELL ME WHICH IS THE CHEAPEST. AFTER ALL, IT'S JUST RONNIE'S MOTHER.'"
COULD YOU HOLD THE FORT? I GOTTA CALL HOME...
NO! DON'T LEAVE ME HERE ALONE WITH THIS!

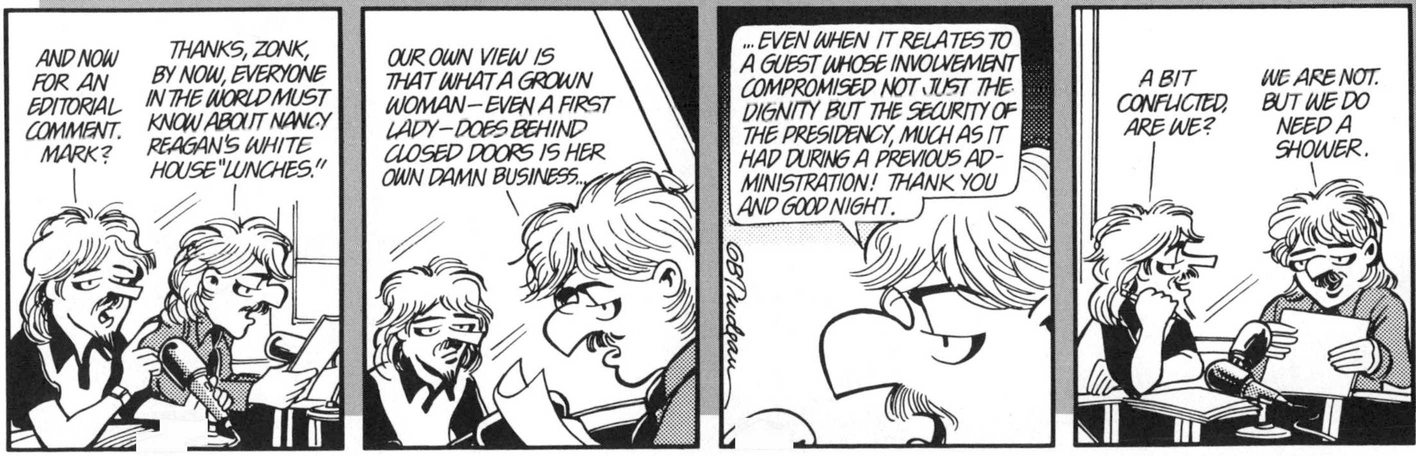
AND NOW FOR AN EDITORIAL COMMENT. MARK?
THANKS, ZONK. BY NOW, EVERYONE IN THE WORLD MUST KNOW ABOUT NANCY REAGAN'S WHITE HOUSE "LUNCHES."
OUR OWN VIEW IS THAT WHAT A GROWN WOMAN — EVEN A FIRST LADY — DOES BEHIND CLOSED DOORS IS HER OWN DAMN BUSINESS...
...EVEN WHEN IT RELATES TO A GUEST WHOSE INVOLVEMENT COMPROMISED NOT JUST THE DIGNITY BUT THE SECURITY OF THE PRESIDENCY, MUCH AS IT HAD DURING A PREVIOUS ADMINISTRATION! THANK YOU AND GOOD NIGHT.
A BIT CONFLICTED, ARE WE?
WE ARE NOT. BUT WE DO NEED A SHOWER.

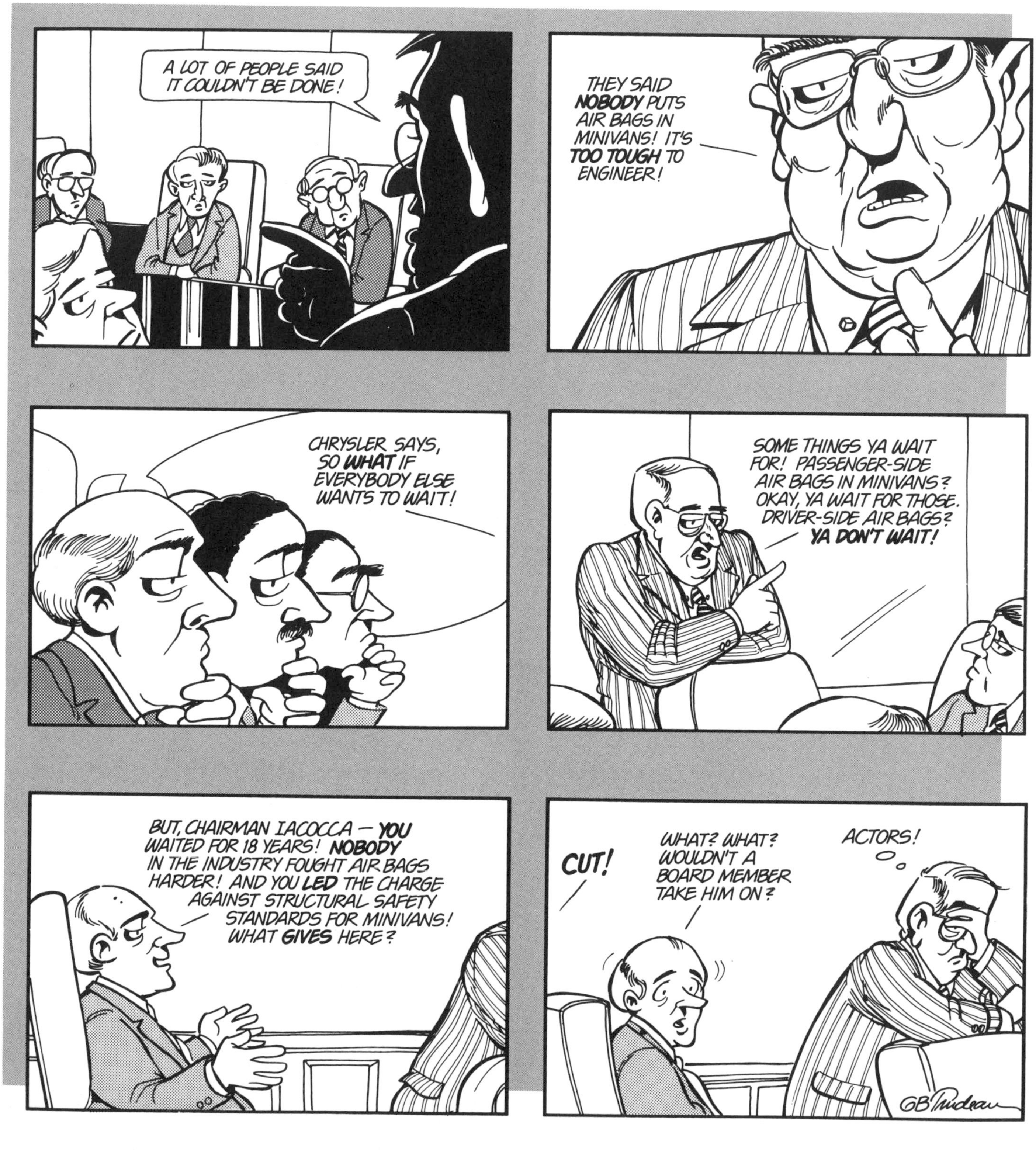

A LOT OF PEOPLE SAID IT COULDN'T BE DONE!
THEY SAID **NOBODY** PUTS AIR BAGS IN MINIVANS! IT'S **TOO TOUGH** TO ENGINEER!
CHRYSLER SAYS, SO **WHAT** IF EVERYBODY ELSE WANTS TO WAIT!
SOME THINGS YA WAIT FOR! PASSENGER-SIDE AIR BAGS IN MINIVANS? OKAY, YA WAIT FOR THOSE. DRIVER-SIDE AIR BAGS? **YA DON'T WAIT!**
BUT, CHAIRMAN IACOCCA — **YOU** WAITED FOR 18 YEARS! **NOBODY** IN THE INDUSTRY FOUGHT AIR BAGS HARDER! AND YOU **LED** THE CHARGE AGAINST STRUCTURAL SAFETY STANDARDS FOR MINIVANS! WHAT **GIVES** HERE?
CUT!
WHAT? WHAT? WOULDN'T A BOARD MEMBER TAKE HIM ON?
ACTORS!
GBTrudeau

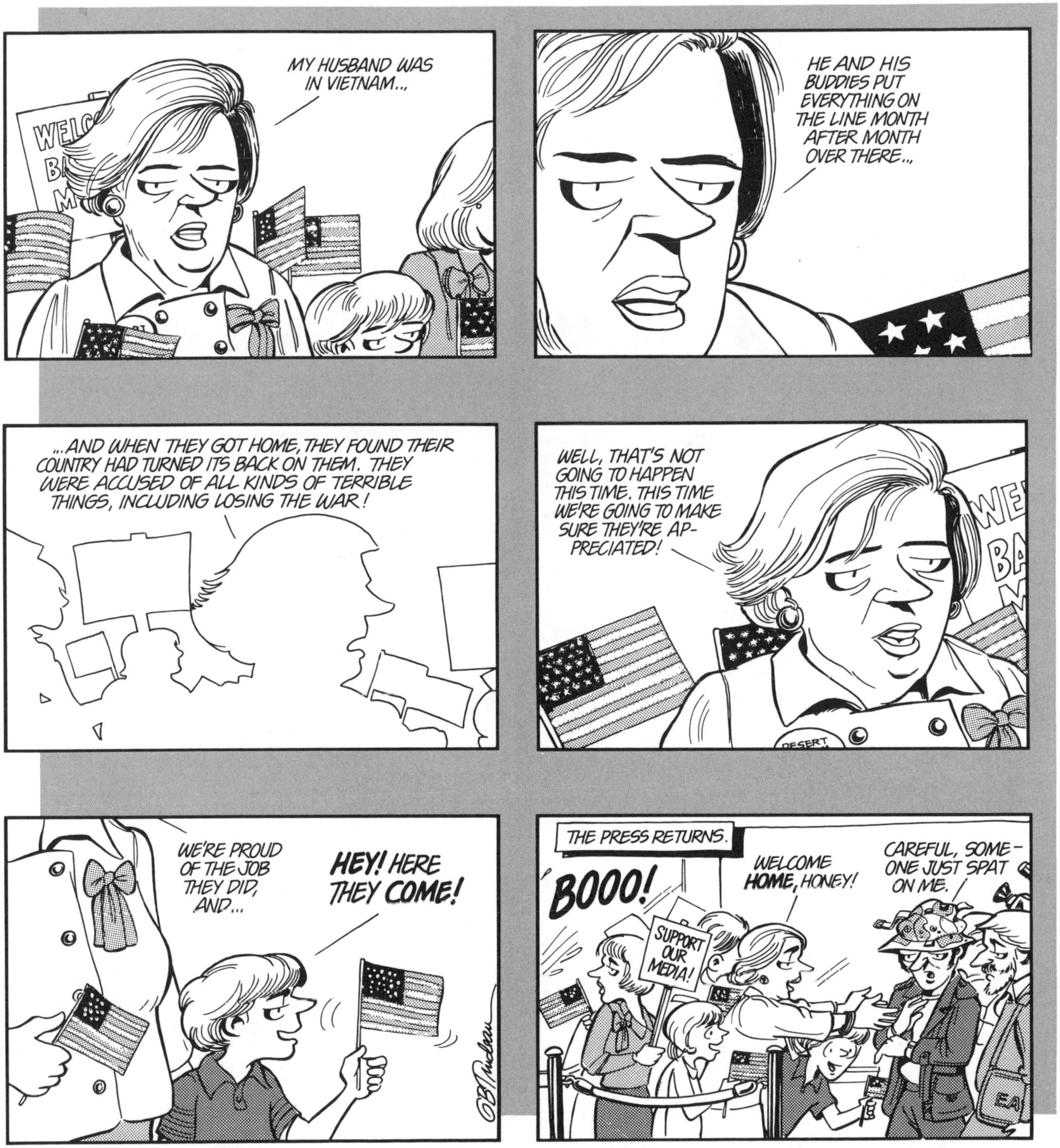
MY HUSBAND WAS IN VIETNAM...
HE AND HIS BUDDIES PUT EVERYTHING ON THE LINE MONTH AFTER MONTH OVER THERE...
...AND WHEN THEY GOT HOME, THEY FOUND THEIR COUNTRY HAD TURNED ITS BACK ON THEM. THEY WERE ACCUSED OF ALL KINDS OF TERRIBLE THINGS, INCLUDING LOSING THE WAR!
WELL, THAT'S NOT GOING TO HAPPEN THIS TIME. THIS TIME WE'RE GOING TO MAKE SURE THEY'RE AP-PRECIATED!
WE'RE PROUD OF THE JOB THEY DID, AND...
HEY! HERE THEY COME!
THE PRESS RETURNS.
BOOO!
SUPPORT OUR MEDIA!
WELCOME HOME, HONEY!
CAREFUL, SOME-ONE JUST SPAT ON ME.

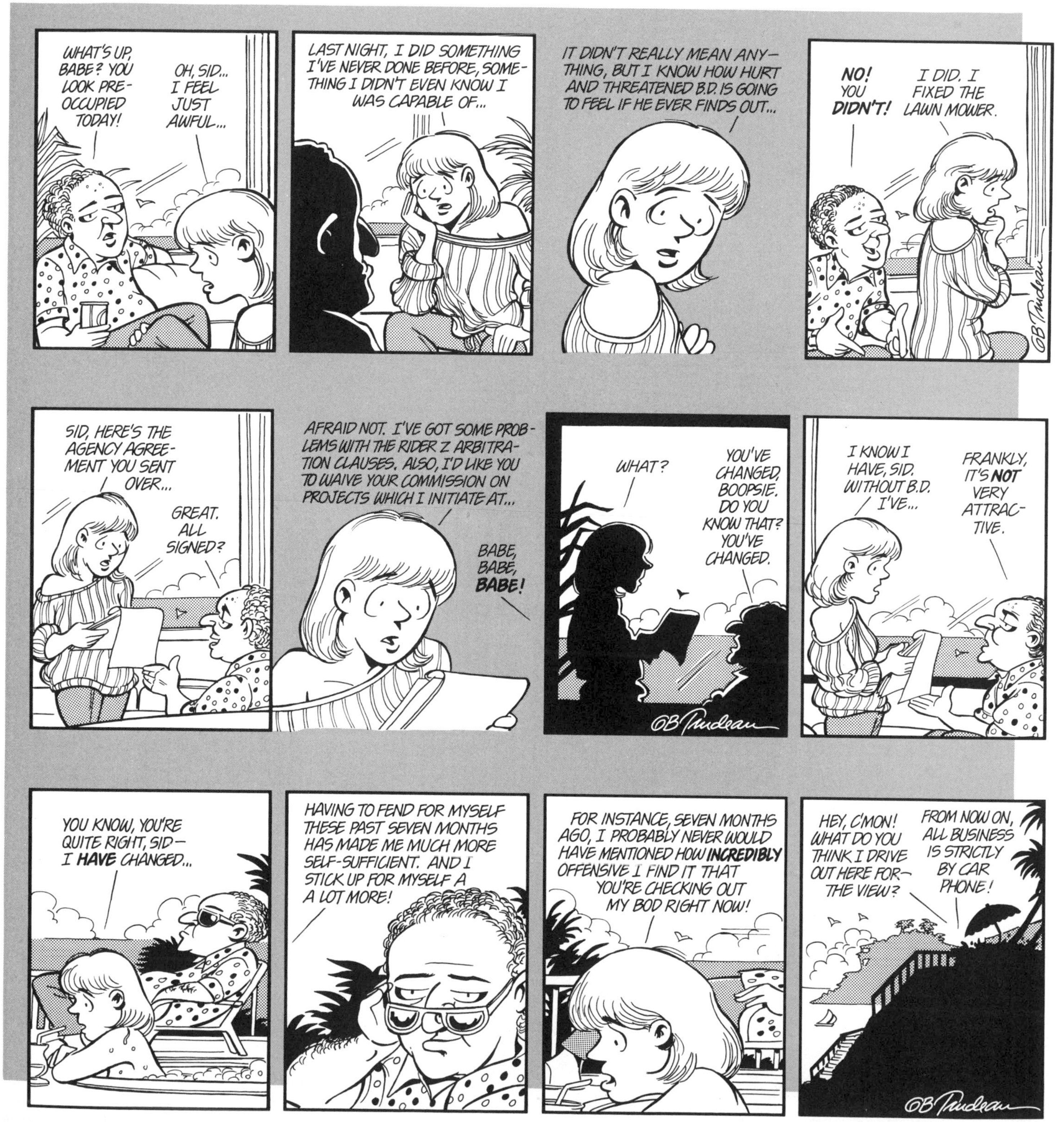
WHAT'S UP, BABE? YOU LOOK PRE-OCCUPIED TODAY!
OH, SID... I FEEL JUST AWFUL...
LAST NIGHT, I DID SOMETHING I'VE NEVER DONE BEFORE, SOMETHING I DIDN'T EVEN KNOW I WAS CAPABLE OF...
IT DIDN'T REALLY MEAN ANYTHING, BUT I KNOW HOW HURT AND THREATENED B.D. IS GOING TO FEEL IF HE EVER FINDS OUT...
NO! YOU DIDN'T!
I DID. I FIXED THE LAWN MOWER.
SID, HERE'S THE AGENCY AGREEMENT YOU SENT OVER...
GREAT. ALL SIGNED?
AFRAID NOT. I'VE GOT SOME PROBLEMS WITH THE RIDER Z ARBITRATION CLAUSES. ALSO, I'D LIKE YOU TO WAIVE YOUR COMMISSION ON PROJECTS WHICH I INITIATE AT...
BABE, BABE, BABE!
WHAT?
YOU'VE CHANGED, BOOPSIE. DO YOU KNOW THAT? YOU'VE CHANGED.
I KNOW I HAVE, SID. WITHOUT B.D. I'VE...
FRANKLY, IT'S NOT VERY ATTRACTIVE.
YOU KNOW, YOU'RE QUITE RIGHT, SID— I HAVE CHANGED...
HAVING TO FEND FOR MYSELF THESE PAST SEVEN MONTHS HAS MADE ME MUCH MORE SELF-SUFFICIENT. AND I STICK UP FOR MYSELF A A LOT MORE!
FOR INSTANCE, SEVEN MONTHS AGO, I PROBABLY NEVER WOULD HAVE MENTIONED HOW INCREDIBLY OFFENSIVE I FIND IT THAT YOU'RE CHECKING OUT MY BOD RIGHT NOW!
HEY, C'MON! WHAT DO YOU THINK I DRIVE OUT HERE FOR— THE VIEW?
FROM NOW ON, ALL BUSINESS IS STRICTLY BY CAR PHONE!

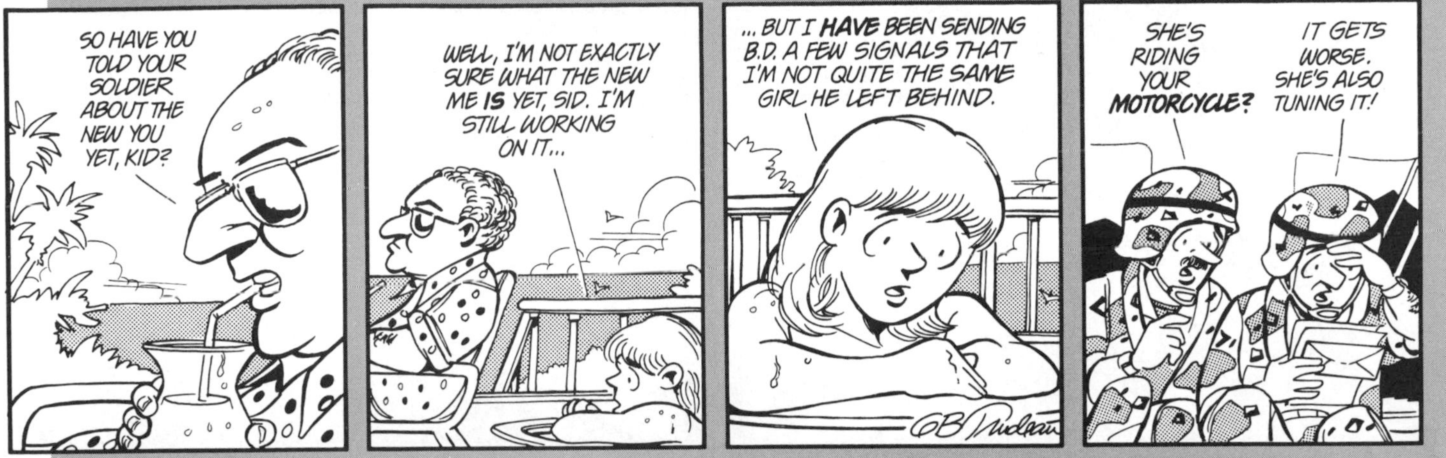
SO HAVE YOU TOLD YOUR SOLDIER ABOUT THE NEW YOU YET, KID?
WELL, I'M NOT EXACTLY SURE WHAT THE NEW ME IS YET, SID. I'M STILL WORKING ON IT...
... BUT I HAVE BEEN SENDING B.D. A FEW SIGNALS THAT I'M NOT QUITE THE SAME GIRL HE LEFT BEHIND.
SHE'S RIDING YOUR MOTORCYCLE?
IT GETS WORSE. SHE'S ALSO TUNING IT!

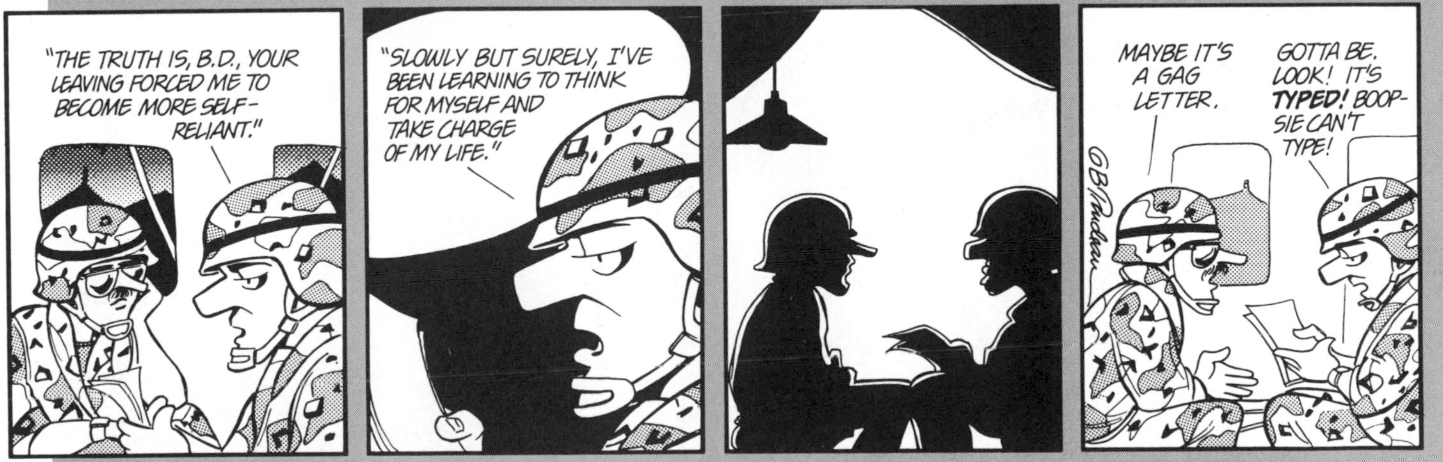
"THE TRUTH IS, B.D., YOUR LEAVING FORCED ME TO BECOME MORE SELF-RELIANT."
"SLOWLY BUT SURELY, I'VE BEEN LEARNING TO THINK FOR MYSELF AND TAKE CHARGE OF MY LIFE."
MAYBE IT'S A GAG LETTER.
GOTTA BE. LOOK! IT'S TYPED! BOOPSIE CAN'T TYPE!

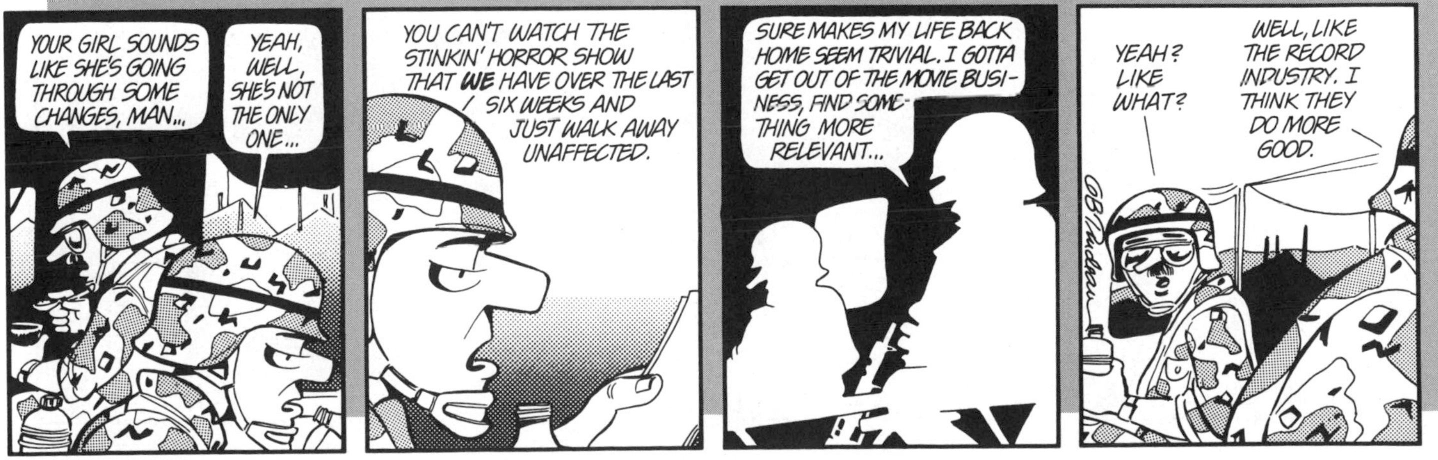
YOUR GIRL SOUNDS LIKE SHE'S GOING THROUGH SOME CHANGES, MAN...
YEAH, WELL, SHE'S NOT THE ONLY ONE...
YOU CAN'T WATCH THE STINKIN' HORROR SHOW THAT WE HAVE OVER THE LAST SIX WEEKS AND JUST WALK AWAY UNAFFECTED.
SURE MAKES MY LIFE BACK HOME SEEM TRIVIAL. I GOTTA GET OUT OF THE MOVIE BUSINESS, FIND SOMETHING MORE RELEVANT...
YEAH? LIKE WHAT?
WELL, LIKE THE RECORD INDUSTRY. I THINK THEY DO MORE GOOD.

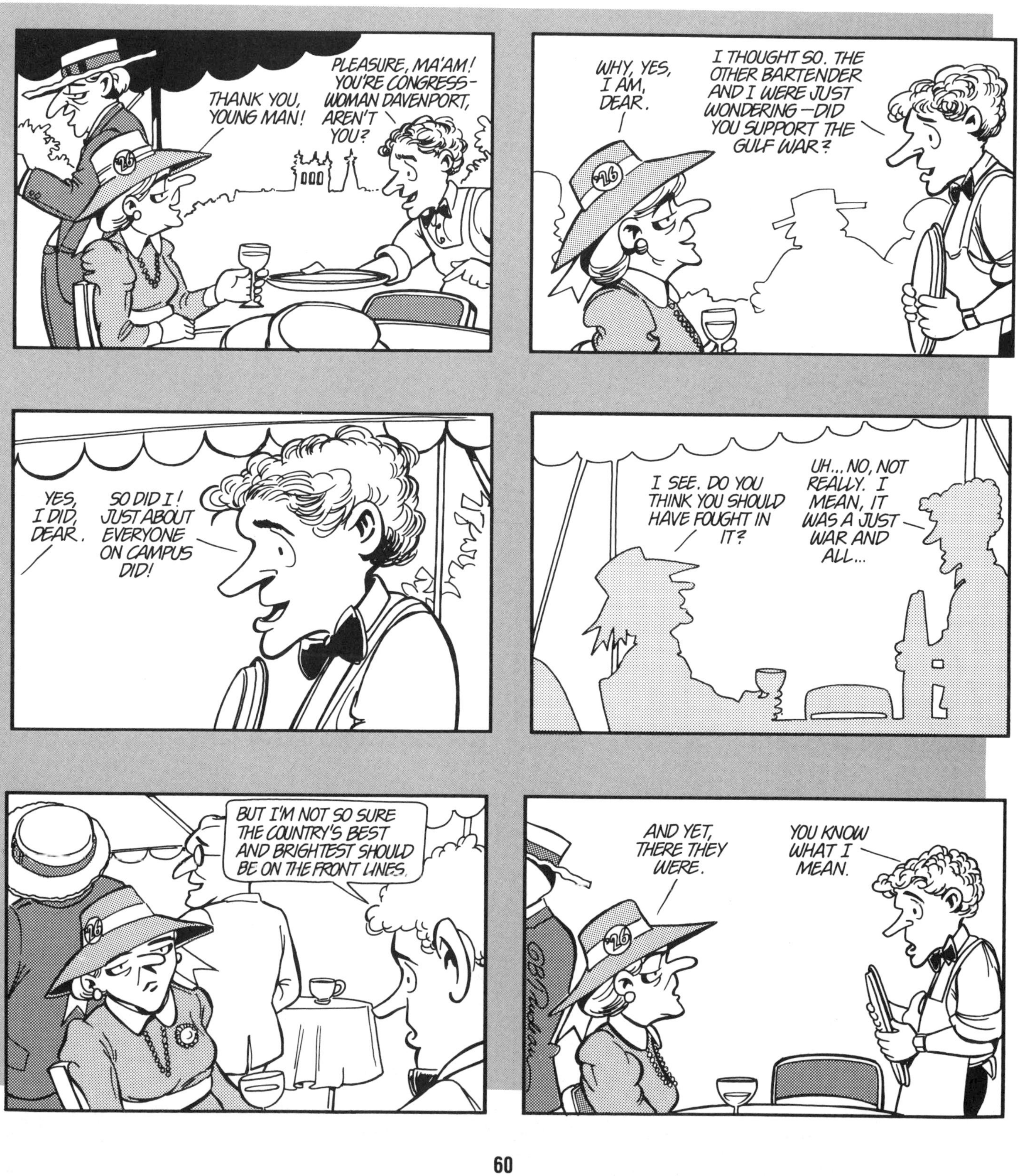
THANK YOU, YOUNG MAN!
PLEASURE, MA'AM! YOU'RE CONGRESSWOMAN DAVENPORT, AREN'T YOU?
WHY, YES, I AM, DEAR.
I THOUGHT SO. THE OTHER BARTENDER AND I WERE JUST WONDERING—DID YOU SUPPORT THE GULF WAR?
YES, I DID, DEAR.
SO DID I! JUST ABOUT EVERYONE ON CAMPUS DID!
I SEE. DO YOU THINK YOU SHOULD HAVE FOUGHT IN IT?
UH.., NO, NOT REALLY. I MEAN, IT WAS A JUST WAR AND ALL...
BUT I'M NOT SO SURE THE COUNTRY'S BEST AND BRIGHTEST SHOULD BE ON THE FRONT LINES.
AND YET, THERE THEY WERE.
YOU KNOW WHAT I MEAN.

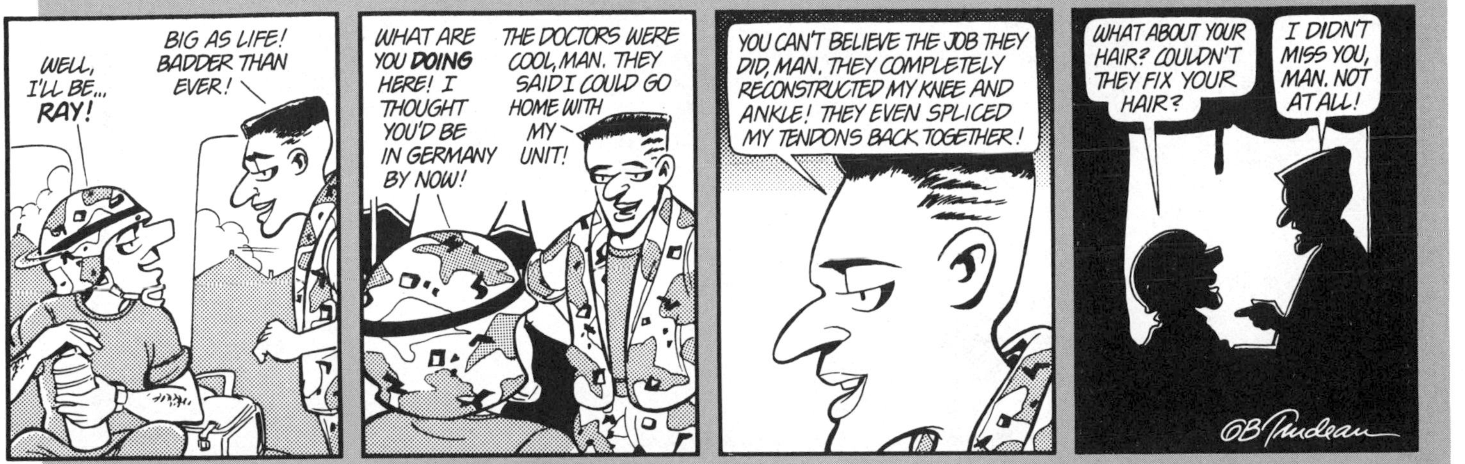
WELL, I'LL BE... RAY!
BIG AS LIFE! BADDER THAN EVER!
WHAT ARE YOU DOING HERE! I THOUGHT YOU'D BE IN GERMANY BY NOW!
THE DOCTORS WERE COOL, MAN. THEY SAID I COULD GO HOME WITH MY UNIT!
YOU CAN'T BELIEVE THE JOB THEY DID, MAN. THEY COMPLETELY RECONSTRUCTED MY KNEE AND ANKLE! THEY EVEN SPLICED MY TENDONS BACK TOGETHER!
WHAT ABOUT YOUR HAIR? COULDN'T THEY FIX YOUR HAIR?
I DIDN'T MISS YOU, MAN. NOT AT ALL!
©B Trudeau

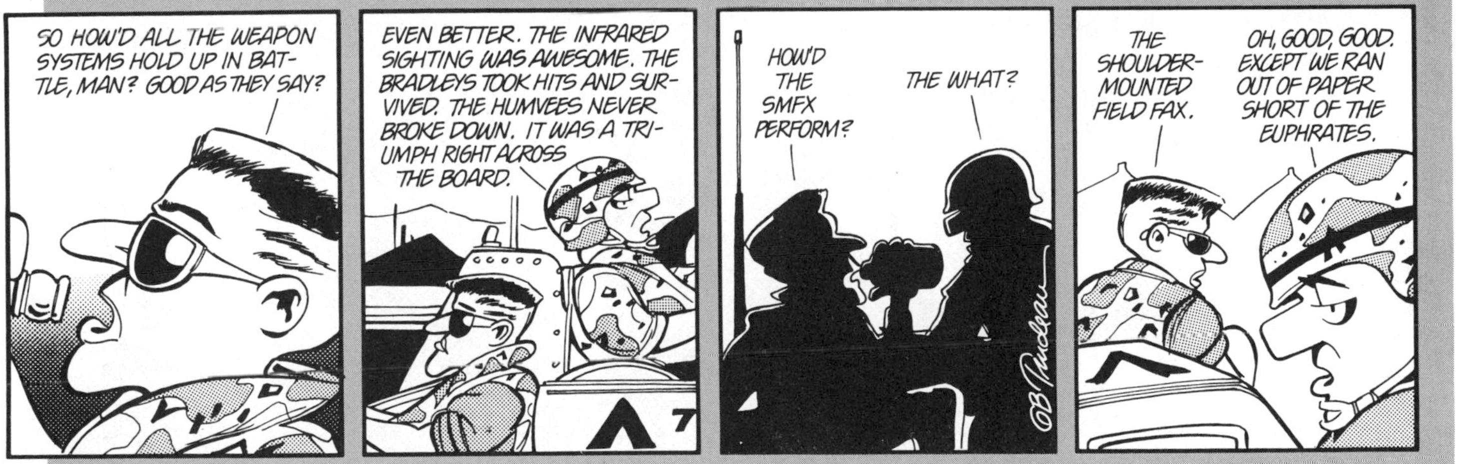
SO HOW'D ALL THE WEAPON SYSTEMS HOLD UP IN BATTLE, MAN? GOOD AS THEY SAY?
EVEN BETTER. THE INFRARED SIGHTING WAS AWESOME. THE BRADLEYS TOOK HITS AND SURVIVED. THE HUMVEES NEVER BROKE DOWN. IT WAS A TRIUMPH RIGHT ACROSS THE BOARD.
HOW'D THE SMFX PERFORM?
THE WHAT?
©B Trudeau
THE SHOULDER-MOUNTED FIELD FAX.
OH, GOOD, GOOD. EXCEPT WE RAN OUT OF PAPER SHORT OF THE EUPHRATES.

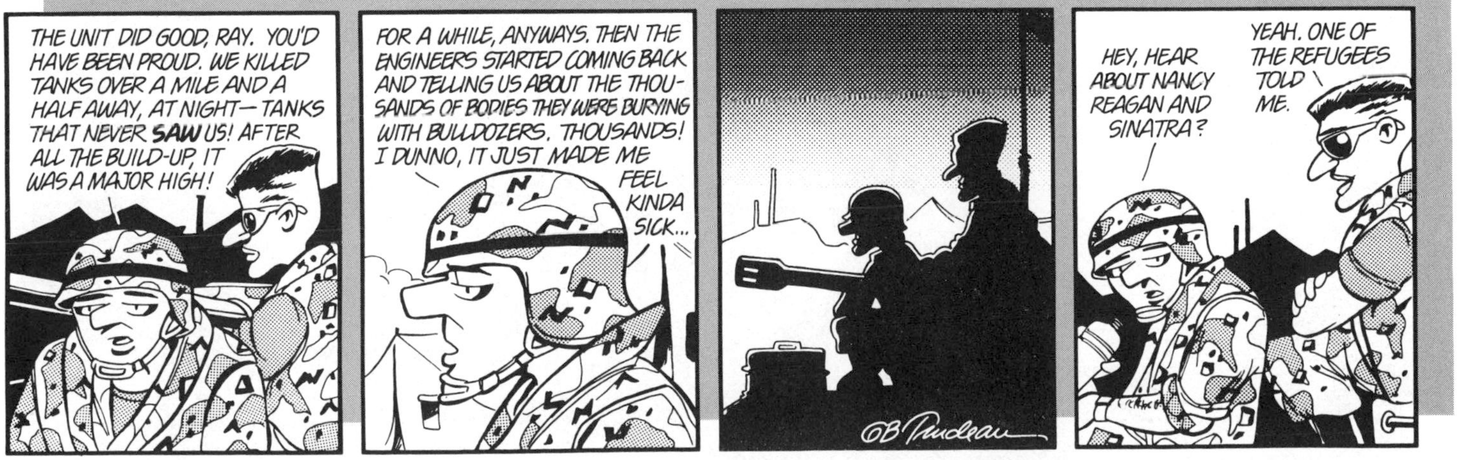
THE UNIT DID GOOD, RAY. YOU'D HAVE BEEN PROUD. WE KILLED TANKS OVER A MILE AND A HALF AWAY, AT NIGHT— TANKS THAT NEVER SAW US! AFTER ALL THE BUILD-UP, IT WAS A MAJOR HIGH!
FOR A WHILE, ANYWAYS. THEN THE ENGINEERS STARTED COMING BACK AND TELLING US ABOUT THE THOUSANDS OF BODIES THEY WERE BURYING WITH BULLDOZERS. THOUSANDS! I DUNNO, IT JUST MADE ME FEEL KINDA SICK...
©B Trudeau
HEY, HEAR ABOUT NANCY REAGAN AND SINATRA?
YEAH. ONE OF THE REFUGEES TOLD ME.

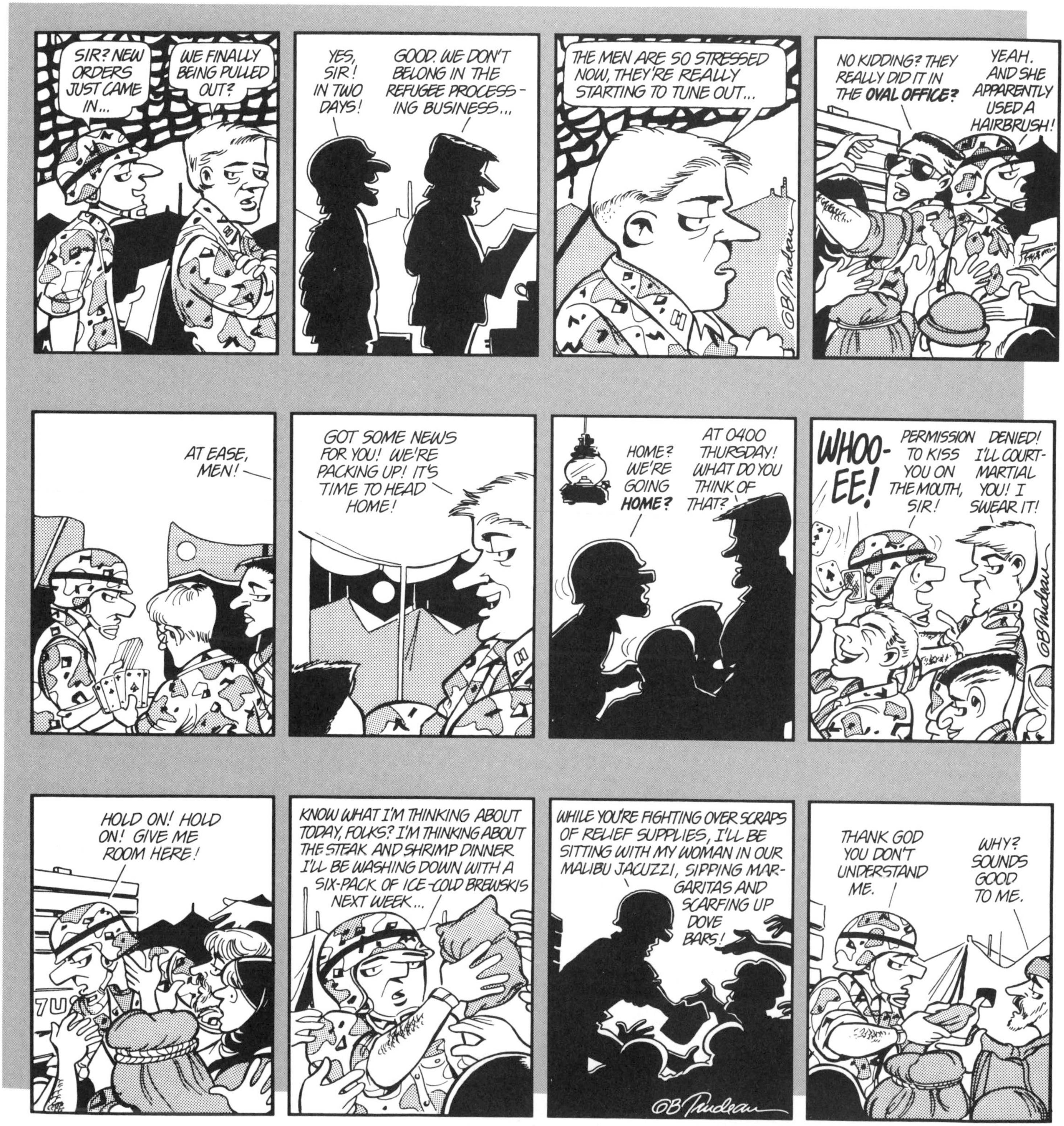

SIR? NEW ORDERS JUST CAME IN...
WE FINALLY BEING PULLED OUT?
YES, SIR! IN TWO DAYS!
GOOD. WE DON'T BELONG IN THE REFUGEE PROCESSING BUSINESS...
THE MEN ARE SO STRESSED NOW, THEY'RE REALLY STARTING TO TUNE OUT...
NO KIDDING? THEY REALLY DID IT IN THE OVAL OFFICE?
YEAH. AND SHE APPARENTLY USED A HAIRBRUSH!
AT EASE, MEN!
GOT SOME NEWS FOR YOU! WE'RE PACKING UP! IT'S TIME TO HEAD HOME!
HOME? WE'RE GOING HOME?
AT 0400 THURSDAY! WHAT DO YOU THINK OF THAT?
WHOO-EE!
PERMISSION TO KISS YOU ON THE MOUTH, SIR!
DENIED! I'LL COURT-MARTIAL YOU! I SWEAR IT!
HOLD ON! HOLD ON! GIVE ME ROOM HERE!
7U
KNOW WHAT I'M THINKING ABOUT TODAY, FOLKS? I'M THINKING ABOUT THE STEAK AND SHRIMP DINNER I'LL BE WASHING DOWN WITH A SIX-PACK OF ICE-COLD BREWSKIS NEXT WEEK...
WHILE YOU'RE FIGHTING OVER SCRAPS OF RELIEF SUPPLIES, I'LL BE SITTING WITH MY WOMAN IN OUR MALIBU JACUZZI, SIPPING MARGARITAS AND SCARFING UP DOVE BARS!
THANK GOD YOU DON'T UNDERSTAND ME.
WHY? SOUNDS GOOD TO ME.

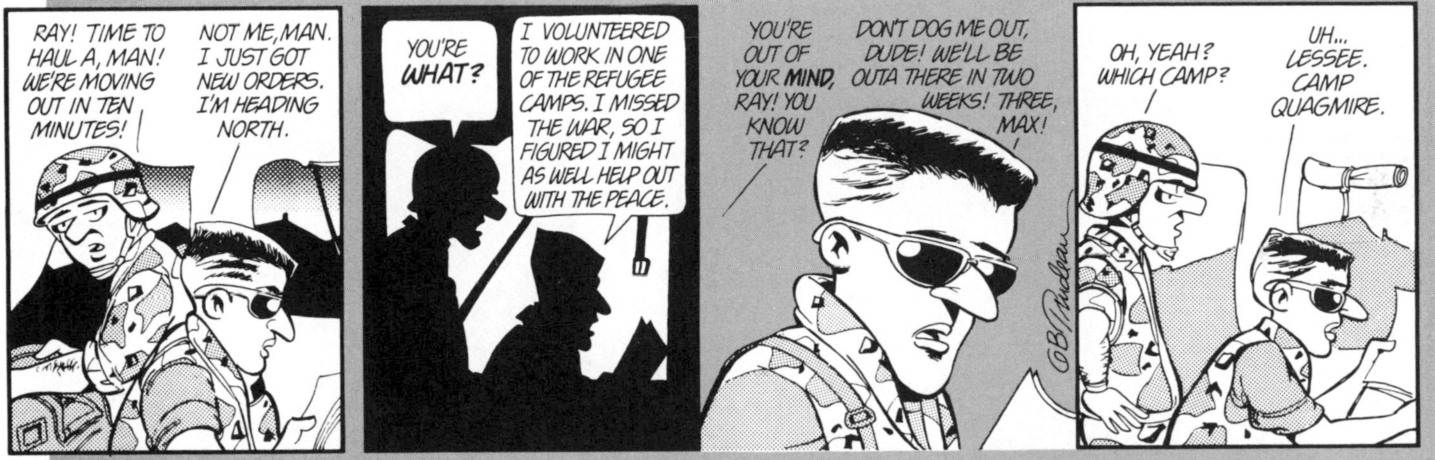
RAY! TIME TO HAUL A, MAN! WE'RE MOVING OUT IN TEN MINUTES!
NOT ME, MAN. I JUST GOT NEW ORDERS. I'M HEADING NORTH.
YOU'RE WHAT?
I VOLUNTEERED TO WORK IN ONE OF THE REFUGEE CAMPS. I MISSED THE WAR, SO I FIGURED I MIGHT AS WELL HELP OUT WITH THE PEACE.
YOU'RE OUT OF YOUR MIND, RAY! YOU KNOW THAT?
DON'T DOG ME OUT, DUDE! WE'LL BE OUTA THERE IN TWO WEEKS! THREE, MAX!
OH, YEAH? WHICH CAMP?
UH... LESSEE. CAMP QUAGMIRE.

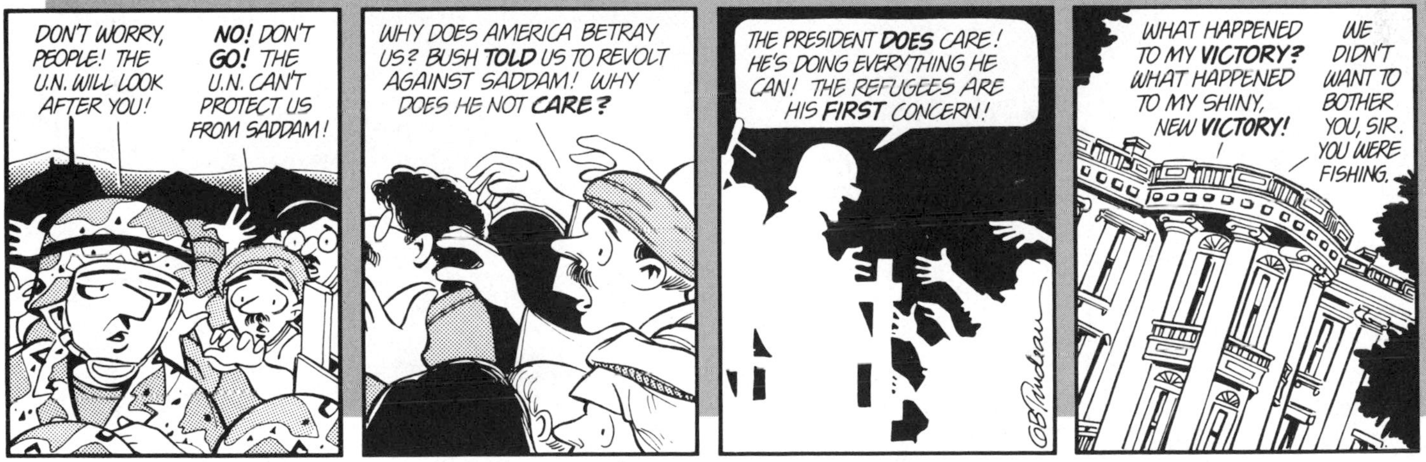
DON'T WORRY, PEOPLE! THE U.N. WILL LOOK AFTER YOU!
NO! DON'T GO! THE U.N. CAN'T PROTECT US FROM SADDAM!
WHY DOES AMERICA BETRAY US? BUSH TOLD US TO REVOLT AGAINST SADDAM! WHY DOES HE NOT CARE?
THE PRESIDENT DOES CARE! HE'S DOING EVERYTHING HE CAN! THE REFUGEES ARE HIS FIRST CONCERN!
WHAT HAPPENED TO MY VICTORY? WHAT HAPPENED TO MY SHINY, NEW VICTORY!
WE DIDN'T WANT TO BOTHER YOU, SIR. YOU WERE FISHING.

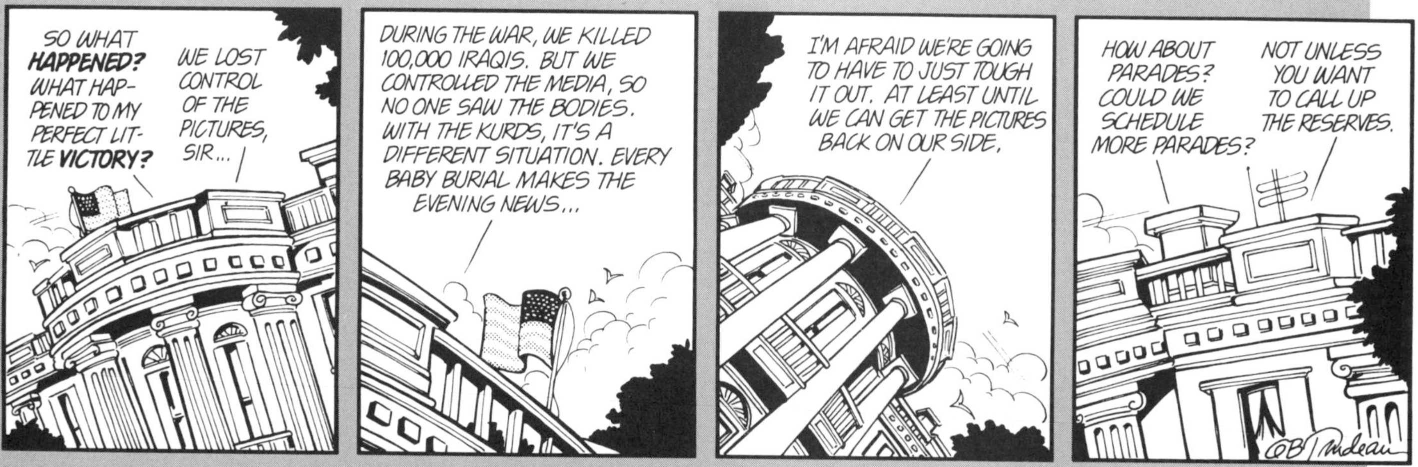
SO WHAT **HAPPENED?** WHAT HAPPENED TO MY PERFECT LITTLE **VICTORY?**
WE LOST CONTROL OF THE PICTURES, SIR...
DURING THE WAR, WE KILLED 100,000 IRAQIS. BUT WE CONTROLLED THE MEDIA, SO NO ONE SAW THE BODIES. WITH THE KURDS, IT'S A DIFFERENT SITUATION. EVERY BABY BURIAL MAKES THE EVENING NEWS...
I'M AFRAID WE'RE GOING TO HAVE TO JUST TOUGH IT OUT. AT LEAST UNTIL WE CAN GET THE PICTURES BACK ON OUR SIDE.
HOW ABOUT PARADES? COULD WE SCHEDULE MORE PARADES?
NOT UNLESS YOU WANT TO CALL UP THE RESERVES.

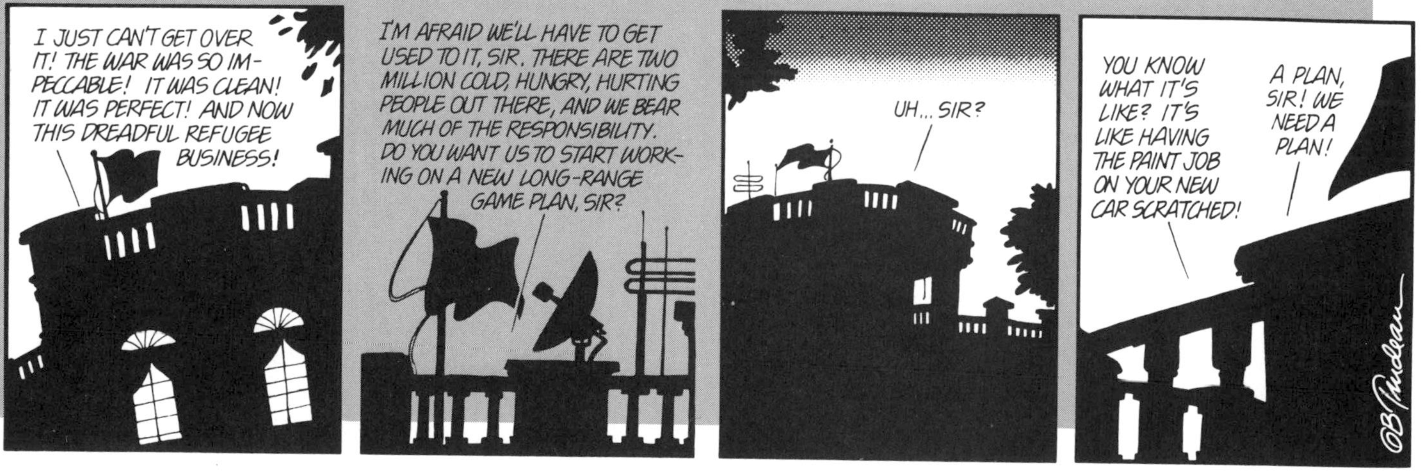
I JUST CAN'T GET OVER IT! THE WAR WAS SO IMPECCABLE! IT WAS CLEAN! IT WAS PERFECT! AND NOW THIS DREADFUL REFUGEE BUSINESS!
I'M AFRAID WE'LL HAVE TO GET USED TO IT, SIR. THERE ARE TWO MILLION COLD, HUNGRY, HURTING PEOPLE OUT THERE, AND WE BEAR MUCH OF THE RESPONSIBILITY. DO YOU WANT US TO START WORKING ON A NEW LONG-RANGE GAME PLAN, SIR?
UH... SIR?
YOU KNOW WHAT IT'S LIKE? IT'S LIKE HAVING THE PAINT JOB ON YOUR NEW CAR SCRATCHED!
A PLAN, SIR! WE NEED A PLAN!

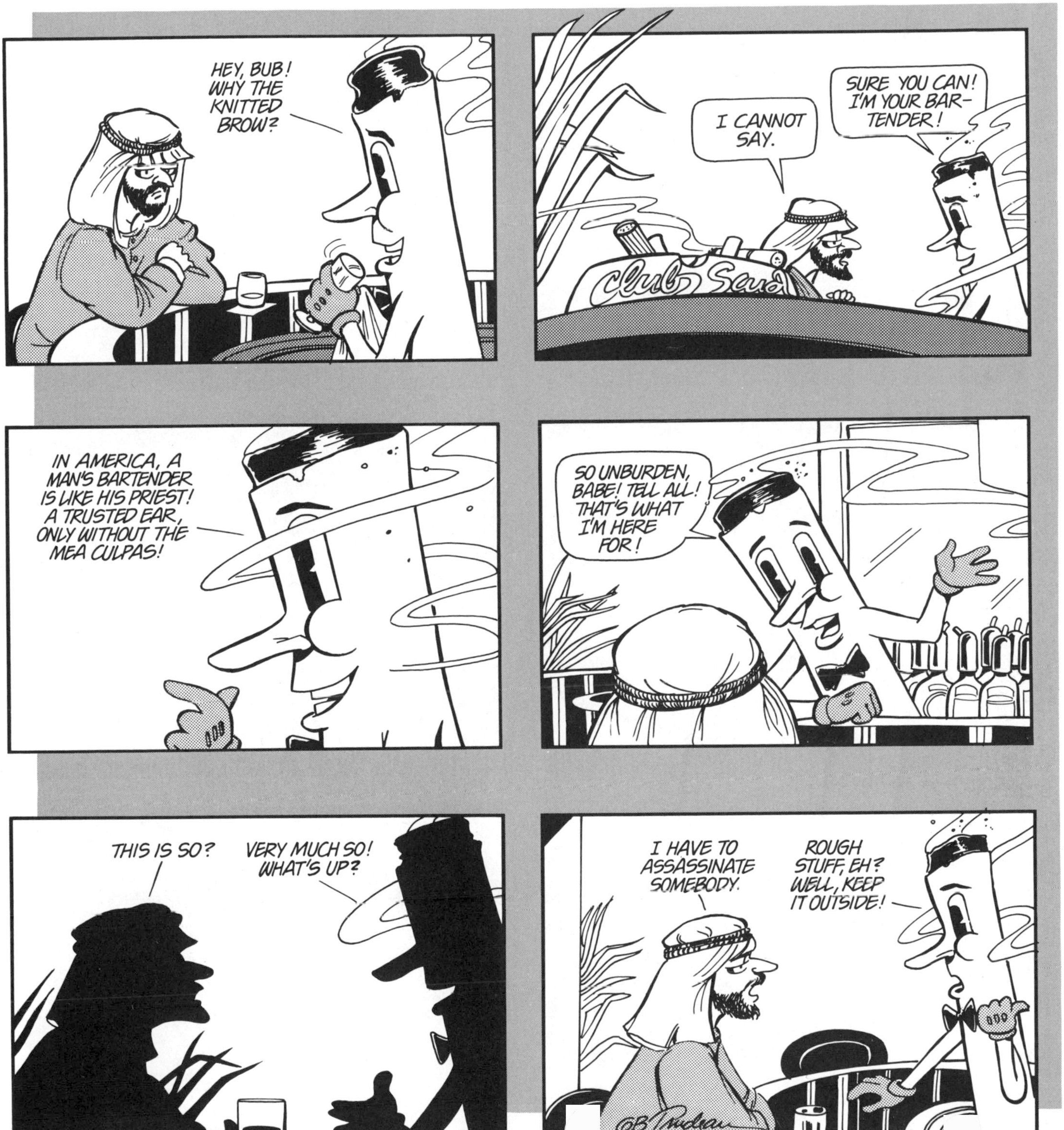
HEY, BUB! WHY THE KNITTED BROW?
I CANNOT SAY.
SURE YOU CAN! I'M YOUR BARTENDER!
IN AMERICA, A MAN'S BARTENDER IS LIKE HIS PRIEST! A TRUSTED EAR, ONLY WITHOUT THE MEA CULPAS!
SO UNBURDEN, BABE! TELL ALL! THAT'S WHAT I'M HERE FOR!
THIS IS SO?
VERY MUCH SO! WHAT'S UP?
I HAVE TO ASSASSINATE SOMEBODY.
ROUGH STUFF, EH? WELL, KEEP IT OUTSIDE!

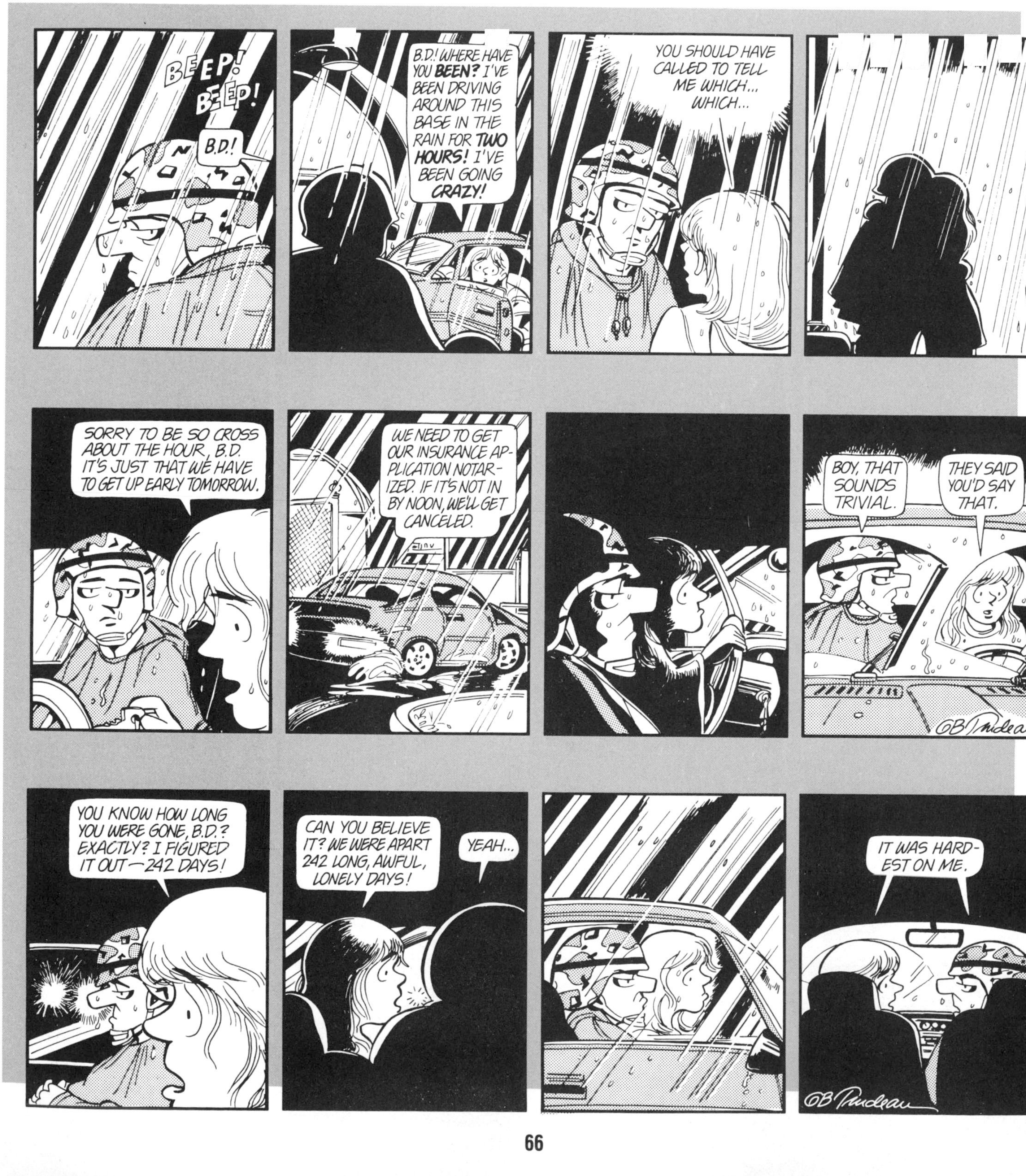
BEEP! BEEP!
B.D.!
B.D.! WHERE HAVE YOU BEEN? I'VE BEEN DRIVING AROUND THIS BASE IN THE RAIN FOR TWO HOURS! I'VE BEEN GOING CRAZY!
YOU SHOULD HAVE CALLED TO TELL ME WHICH... WHICH...
SORRY TO BE SO CROSS ABOUT THE HOUR, B.D. IT'S JUST THAT WE HAVE TO GET UP EARLY TOMORROW.
WE NEED TO GET OUR INSURANCE APPLICATION NOTARIZED. IF IT'S NOT IN BY NOON, WE'LL GET CANCELED.
BOY, THAT SOUNDS TRIVIAL.
THEY SAID YOU'D SAY THAT.
YOU KNOW HOW LONG YOU WERE GONE, B.D.? EXACTLY? I FIGURED IT OUT — 242 DAYS!
CAN YOU BELIEVE IT? WE WERE APART 242 LONG, AWFUL, LONELY DAYS!
YEAH...
IT WAS HARDEST ON ME.

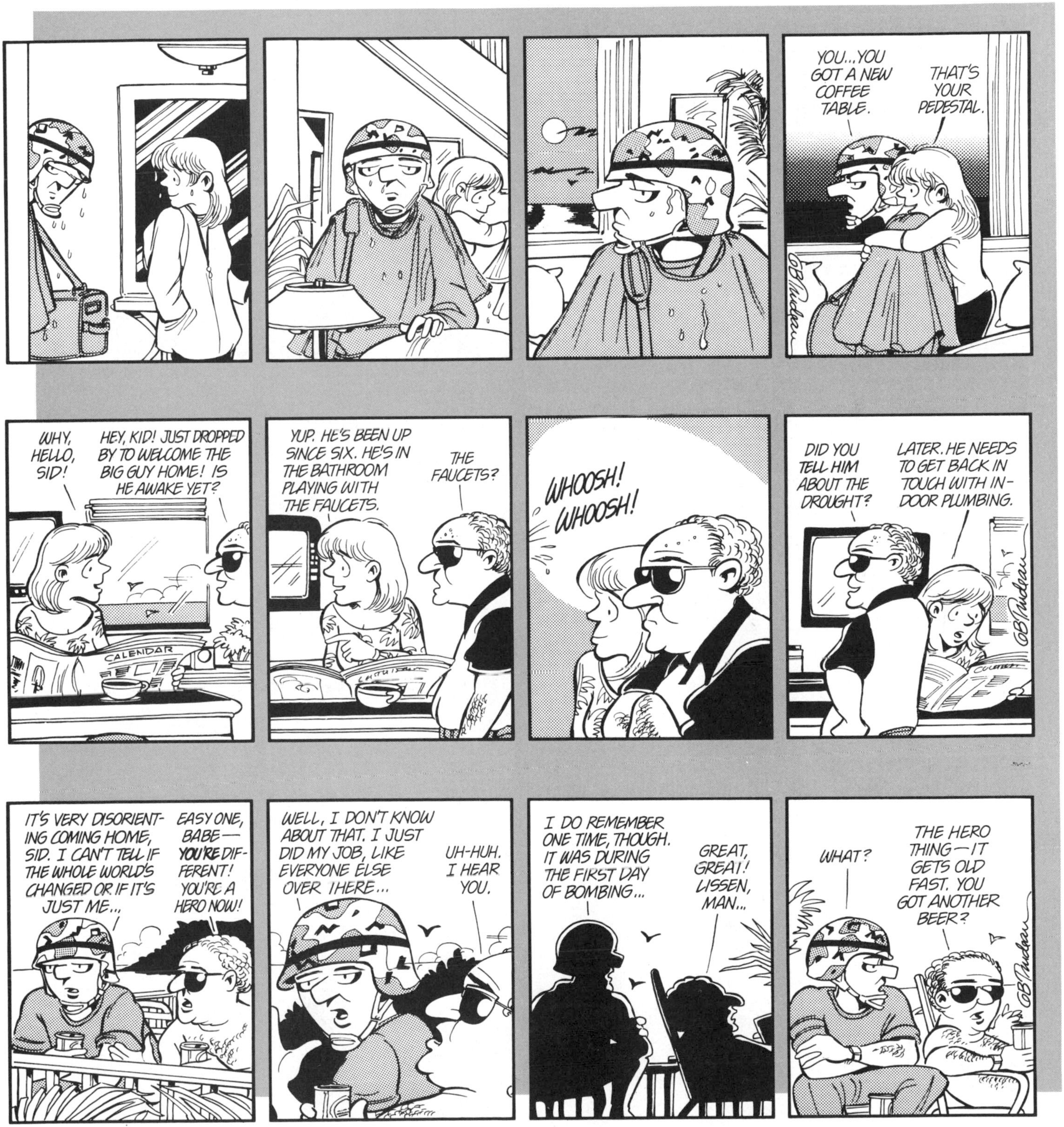
YOU...YOU GOT A NEW COFFEE TABLE.
THAT'S YOUR PEDESTAL.
WHY, HELLO, SID!
HEY, KID! JUST DROPPED BY TO WELCOME THE BIG GUY HOME! IS HE AWAKE YET?
CALENDAR
YUP. HE'S BEEN UP SINCE SIX. HE'S IN THE BATHROOM PLAYING WITH THE FAUCETS.
THE FAUCETS?
WHOOSH! WHOOSH!
DID YOU TELL HIM ABOUT THE DROUGHT?
LATER. HE NEEDS TO GET BACK IN TOUCH WITH IN-DOOR PLUMBING.
IT'S VERY DISORIENT-ING COMING HOME, SID. I CAN'T TELL IF THE WHOLE WORLD'S CHANGED OR IF IT'S JUST ME...
EASY ONE, BABE— YOU'RE DIF-FERENT! YOU'RE A HERO NOW!
WELL, I DON'T KNOW ABOUT THAT. I JUST DID MY JOB, LIKE EVERYONE ELSE OVER THERE...
UH-HUH. I HEAR YOU.
I DO REMEMBER ONE TIME, THOUGH. IT WAS DURING THE FIRST DAY OF BOMBING...
GREAT, GREAT! LISSEN, MAN...
WHAT?
THE HERO THING—IT GETS OLD FAST. YOU GOT ANOTHER BEER?

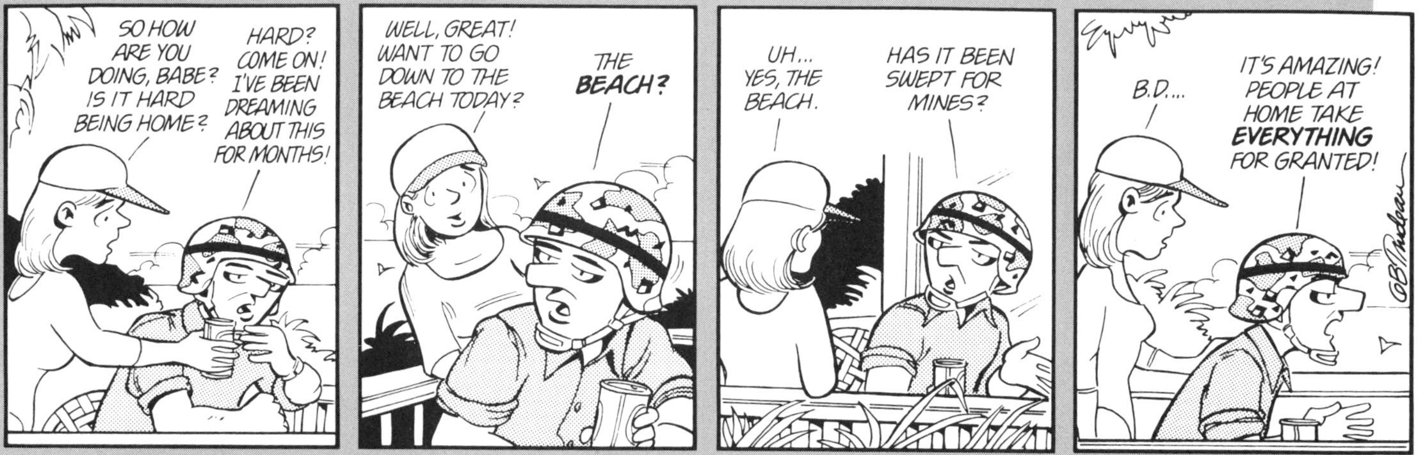
SO HOW ARE YOU DOING, BABE? IS IT HARD BEING HOME?
HARD? COME ON! I'VE BEEN DREAMING ABOUT THIS FOR MONTHS!
WELL, GREAT! WANT TO GO DOWN TO THE BEACH TODAY?
THE **BEACH?**
UH... YES, THE BEACH.
HAS IT BEEN SWEPT FOR MINES?
B.D....
IT'S AMAZING! PEOPLE AT HOME TAKE **EVERYTHING** FOR GRANTED!
GB Trudeau

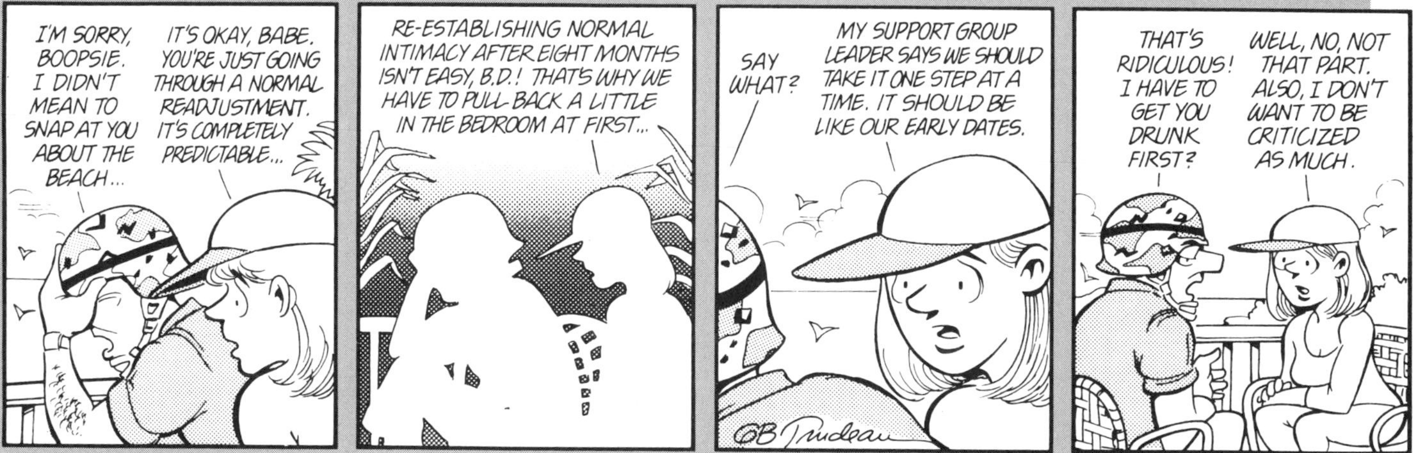
I'M SORRY, BOOPSIE. I DIDN'T MEAN TO SNAP AT YOU ABOUT THE BEACH...
IT'S OKAY, BABE. YOU'RE JUST GOING THROUGH A NORMAL READJUSTMENT. IT'S COMPLETELY PREDICTABLE...
RE-ESTABLISHING NORMAL INTIMACY AFTER EIGHT MONTHS ISN'T EASY, B.D.! THAT'S WHY WE HAVE TO PULL BACK A LITTLE IN THE BEDROOM AT FIRST...
SAY WHAT?
MY SUPPORT GROUP LEADER SAYS WE SHOULD TAKE IT ONE STEP AT A TIME. IT SHOULD BE LIKE OUR EARLY DATES.
GB Trudeau
THAT'S RIDICULOUS! I HAVE TO GET YOU DRUNK FIRST?
WELL, NO, NOT THAT PART. ALSO, I DON'T WANT TO BE CRITICIZED AS MUCH.

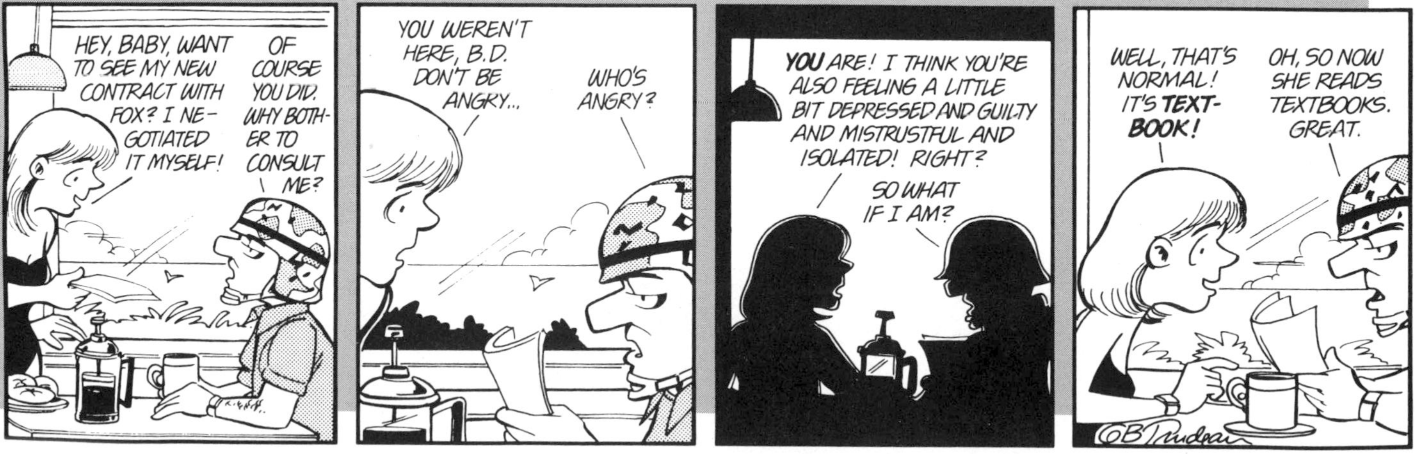
HEY, BABY, WANT TO SEE MY NEW CONTRACT WITH FOX? I NEGOTIATED IT MYSELF!
OF COURSE YOU DID. WHY BOTHER TO CONSULT ME?
YOU WEREN'T HERE, B.D. DON'T BE ANGRY...
WHO'S ANGRY?
YOU ARE! I THINK YOU'RE ALSO FEELING A LITTLE BIT DEPRESSED AND GUILTY AND MISTRUSTFUL AND ISOLATED! RIGHT?
SO WHAT IF I AM?
WELL, THAT'S NORMAL! IT'S **TEXTBOOK!**
OH, SO NOW SHE READS TEXTBOOKS. GREAT.
GB Trudeau

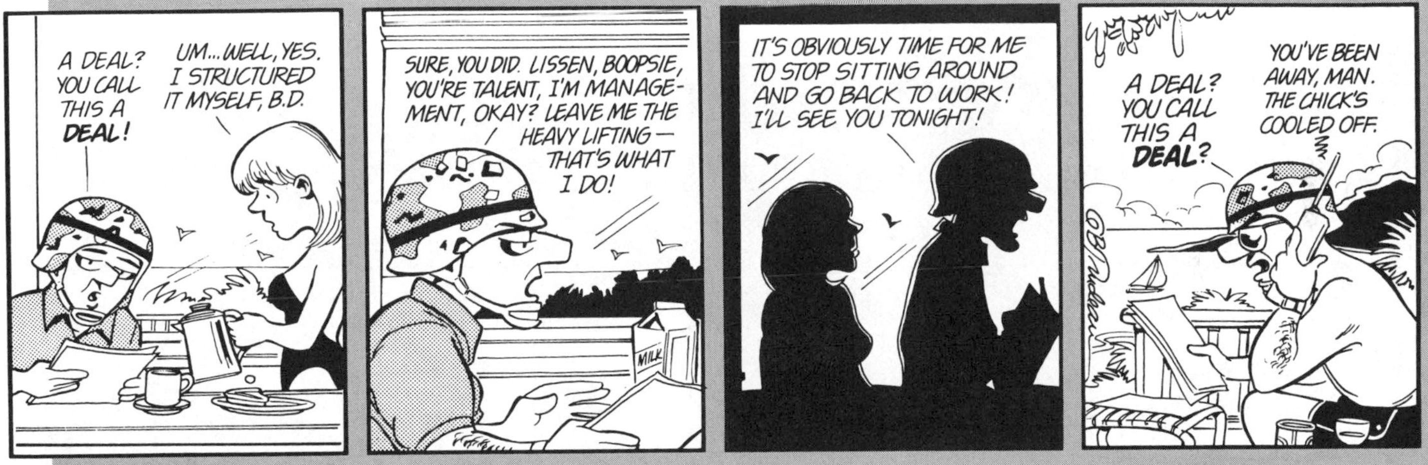
A DEAL? YOU CALL THIS A **DEAL**!
UM... WELL, YES. I STRUCTURED IT MYSELF, B.D.
SURE, YOU DID. LISSEN, BOOPSIE, YOU'RE TALENT, I'M MANAGEMENT, OKAY? LEAVE ME THE HEAVY LIFTING — THAT'S WHAT I DO!
IT'S OBVIOUSLY TIME FOR ME TO STOP SITTING AROUND AND GO BACK TO WORK! I'LL SEE YOU TONIGHT!
A DEAL? YOU CALL THIS A **DEAL**?
YOU'VE BEEN AWAY, MAN. THE CHICK'S COOLED OFF.
MILK

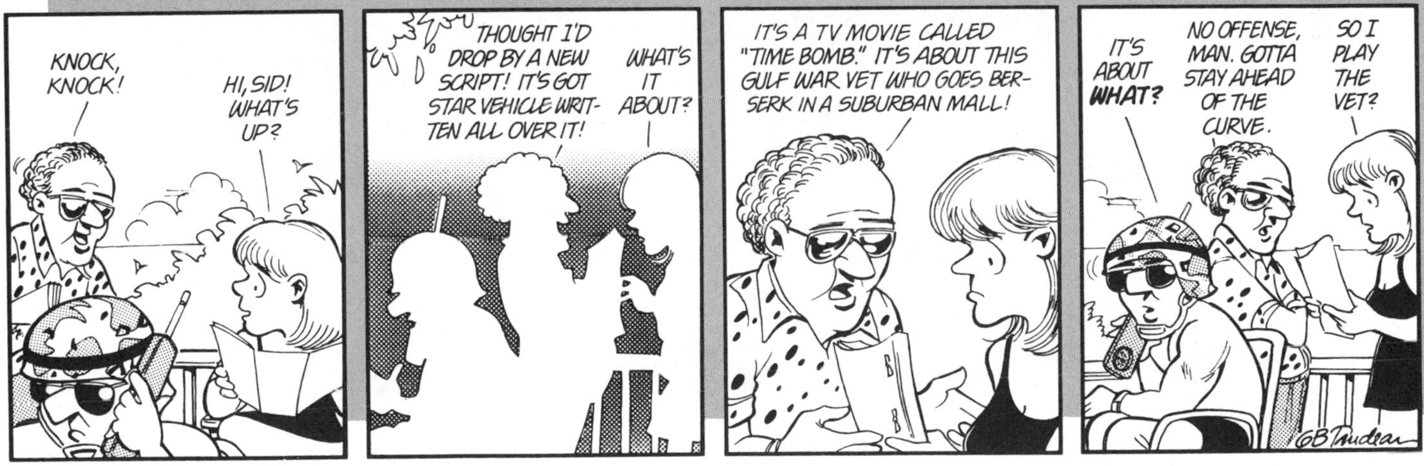
KNOCK, KNOCK!
HI, SID! WHAT'S UP?
THOUGHT I'D DROP BY A NEW SCRIPT! IT'S GOT STAR VEHICLE WRITTEN ALL OVER IT!
WHAT'S IT ABOUT?
IT'S A TV MOVIE CALLED "TIME BOMB." IT'S ABOUT THIS GULF WAR VET WHO GOES BERSERK IN A SUBURBAN MALL!
IT'S ABOUT **WHAT**?
NO OFFENSE, MAN. GOTTA STAY AHEAD OF THE CURVE.
SO I PLAY THE VET?

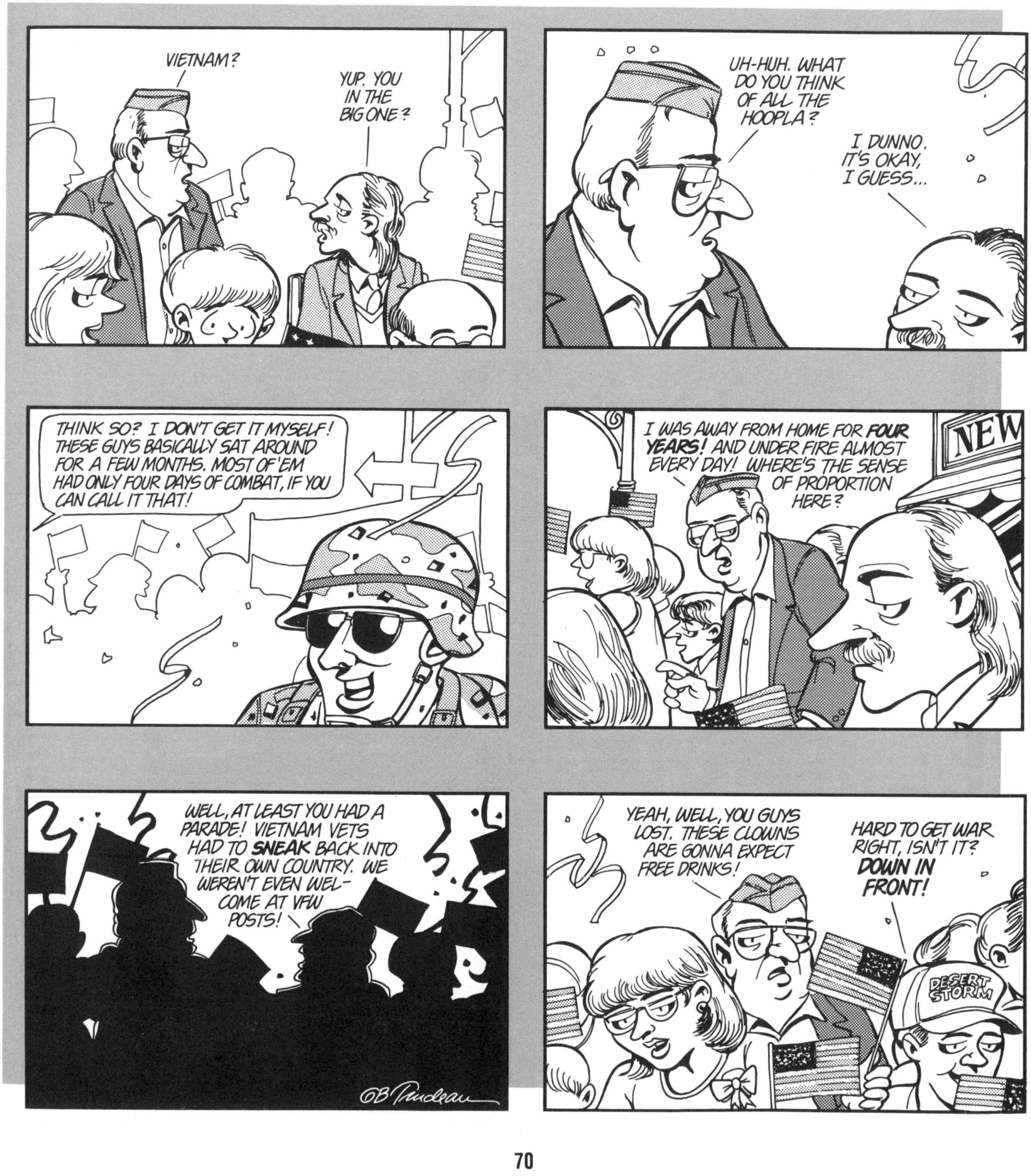
VIETNAM?
YUP. YOU IN THE BIG ONE?
UH-HUH. WHAT DO YOU THINK OF ALL THE HOOPLA?
I DUNNO. IT'S OKAY, I GUESS...
THINK SO? I DON'T GET IT MYSELF! THESE GUYS BASICALLY SAT AROUND FOR A FEW MONTHS. MOST OF 'EM HAD ONLY FOUR DAYS OF COMBAT, IF YOU CAN CALL IT THAT!
I WAS AWAY FROM HOME FOR FOUR YEARS! AND UNDER FIRE ALMOST EVERY DAY! WHERE'S THE SENSE OF PROPORTION HERE?
NEW
WELL, AT LEAST YOU HAD A PARADE! VIETNAM VETS HAD TO SNEAK BACK INTO THEIR OWN COUNTRY. WE WEREN'T EVEN WEL-COME AT VFW POSTS!
©B Trudeau
YEAH, WELL, YOU GUYS LOST. THESE CLOWNS ARE GONNA EXPECT FREE DRINKS!
HARD TO GET WAR RIGHT, ISN'T IT? DOWN IN FRONT!
DESERT STORM

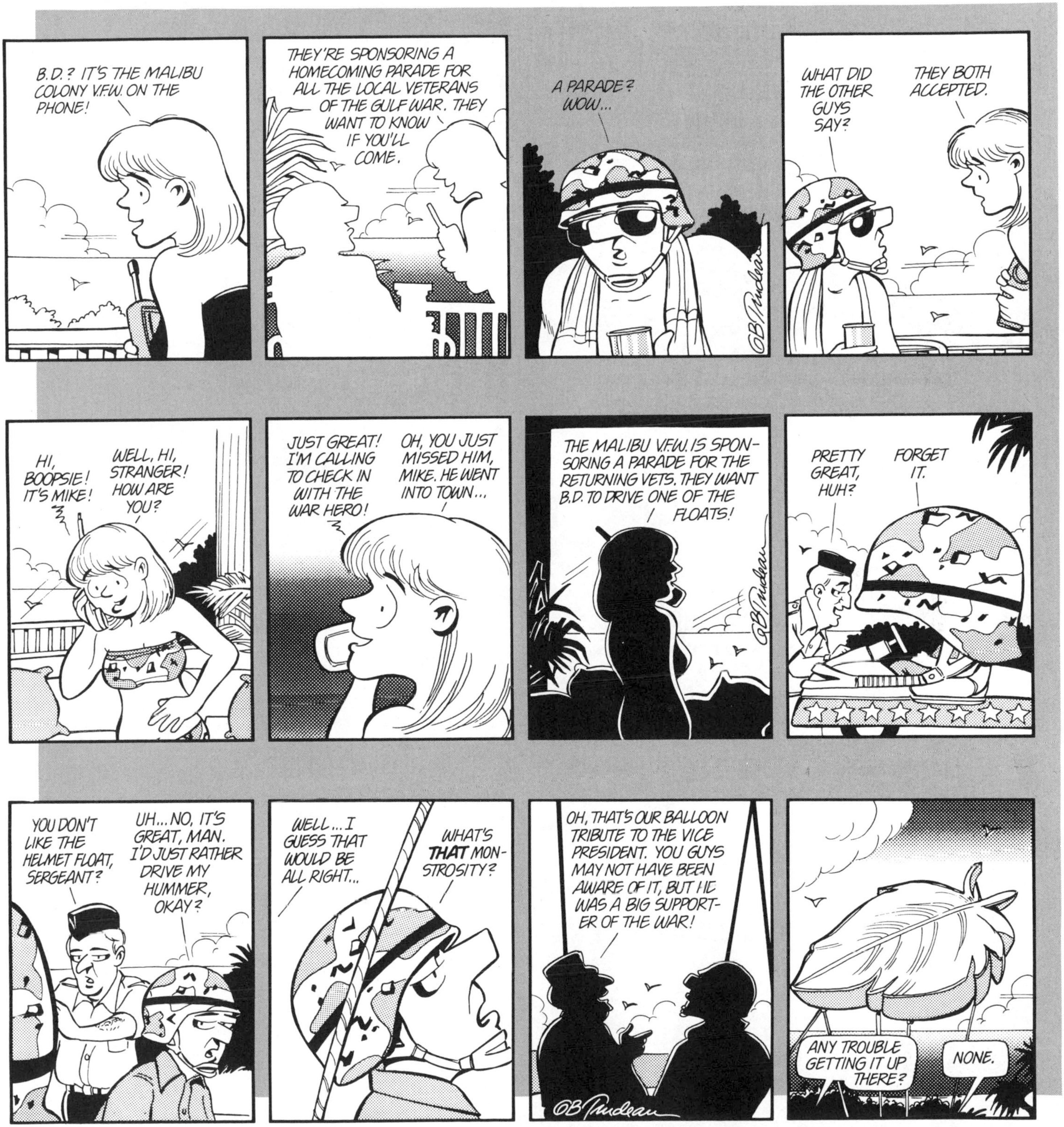
B.D.? IT'S THE MALIBU COLONY V.F.W. ON THE PHONE!
THEY'RE SPONSORING A HOMECOMING PARADE FOR ALL THE LOCAL VETERANS OF THE GULF WAR. THEY WANT TO KNOW IF YOU'LL COME.
A PARADE? WOW...
WHAT DID THE OTHER GUYS SAY?
THEY BOTH ACCEPTED.
HI, BOOPSIE! IT'S MIKE!
WELL, HI, STRANGER! HOW ARE YOU?
JUST GREAT! I'M CALLING TO CHECK IN WITH THE WAR HERO!
OH, YOU JUST MISSED HIM, MIKE. HE WENT INTO TOWN...
THE MALIBU V.F.W. IS SPONSORING A PARADE FOR THE RETURNING VETS. THEY WANT B.D. TO DRIVE ONE OF THE FLOATS!
PRETTY GREAT, HUH?
FORGET IT.
YOU DON'T LIKE THE HELMET FLOAT, SERGEANT?
UH... NO, IT'S GREAT, MAN. I'D JUST RATHER DRIVE MY HUMMER, OKAY?
WELL... I GUESS THAT WOULD BE ALL RIGHT...
WHAT'S THAT MONSTROSITY?
OH, THAT'S OUR BALLOON TRIBUTE TO THE VICE PRESIDENT. YOU GUYS MAY NOT HAVE BEEN AWARE OF IT, BUT HE WAS A BIG SUPPORTER OF THE WAR!
ANY TROUBLE GETTING IT UP THERE?
NONE.

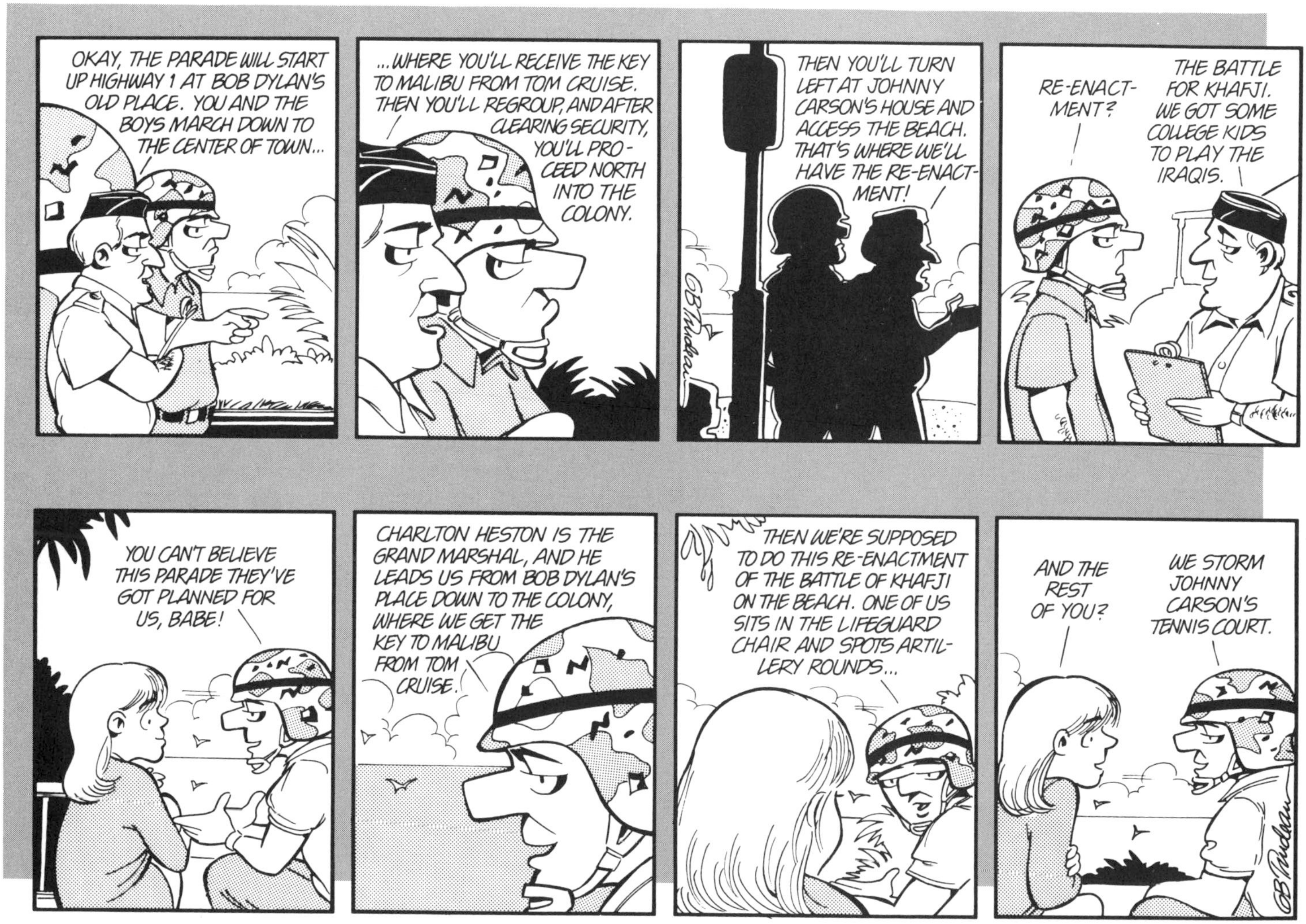
OKAY, THE PARADE WILL START UP HIGHWAY 1 AT BOB DYLAN'S OLD PLACE. YOU AND THE BOYS MARCH DOWN TO THE CENTER OF TOWN...
...WHERE YOU'LL RECEIVE THE KEY TO MALIBU FROM TOM CRUISE. THEN YOU'LL REGROUP, AND AFTER CLEARING SECURITY, YOU'LL PROCEED NORTH INTO THE COLONY.
THEN YOU'LL TURN LEFT AT JOHNNY CARSON'S HOUSE AND ACCESS THE BEACH. THAT'S WHERE WE'LL HAVE THE RE-ENACTMENT!
RE-ENACTMENT?
THE BATTLE FOR KHAFJI. WE GOT SOME COLLEGE KIDS TO PLAY THE IRAQIS.
YOU CAN'T BELIEVE THIS PARADE THEY'VE GOT PLANNED FOR US, BABE!
CHARLTON HESTON IS THE GRAND MARSHAL, AND HE LEADS US FROM BOB DYLAN'S PLACE DOWN TO THE COLONY, WHERE WE GET THE KEY TO MALIBU FROM TOM CRUISE.
THEN WE'RE SUPPOSED TO DO THIS RE-ENACTMENT OF THE BATTLE OF KHAFJI ON THE BEACH. ONE OF US SITS IN THE LIFEGUARD CHAIR AND SPOTS ARTILLERY ROUNDS...
AND THE REST OF YOU?
WE STORM JOHNNY CARSON'S TENNIS COURT.

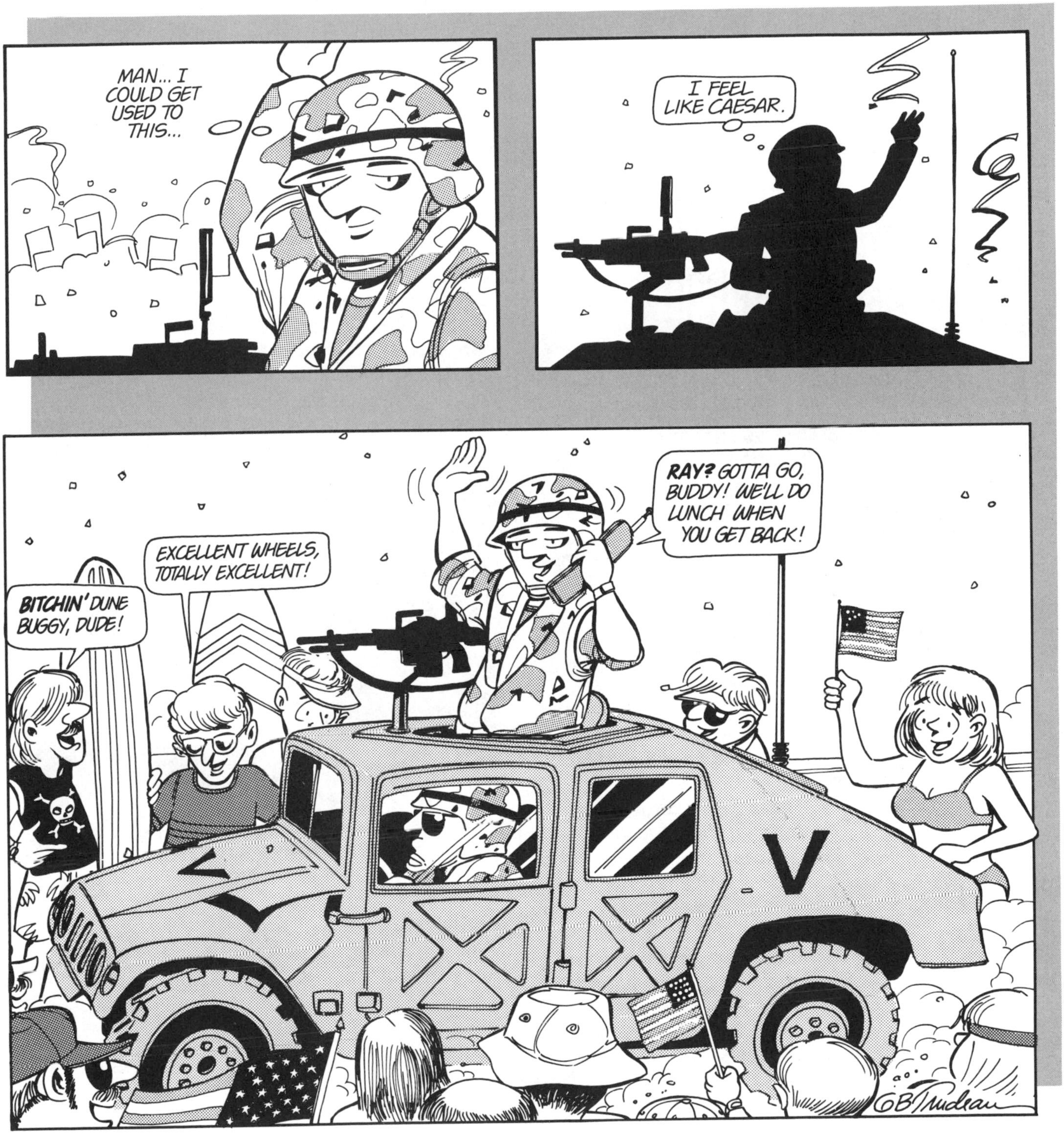
MAN... I COULD GET USED TO THIS...
I FEEL LIKE CAESAR.
BITCHIN' DUNE BUGGY, DUDE!
EXCELLENT WHEELS, TOTALLY EXCELLENT!
RAY? GOTTA GO, BUDDY! WE'LL DO LUNCH WHEN YOU GET BACK!
V
GB Trudeau

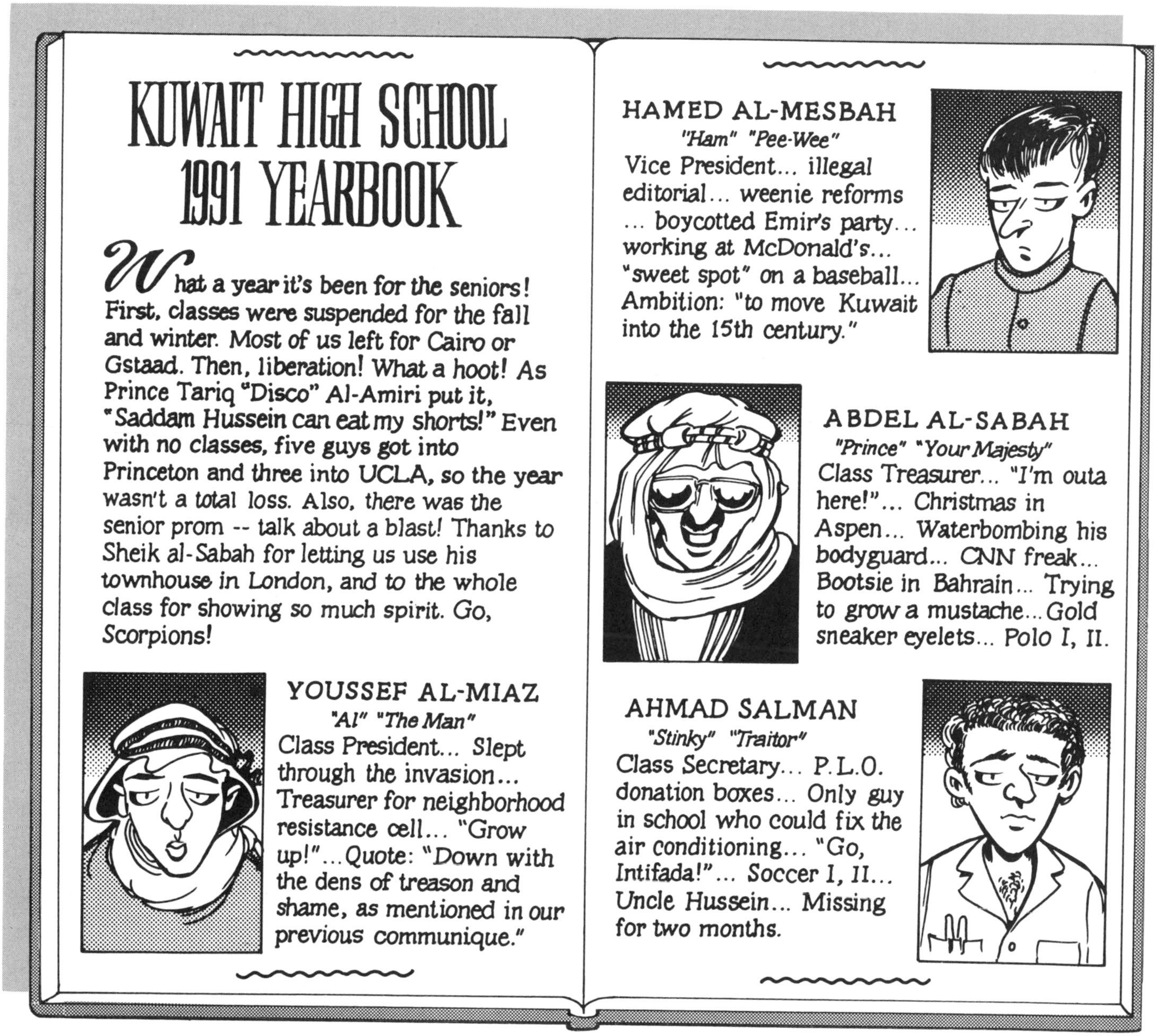
KUWAIT HIGH SCHOOL
1991 YEARBOOK
What a year it's been for the seniors! First, classes were suspended for the fall and winter. Most of us left for Cairo or Gstaad. Then, liberation! What a hoot! As Prince Tariq "Disco" Al-Amiri put it, "Saddam Hussein can eat my shorts!" Even with no classes, five guys got into Princeton and three into UCLA, so the year wasn't a total loss. Also, there was the senior prom -- talk about a blast! Thanks to Sheik al-Sabah for letting us use his townhouse in London, and to the whole class for showing so much spirit. Go, Scorpions!
YOUSSEF AL-MIAZ
"Al" "The Man"
Class President... Slept through the invasion... Treasurer for neighborhood resistance cell... "Grow up!"... Quote: "Down with the dens of treason and shame, as mentioned in our previous communique."
HAMED AL-MESBAH
"Ham" "Pee-Wee"
Vice President... illegal editorial... weenie reforms ... boycotted Emir's party... working at McDonald's... "sweet spot" on a baseball... Ambition: "to move Kuwait into the 15th century."
ABDEL AL-SABAH
"Prince" "Your Majesty"
Class Treasurer... "I'm outa here!"... Christmas in Aspen... Waterbombing his bodyguard... CNN freak... Bootsie in Bahrain... Trying to grow a mustache... Gold sneaker eyelets... Polo I, II.
AHMAD SALMAN
"Stinky" "Traitor"
Class Secretary... P.L.O. donation boxes... Only guy in school who could fix the air conditioning... "Go, Intifada!"... Soccer I, II... Uncle Hussein... Missing for two months.

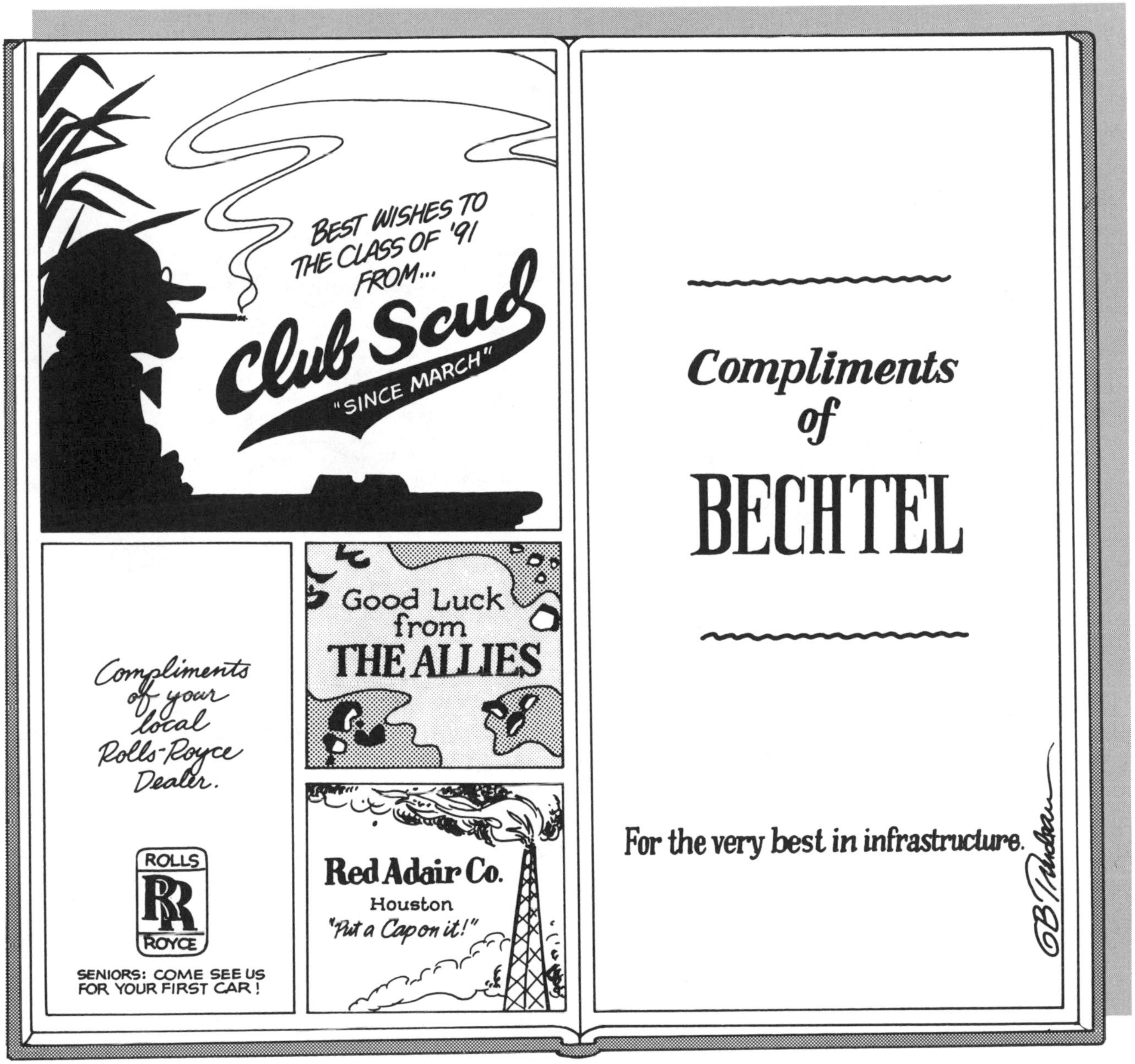
BEST WISHES TO THE CLASS OF '91 FROM...
Club Scud
"SINCE MARCH"
Compliments of your local Rolls-Royce Dealer.
ROLLS RR ROYCE
SENIORS: COME SEE US FOR YOUR FIRST CAR!
Good Luck from THE ALLIES
Red Adair Co.
Houston
"Put a Cap on it!"
Compliments of
BECHTEL
For the very best in infrastructure.

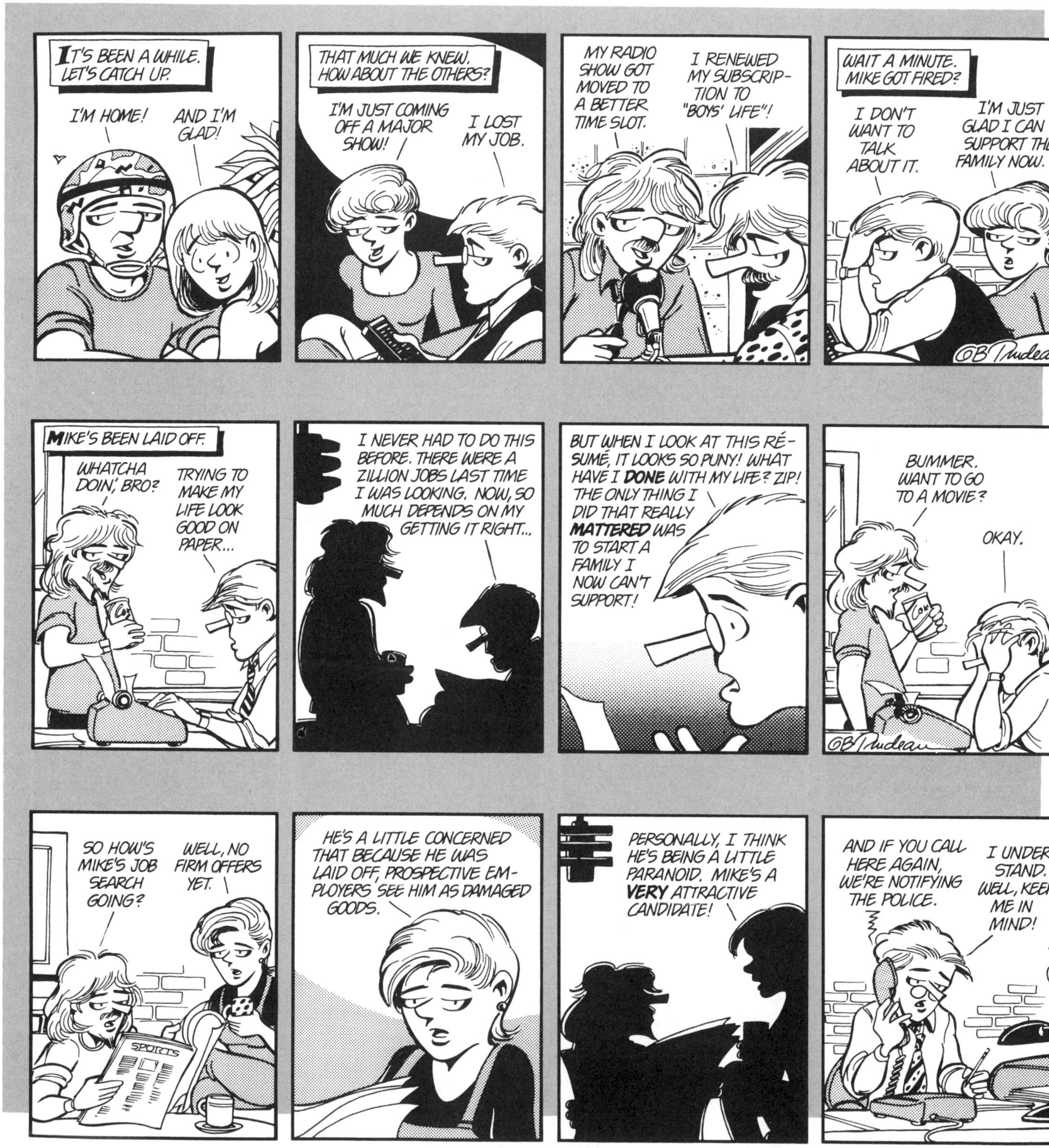
IT'S BEEN A WHILE. LET'S CATCH UP.
I'M HOME!
AND I'M GLAD!
THAT MUCH WE KNEW. HOW ABOUT THE OTHERS?
I'M JUST COMING OFF A MAJOR SHOW!
I LOST MY JOB.
MY RADIO SHOW GOT MOVED TO A BETTER TIME SLOT.
I RENEWED MY SUBSCRIPTION TO "BOYS' LIFE"!
WAIT A MINUTE. MIKE GOT FIRED?
I DON'T WANT TO TALK ABOUT IT.
I'M JUST GLAD I CAN SUPPORT THE FAMILY NOW.
©B Trudeau
MIKE'S BEEN LAID OFF.
WHATCHA DOIN', BRO?
TRYING TO MAKE MY LIFE LOOK GOOD ON PAPER...
I NEVER HAD TO DO THIS BEFORE. THERE WERE A ZILLION JOBS LAST TIME I WAS LOOKING. NOW, SO MUCH DEPENDS ON MY GETTING IT RIGHT...
BUT WHEN I LOOK AT THIS RÉSUMÉ, IT LOOKS SO PUNY! WHAT HAVE I DONE WITH MY LIFE? ZIP! THE ONLY THING I DID THAT REALLY MATTERED WAS TO START A FAMILY I NOW CAN'T SUPPORT!
BUMMER. WANT TO GO TO A MOVIE?
OKAY.
©B Trudeau
SO HOW'S MIKE'S JOB SEARCH GOING?
WELL, NO FIRM OFFERS YET.
SPORTS
HE'S A LITTLE CONCERNED THAT BECAUSE HE WAS LAID OFF, PROSPECTIVE EMPLOYERS SEE HIM AS DAMAGED GOODS.
PERSONALLY, I THINK HE'S BEING A LITTLE PARANOID. MIKE'S A VERY ATTRACTIVE CANDIDATE!
AND IF YOU CALL HERE AGAIN, WE'RE NOTIFYING THE POLICE.
I UNDERSTAND. WELL, KEEP ME IN MIND!
©B Trudeau

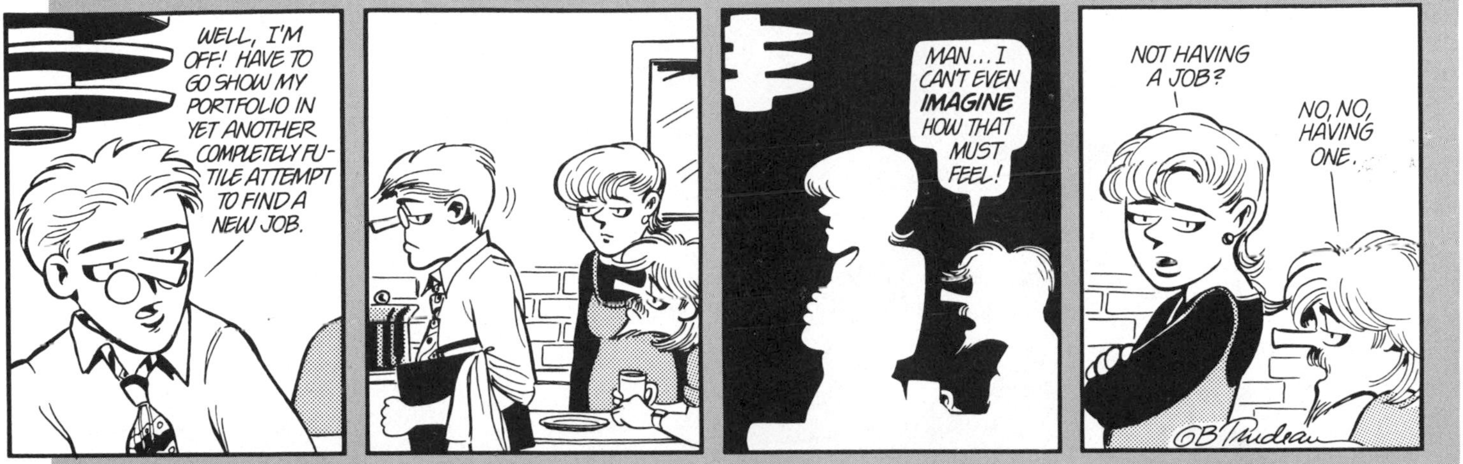
WELL, I'M OFF! HAVE TO GO SHOW MY PORTFOLIO IN YET ANOTHER COMPLETELY FUTILE ATTEMPT TO FIND A NEW JOB.
MAN... I CAN'T EVEN IMAGINE HOW THAT MUST FEEL!
NOT HAVING A JOB?
NO, NO, HAVING ONE.

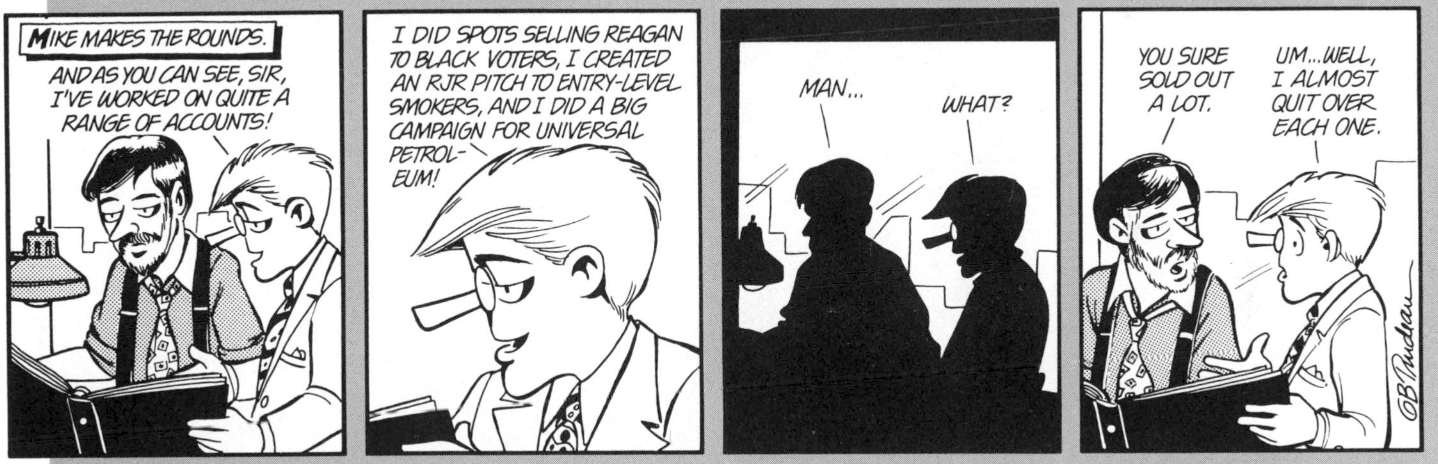
MIKE MAKES THE ROUNDS.
AND AS YOU CAN SEE, SIR, I'VE WORKED ON QUITE A RANGE OF ACCOUNTS!
I DID SPOTS SELLING REAGAN TO BLACK VOTERS, I CREATED AN RJR PITCH TO ENTRY-LEVEL SMOKERS, AND I DID A BIG CAMPAIGN FOR UNIVERSAL PETROLEUM!
MAN...
WHAT?
YOU SURE SOLD OUT A LOT.
UM... WELL, I ALMOST QUIT OVER EACH ONE.

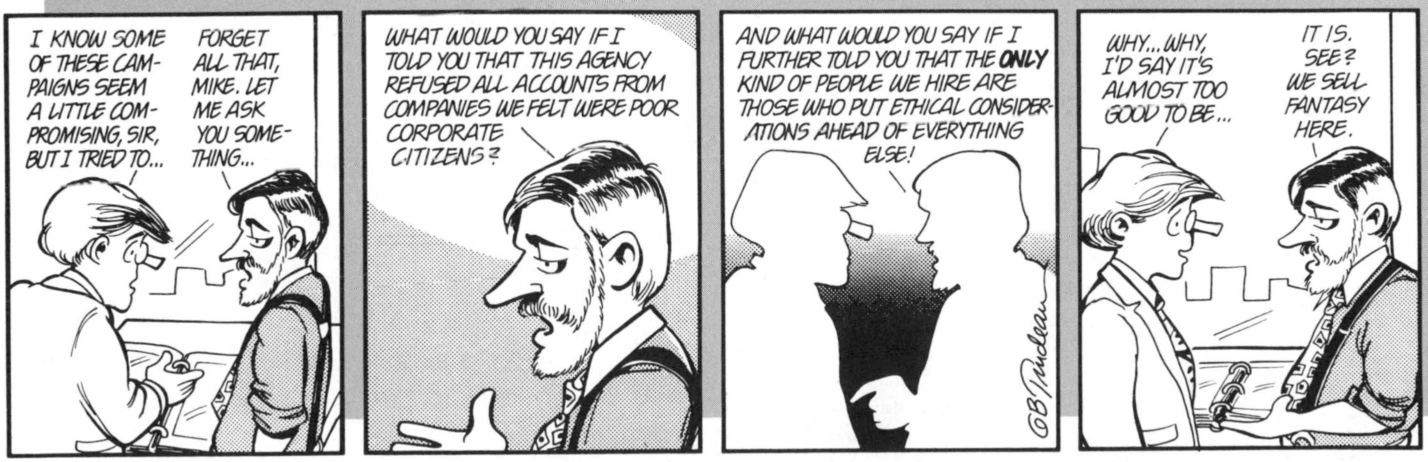
I KNOW SOME OF THESE CAMPAIGNS SEEM A LITTLE COMPROMISING, SIR, BUT I TRIED TO...
FORGET ALL THAT, MIKE. LET ME ASK YOU SOMETHING...
WHAT WOULD YOU SAY IF I TOLD YOU THAT THIS AGENCY REFUSED ALL ACCOUNTS FROM COMPANIES WE FELT WERE POOR CORPORATE CITIZENS?
AND WHAT WOULD YOU SAY IF I FURTHER TOLD YOU THAT THE ONLY KIND OF PEOPLE WE HIRE ARE THOSE WHO PUT ETHICAL CONSIDERATIONS AHEAD OF EVERYTHING ELSE!
WHY... WHY, I'D SAY IT'S ALMOST TOO GOOD TO BE...
IT IS. SEE? WE SELL FANTASY HERE.

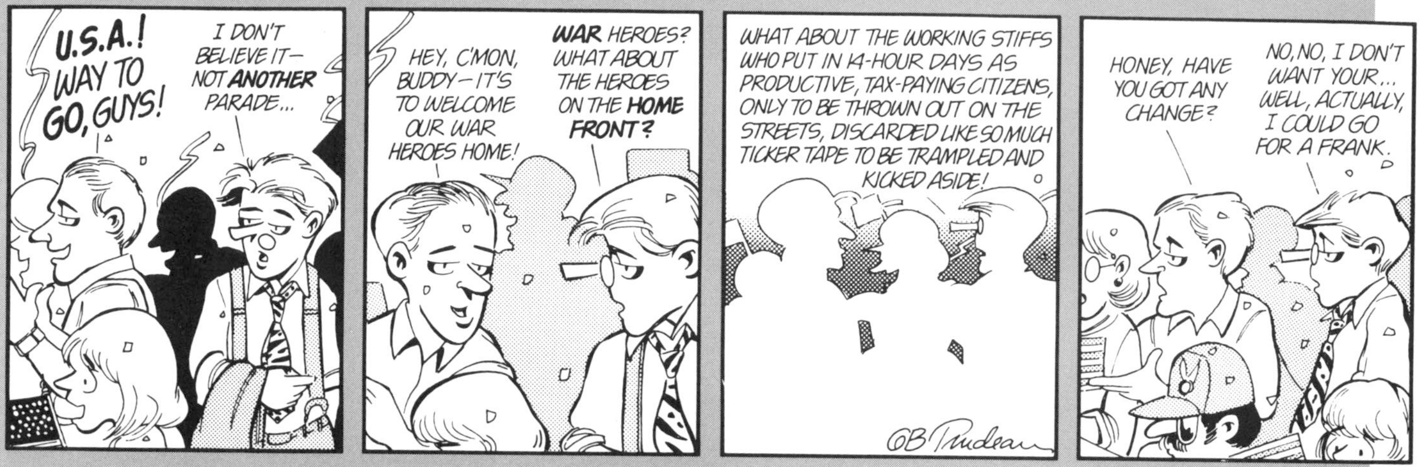
U.S.A.! WAY TO GO, GUYS!
I DON'T BELIEVE IT— NOT ANOTHER PARADE...
HEY, C'MON, BUDDY—IT'S TO WELCOME OUR WAR HEROES HOME!
WAR HEROES? WHAT ABOUT THE HEROES ON THE HOME FRONT?
WHAT ABOUT THE WORKING STIFFS WHO PUT IN 14-HOUR DAYS AS PRODUCTIVE, TAX-PAYING CITIZENS, ONLY TO BE THROWN OUT ON THE STREETS, DISCARDED LIKE SO MUCH TICKER TAPE TO BE TRAMPLED AND KICKED ASIDE!
HONEY, HAVE YOU GOT ANY CHANGE?
NO, NO, I DON'T WANT YOUR... WELL, ACTUALLY, I COULD GO FOR A FRANK.

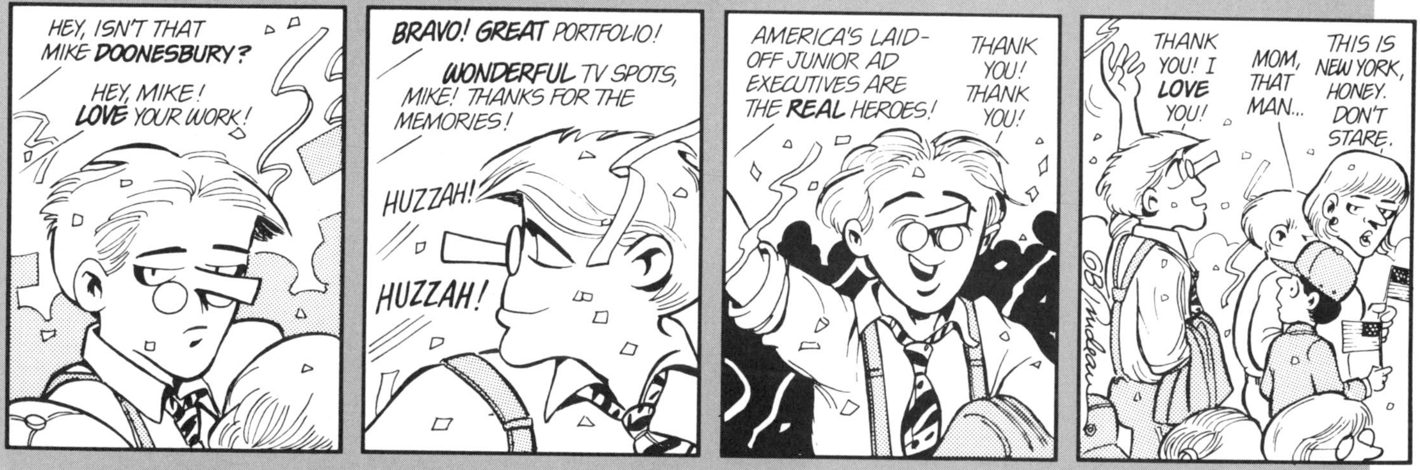
HEY, ISN'T THAT MIKE DOONESBURY?
HEY, MIKE! LOVE YOUR WORK!
BRAVO! GREAT PORTFOLIO!
WONDERFUL TV SPOTS, MIKE! THANKS FOR THE MEMORIES!
HUZZAH!
HUZZAH!
AMERICA'S LAID-OFF JUNIOR AD EXECUTIVES ARE THE REAL HEROES!
THANK YOU! THANK YOU!
THANK YOU! I LOVE YOU!
MOM, THAT MAN...
THIS IS NEW YORK, HONEY. DON'T STARE.

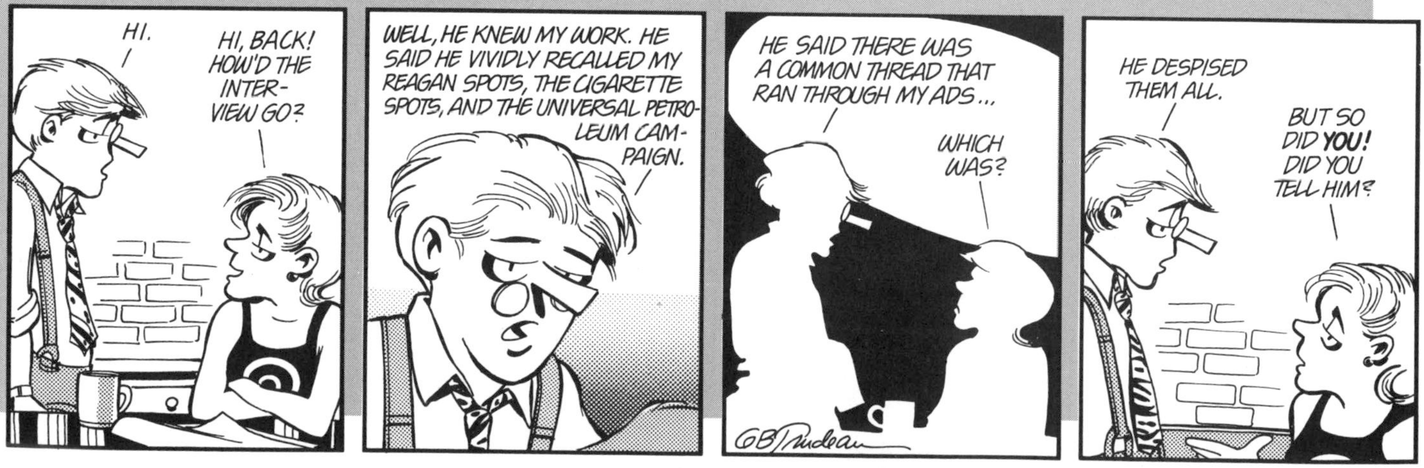
HI.
HI, BACK! HOW'D THE INTERVIEW GO?
WELL, HE KNEW MY WORK. HE SAID HE VIVIDLY RECALLED MY REAGAN SPOTS, THE CIGARETTE SPOTS, AND THE UNIVERSAL PETROLEUM CAMPAIGN.
HE SAID THERE WAS A COMMON THREAD THAT RAN THROUGH MY ADS...
WHICH WAS?
HE DESPISED THEM ALL.
BUT SO DID YOU! DID YOU TELL HIM?

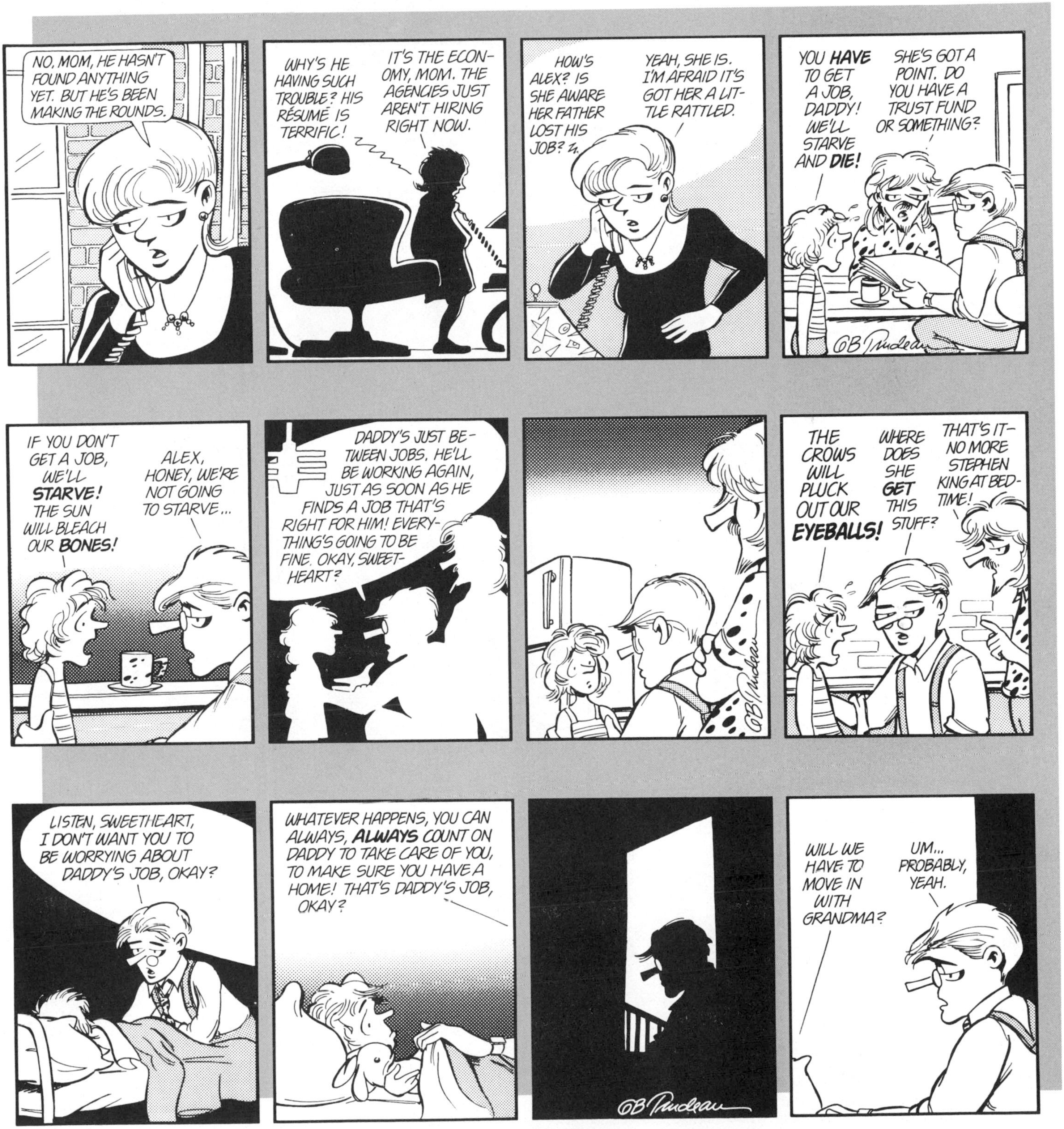
NO, MOM, HE HASN'T FOUND ANYTHING YET. BUT HE'S BEEN MAKING THE ROUNDS.
WHY'S HE HAVING SUCH TROUBLE? HIS RÉSUMÉ IS TERRIFIC!
IT'S THE ECONOMY, MOM. THE AGENCIES JUST AREN'T HIRING RIGHT NOW.
HOW'S ALEX? IS SHE AWARE HER FATHER LOST HIS JOB?
YEAH, SHE IS. I'M AFRAID IT'S GOT HER A LITTLE RATTLED.
YOU HAVE TO GET A JOB, DADDY! WE'LL STARVE AND DIE!
SHE'S GOT A POINT. DO YOU HAVE A TRUST FUND OR SOMETHING?
IF YOU DON'T GET A JOB, WE'LL STARVE! THE SUN WILL BLEACH OUR BONES!
ALEX, HONEY, WE'RE NOT GOING TO STARVE...
DADDY'S JUST BETWEEN JOBS. HE'LL BE WORKING AGAIN, JUST AS SOON AS HE FINDS A JOB THAT'S RIGHT FOR HIM! EVERYTHING'S GOING TO BE FINE. OKAY, SWEETHEART?
THE CROWS WILL PLUCK OUT OUR EYEBALLS!
WHERE DOES SHE GET THIS STUFF?
THAT'S IT—NO MORE STEPHEN KING AT BEDTIME!
LISTEN, SWEETHEART, I DON'T WANT YOU TO BE WORRYING ABOUT DADDY'S JOB, OKAY?
WHATEVER HAPPENS, YOU CAN ALWAYS, ALWAYS COUNT ON DADDY TO TAKE CARE OF YOU, TO MAKE SURE YOU HAVE A HOME! THAT'S DADDY'S JOB, OKAY?
WILL WE HAVE TO MOVE IN WITH GRANDMA?
UM... PROBABLY, YEAH.

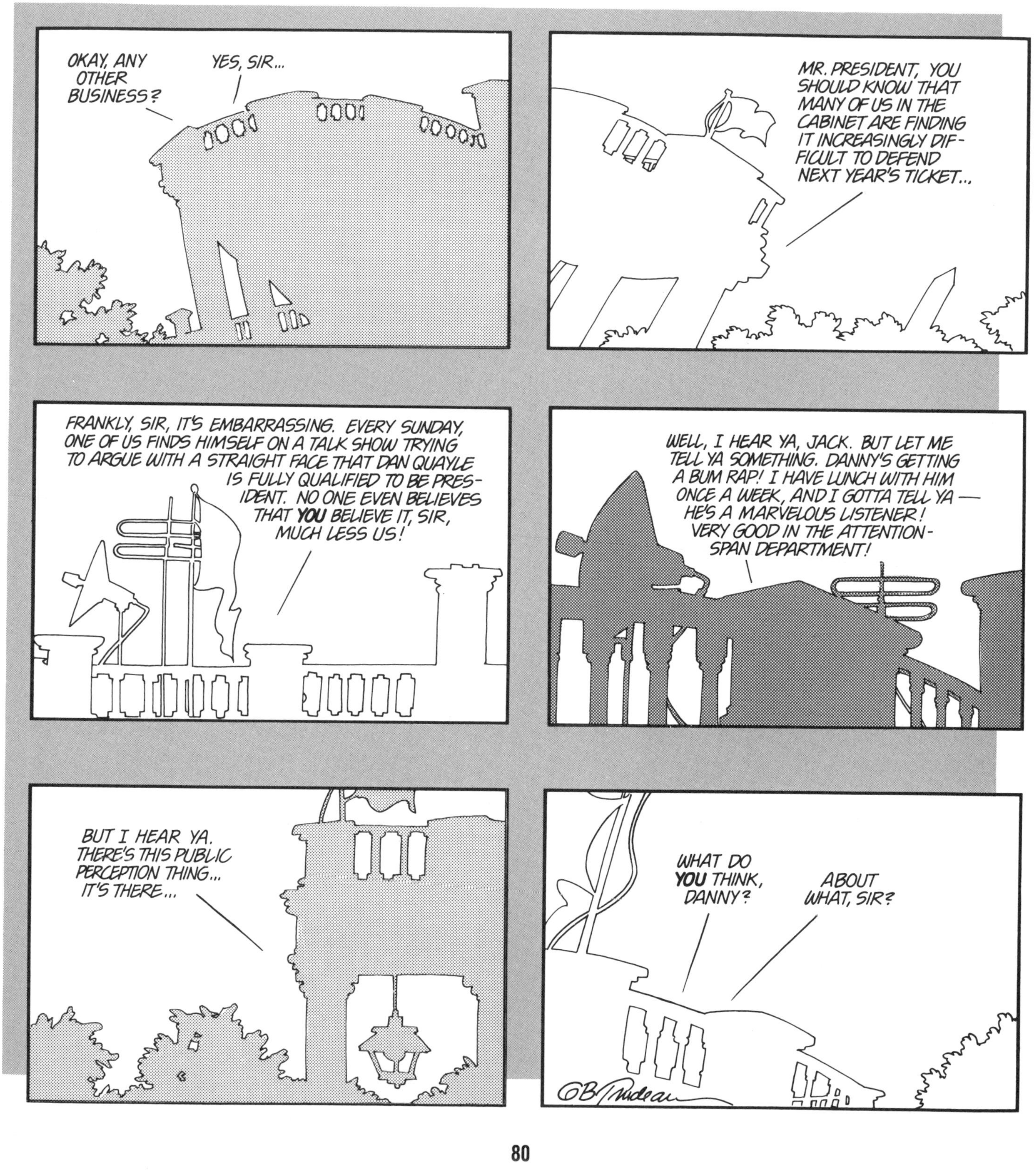
OKAY, ANY OTHER BUSINESS?
YES, SIR...
MR. PRESIDENT, YOU SHOULD KNOW THAT MANY OF US IN THE CABINET ARE FINDING IT INCREASINGLY DIF-FICULT TO DEFEND NEXT YEAR'S TICKET...
FRANKLY, SIR, IT'S EMBARRASSING. EVERY SUNDAY, ONE OF US FINDS HIMSELF ON A TALK SHOW TRYING TO ARGUE WITH A STRAIGHT FACE THAT DAN QUAYLE IS FULLY QUALIFIED TO BE PRES-IDENT. NO ONE EVEN BELIEVES THAT **YOU** BELIEVE IT, SIR, MUCH LESS US!
WELL, I HEAR YA, JACK. BUT LET ME TELL YA SOMETHING. DANNY'S GETTING A BUM RAP! I HAVE LUNCH WITH HIM ONCE A WEEK, AND I GOTTA TELL YA — HE'S A MARVELOUS LISTENER! VERY GOOD IN THE ATTENTION-SPAN DEPARTMENT!
BUT I HEAR YA. THERE'S THIS PUBLIC PERCEPTION THING... IT'S THERE...
WHAT DO **YOU** THINK, DANNY?
ABOUT WHAT, SIR?
GB Trudeau

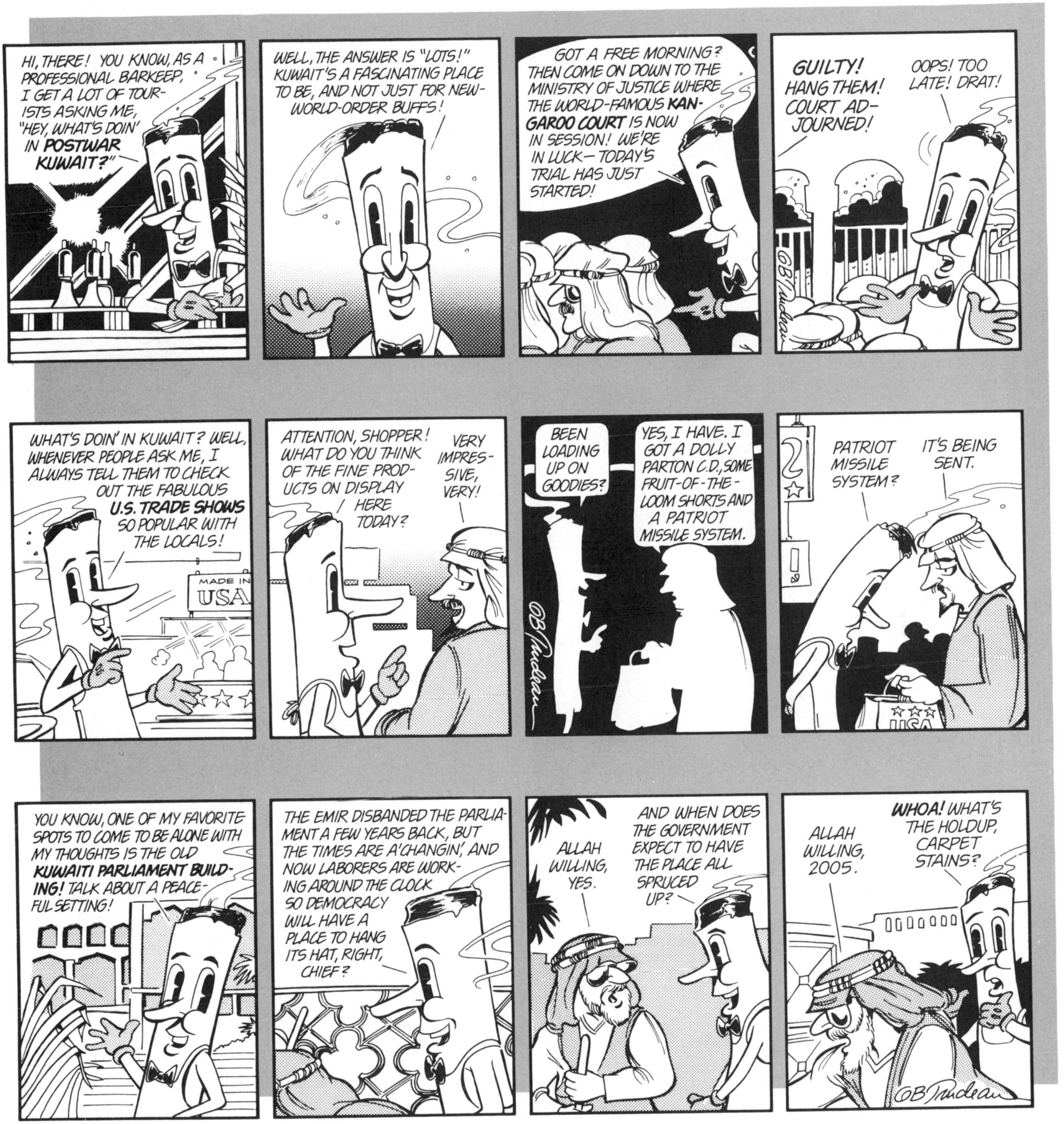
HI, THERE! YOU KNOW, AS A PROFESSIONAL BARKEEP, I GET A LOT OF TOURISTS ASKING ME, "HEY, WHAT'S DOIN' IN POSTWAR KUWAIT?"
WELL, THE ANSWER IS "LOTS!" KUWAIT'S A FASCINATING PLACE TO BE, AND NOT JUST FOR NEW-WORLD-ORDER BUFFS!
GOT A FREE MORNING? THEN COME ON DOWN TO THE MINISTRY OF JUSTICE WHERE THE WORLD-FAMOUS KANGAROO COURT IS NOW IN SESSION! WE'RE IN LUCK—TODAY'S TRIAL HAS JUST STARTED!
GUILTY! HANG THEM! COURT ADJOURNED!
OOPS! TOO LATE! DRAT!
WHAT'S DOIN' IN KUWAIT? WELL, WHENEVER PEOPLE ASK ME, I ALWAYS TELL THEM TO CHECK OUT THE FABULOUS U.S. TRADE SHOWS SO POPULAR WITH THE LOCALS!
MADE IN USA
ATTENTION, SHOPPER! WHAT DO YOU THINK OF THE FINE PRODUCTS ON DISPLAY HERE TODAY?
VERY IMPRESSIVE, VERY!
BEEN LOADING UP ON GOODIES?
YES, I HAVE. I GOT A DOLLY PARTON C.D., SOME FRUIT-OF-THE-LOOM SHORTS AND A PATRIOT MISSILE SYSTEM.
PATRIOT MISSILE SYSTEM?
IT'S BEING SENT.
YOU KNOW, ONE OF MY FAVORITE SPOTS TO COME TO BE ALONE WITH MY THOUGHTS IS THE OLD KUWAITI PARLIAMENT BUILDING! TALK ABOUT A PEACEFUL SETTING!
THE EMIR DISBANDED THE PARLIAMENT A FEW YEARS BACK, BUT THE TIMES ARE A'CHANGIN', AND NOW LABORERS ARE WORKING AROUND THE CLOCK SO DEMOCRACY WILL HAVE A PLACE TO HANG ITS HAT, RIGHT, CHIEF?
AND WHEN DOES THE GOVERNMENT EXPECT TO HAVE THE PLACE ALL SPRUCED UP?
ALLAH WILLING, YES.
WHOA! WHAT'S THE HOLDUP, CARPET STAINS?
ALLAH WILLING, 2005.
GB Trudeau

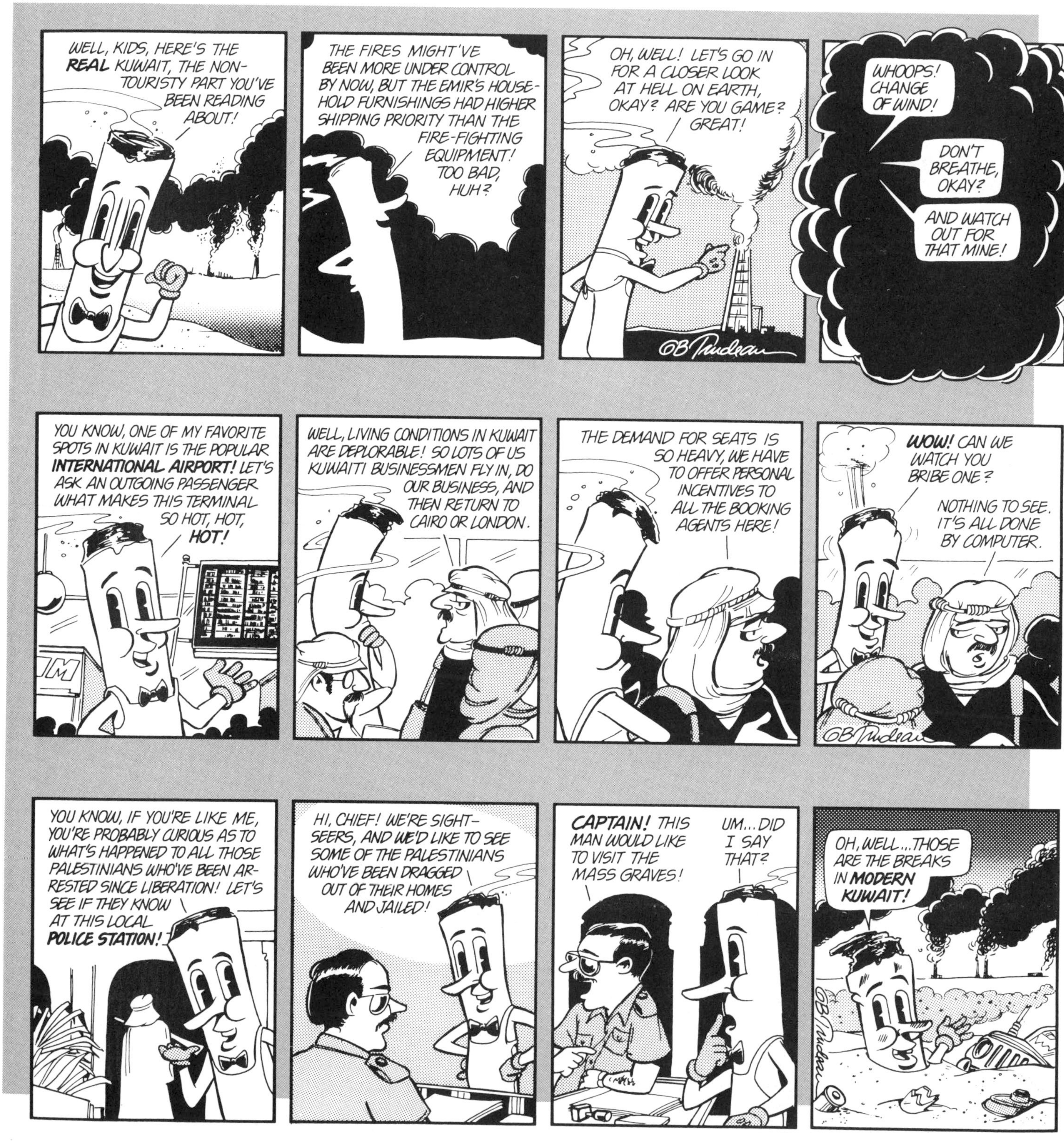
WELL, KIDS, HERE'S THE REAL KUWAIT, THE NON-TOURISTY PART YOU'VE BEEN READING ABOUT!
THE FIRES MIGHT'VE BEEN MORE UNDER CONTROL BY NOW, BUT THE EMIR'S HOUSEHOLD FURNISHINGS HAD HIGHER SHIPPING PRIORITY THAN THE FIRE-FIGHTING EQUIPMENT! TOO BAD, HUH?
OH, WELL! LET'S GO IN FOR A CLOSER LOOK AT HELL ON EARTH, OKAY? ARE YOU GAME? GREAT!
GB Trudeau
WHOOPS! CHANGE OF WIND!
DON'T BREATHE, OKAY?
AND WATCH OUT FOR THAT MINE!
YOU KNOW, ONE OF MY FAVORITE SPOTS IN KUWAIT IS THE POPULAR INTERNATIONAL AIRPORT! LET'S ASK AN OUTGOING PASSENGER WHAT MAKES THIS TERMINAL SO HOT, HOT, HOT!
WELL, LIVING CONDITIONS IN KUWAIT ARE DEPLORABLE! SO LOTS OF US KUWAITI BUSINESSMEN FLY IN, DO OUR BUSINESS, AND THEN RETURN TO CAIRO OR LONDON.
THE DEMAND FOR SEATS IS SO HEAVY, WE HAVE TO OFFER PERSONAL INCENTIVES TO ALL THE BOOKING AGENTS HERE!
WOW! CAN WE WATCH YOU BRIBE ONE?
NOTHING TO SEE. IT'S ALL DONE BY COMPUTER.
GB Trudeau
YOU KNOW, IF YOU'RE LIKE ME, YOU'RE PROBABLY CURIOUS AS TO WHAT'S HAPPENED TO ALL THOSE PALESTINIANS WHO'VE BEEN ARRESTED SINCE LIBERATION! LET'S SEE IF THEY KNOW AT THIS LOCAL POLICE STATION!
HI, CHIEF! WE'RE SIGHTSEERS, AND WE'D LIKE TO SEE SOME OF THE PALESTINIANS WHO'VE BEEN DRAGGED OUT OF THEIR HOMES AND JAILED!
CAPTAIN! THIS MAN WOULD LIKE TO VISIT THE MASS GRAVES!
UM... DID I SAY THAT?
OH, WELL... THOSE ARE THE BREAKS IN MODERN KUWAIT!
GB Trudeau

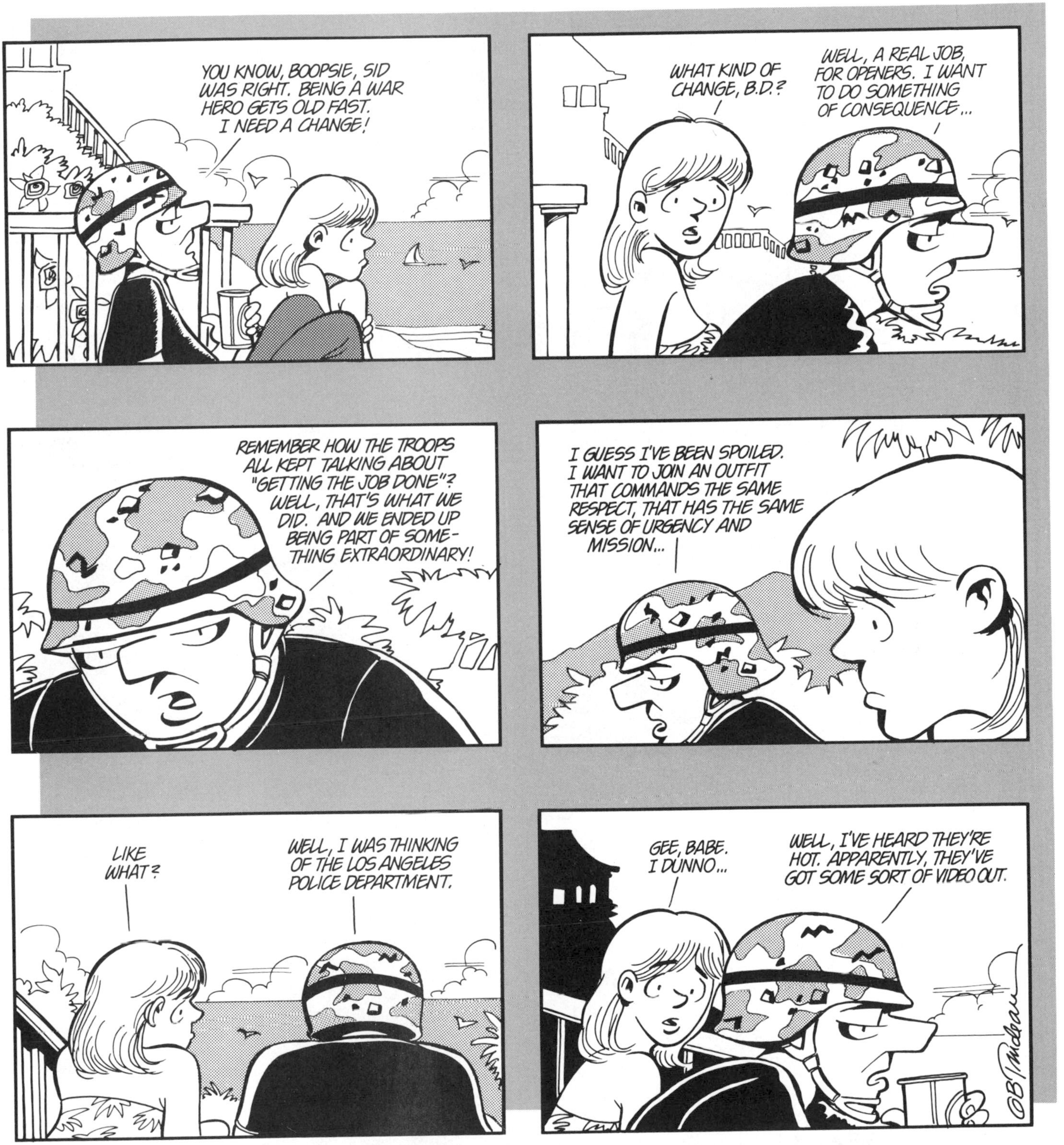
YOU KNOW, BOOPSIE, SID WAS RIGHT. BEING A WAR HERO GETS OLD FAST. I NEED A CHANGE!
WHAT KIND OF CHANGE, B.D.?
WELL, A REAL JOB, FOR OPENERS. I WANT TO DO SOMETHING OF CONSEQUENCE...
REMEMBER HOW THE TROOPS ALL KEPT TALKING ABOUT "GETTING THE JOB DONE"? WELL, THAT'S WHAT WE DID. AND WE ENDED UP BEING PART OF SOME-THING EXTRAORDINARY!
I GUESS I'VE BEEN SPOILED. I WANT TO JOIN AN OUTFIT THAT COMMANDS THE SAME RESPECT, THAT HAS THE SAME SENSE OF URGENCY AND MISSION...
LIKE WHAT?
WELL, I WAS THINKING OF THE LOS ANGELES POLICE DEPARTMENT.
GEE, BABE. I DUNNO...
WELL, I'VE HEARD THEY'RE HOT. APPARENTLY, THEY'VE GOT SOME SORT OF VIDEO OUT.

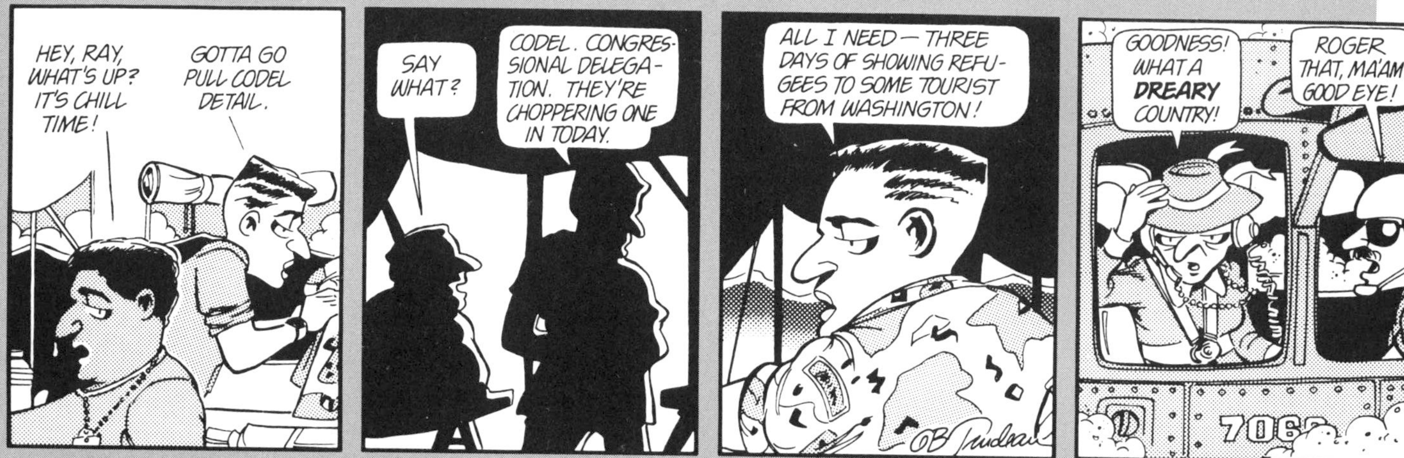
HEY, RAY, WHAT'S UP? IT'S CHILL TIME!
GOTTA GO PULL CODEL DETAIL.
SAY WHAT?
CODEL. CONGRESSIONAL DELEGATION. THEY'RE CHOPPERING ONE IN TODAY.
ALL I NEED — THREE DAYS OF SHOWING REFUGEES TO SOME TOURIST FROM WASHINGTON!
GOODNESS! WHAT A **DREARY** COUNTRY!
ROGER THAT, MA'AM! GOOD EYE!
7068

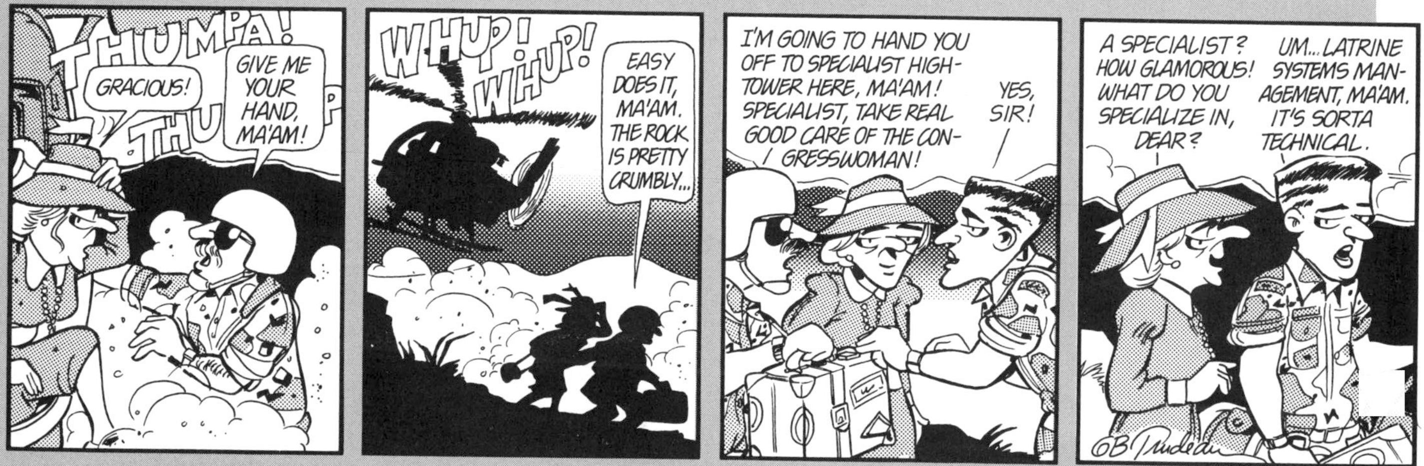
THUMPA! THUMP
GRACIOUS!
GIVE ME YOUR HAND, MA'AM!
WHUP! WHUP!
EASY DOES IT, MA'AM. THE ROCK IS PRETTY CRUMBLY...
I'M GOING TO HAND YOU OFF TO SPECIALIST HIGHTOWER HERE, MA'AM! SPECIALIST, TAKE REAL GOOD CARE OF THE CONGRESSWOMAN!
YES, SIR!
A SPECIALIST? HOW GLAMOROUS! WHAT DO YOU SPECIALIZE IN, DEAR?
UM... LATRINE SYSTEMS MANAGEMENT, MA'AM. IT'S SORTA TECHNICAL.

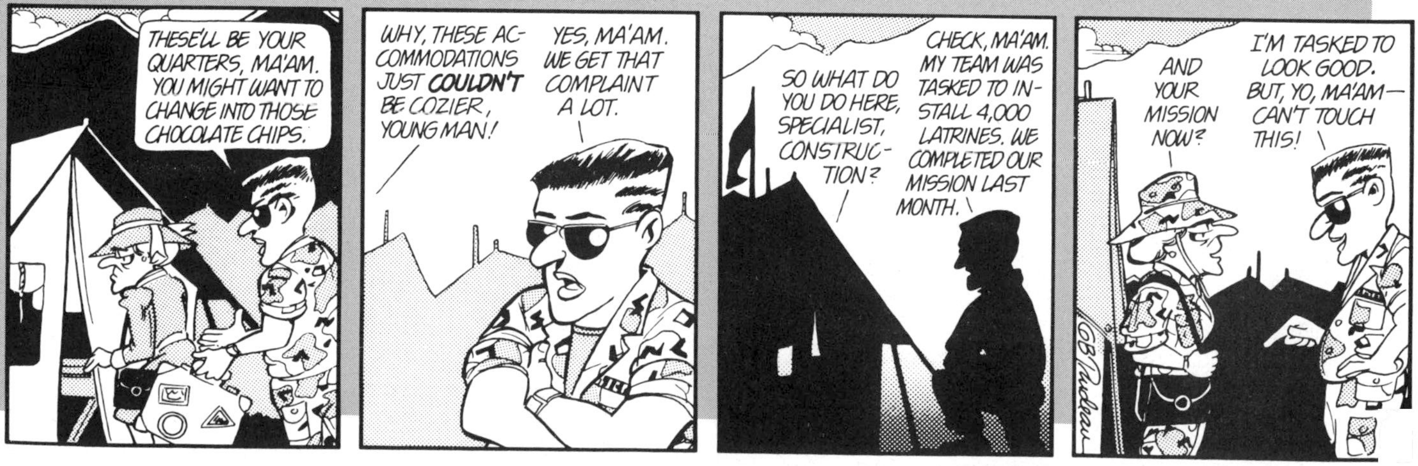
THESE'LL BE YOUR QUARTERS, MA'AM. YOU MIGHT WANT TO CHANGE INTO THOSE CHOCOLATE CHIPS.
WHY, THESE ACCOMMODATIONS JUST **COULDN'T** BE COZIER, YOUNG MAN!
YES, MA'AM. WE GET THAT COMPLAINT A LOT.
SO WHAT DO YOU DO HERE, SPECIALIST, CONSTRUCTION?
CHECK, MA'AM. MY TEAM WAS TASKED TO INSTALL 4,000 LATRINES. WE COMPLETED OUR MISSION LAST MONTH.
AND YOUR MISSION NOW?
I'M TASKED TO LOOK GOOD. BUT, YO, MA'AM — CAN'T TOUCH THIS!

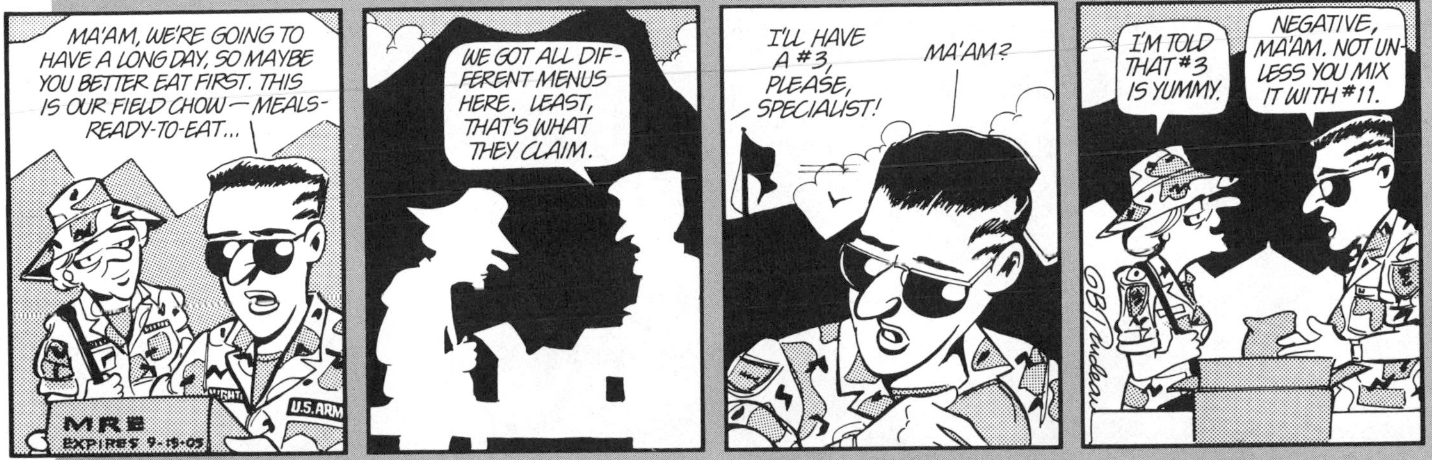
MA'AM, WE'RE GOING TO HAVE A LONG DAY, SO MAYBE YOU BETTER EAT FIRST. THIS IS OUR FIELD CHOW — MEALS-READY-TO-EAT...
MRE
U.S.ARM
WE GOT ALL DIFFERENT MENUS HERE. LEAST, THAT'S WHAT THEY CLAIM.
I'LL HAVE A #3, PLEASE, SPECIALIST!
MA'AM?
I'M TOLD THAT #3 IS YUMMY.
NEGATIVE, MA'AM. NOT UNLESS YOU MIX IT WITH #11.
©B Trudeau

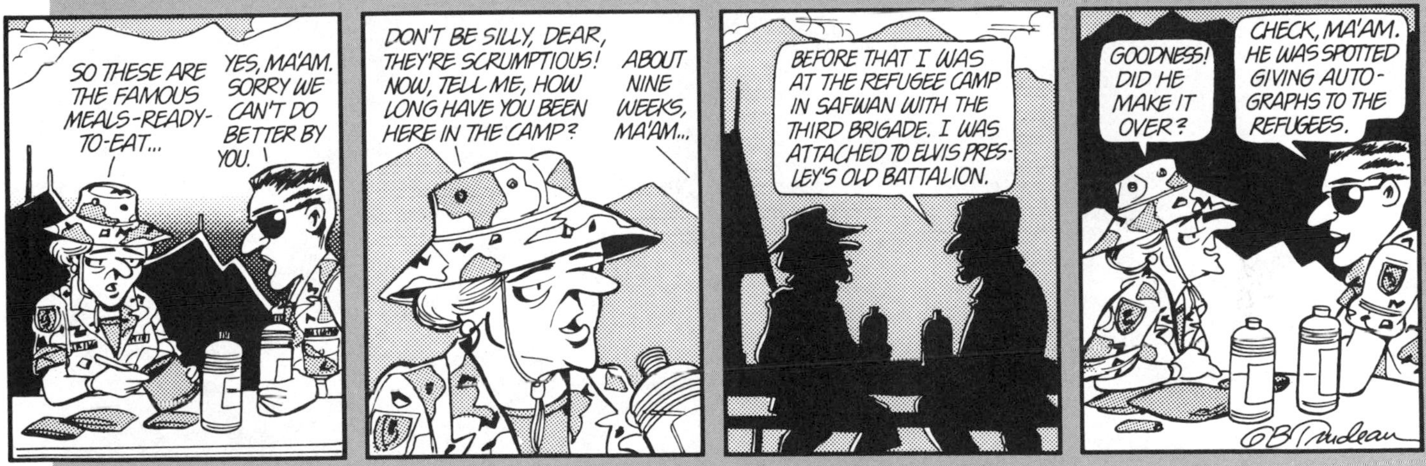
SO THESE ARE THE FAMOUS MEALS-READY-TO-EAT...
YES, MA'AM. SORRY WE CAN'T DO BETTER BY YOU.
DON'T BE SILLY, DEAR, THEY'RE SCRUMPTIOUS! NOW, TELL ME, HOW LONG HAVE YOU BEEN HERE IN THE CAMP?
ABOUT NINE WEEKS, MA'AM...
BEFORE THAT I WAS AT THE REFUGEE CAMP IN SAFWAN WITH THE THIRD BRIGADE. I WAS ATTACHED TO ELVIS PRESLEY'S OLD BATTALION.
GOODNESS! DID HE MAKE IT OVER?
CHECK, MA'AM. HE WAS SPOTTED GIVING AUTOGRAPHS TO THE REFUGEES.
©B Trudeau

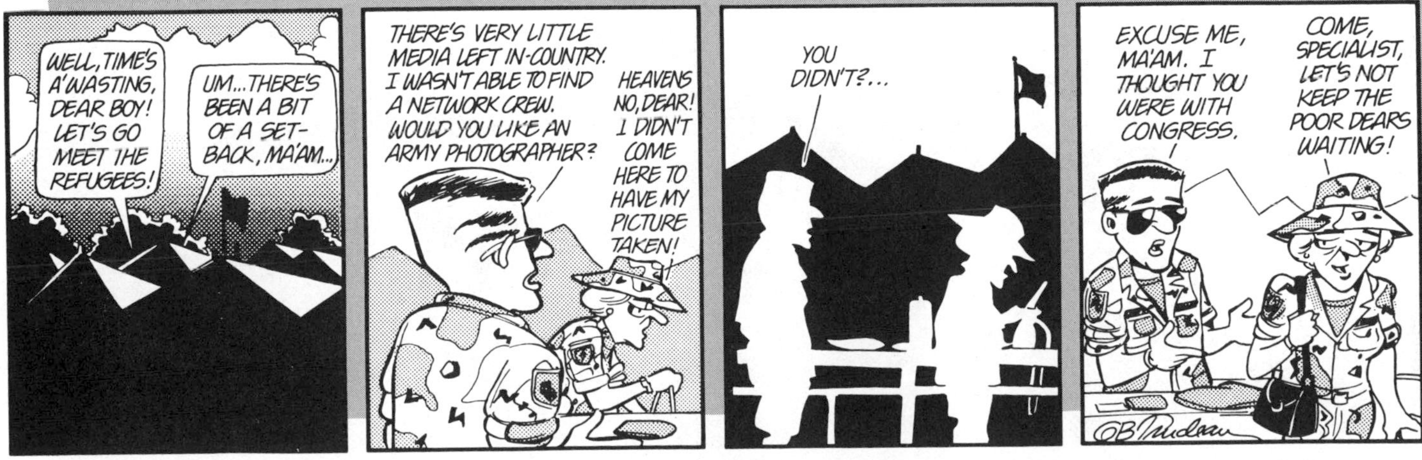
WELL, TIME'S A'WASTING, DEAR BOY! LET'S GO MEET THE REFUGEES!
UM...THERE'S BEEN A BIT OF A SETBACK, MA'AM...
THERE'S VERY LITTLE MEDIA LEFT IN-COUNTRY. I WASN'T ABLE TO FIND A NETWORK CREW. WOULD YOU LIKE AN ARMY PHOTOGRAPHER?
HEAVENS NO, DEAR! I DIDN'T COME HERE TO HAVE MY PICTURE TAKEN!
YOU DIDN'T?...
EXCUSE ME, MA'AM. I THOUGHT YOU WERE WITH CONGRESS.
COME, SPECIALIST, LET'S NOT KEEP THE POOR DEARS WAITING!
©B Trudeau

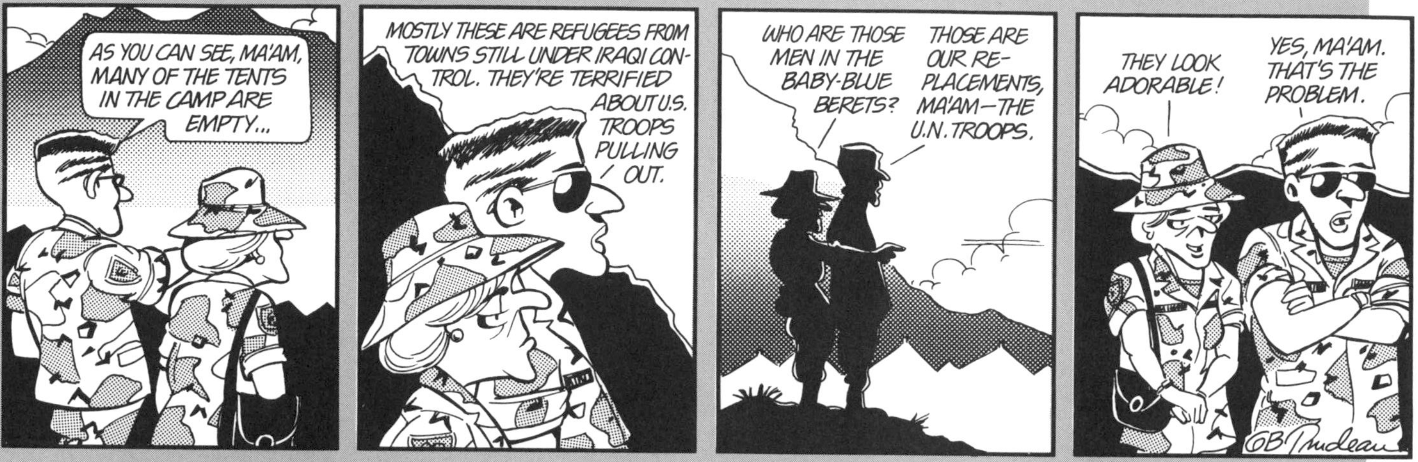
AS YOU CAN SEE, MA'AM, MANY OF THE TENTS IN THE CAMP ARE EMPTY...
MOSTLY THESE ARE REFUGEES FROM TOWNS STILL UNDER IRAQI CONTROL. THEY'RE TERRIFIED ABOUT U.S. TROOPS PULLING OUT.
WHO ARE THOSE MEN IN THE BABY-BLUE BERETS?
THOSE ARE OUR REPLACEMENTS, MA'AM—THE U.N. TROOPS.
THEY LOOK ADORABLE!
YES, MA'AM. THAT'S THE PROBLEM.

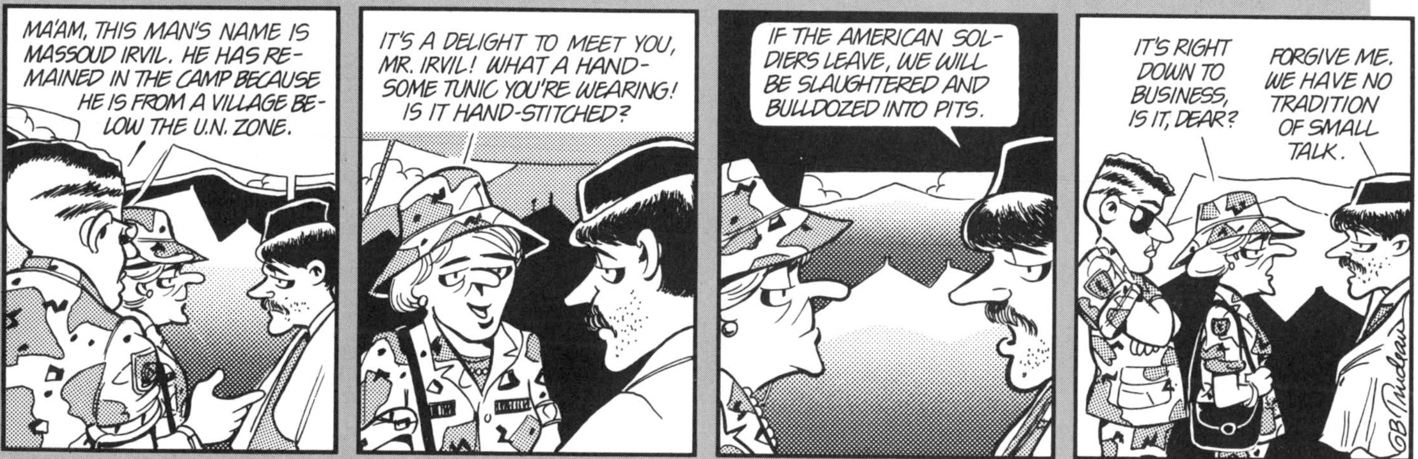
MA'AM, THIS MAN'S NAME IS MASSOUD IRVIL. HE HAS REMAINED IN THE CAMP BECAUSE HE IS FROM A VILLAGE BELOW THE U.N. ZONE.
IT'S A DELIGHT TO MEET YOU, MR. IRVIL! WHAT A HANDSOME TUNIC YOU'RE WEARING! IS IT HAND-STITCHED?
IF THE AMERICAN SOLDIERS LEAVE, WE WILL BE SLAUGHTERED AND BULLDOZED INTO PITS.
IT'S RIGHT DOWN TO BUSINESS, IS IT, DEAR?
FORGIVE ME. WE HAVE NO TRADITION OF SMALL TALK.

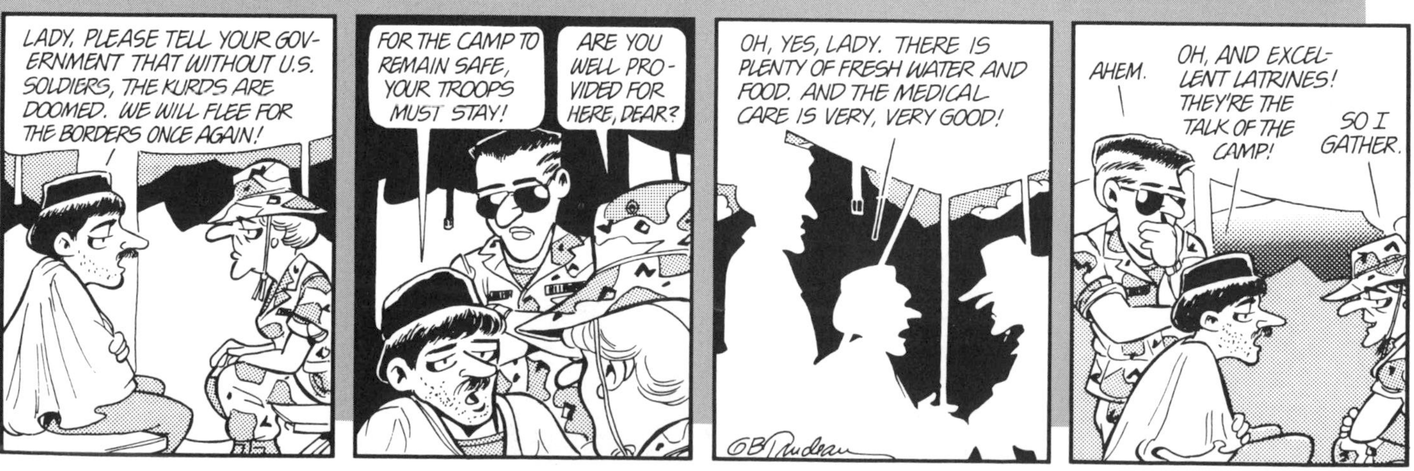
LADY, PLEASE TELL YOUR GOVERNMENT THAT WITHOUT U.S. SOLDIERS, THE KURDS ARE DOOMED. WE WILL FLEE FOR THE BORDERS ONCE AGAIN!
FOR THE CAMP TO REMAIN SAFE, YOUR TROOPS MUST STAY!
ARE YOU WELL PROVIDED FOR HERE, DEAR?
OH, YES, LADY. THERE IS PLENTY OF FRESH WATER AND FOOD. AND THE MEDICAL CARE IS VERY, VERY GOOD!
AHEM.
OH, AND EXCELLENT LATRINES! THEY'RE THE TALK OF THE CAMP!
SO I GATHER.

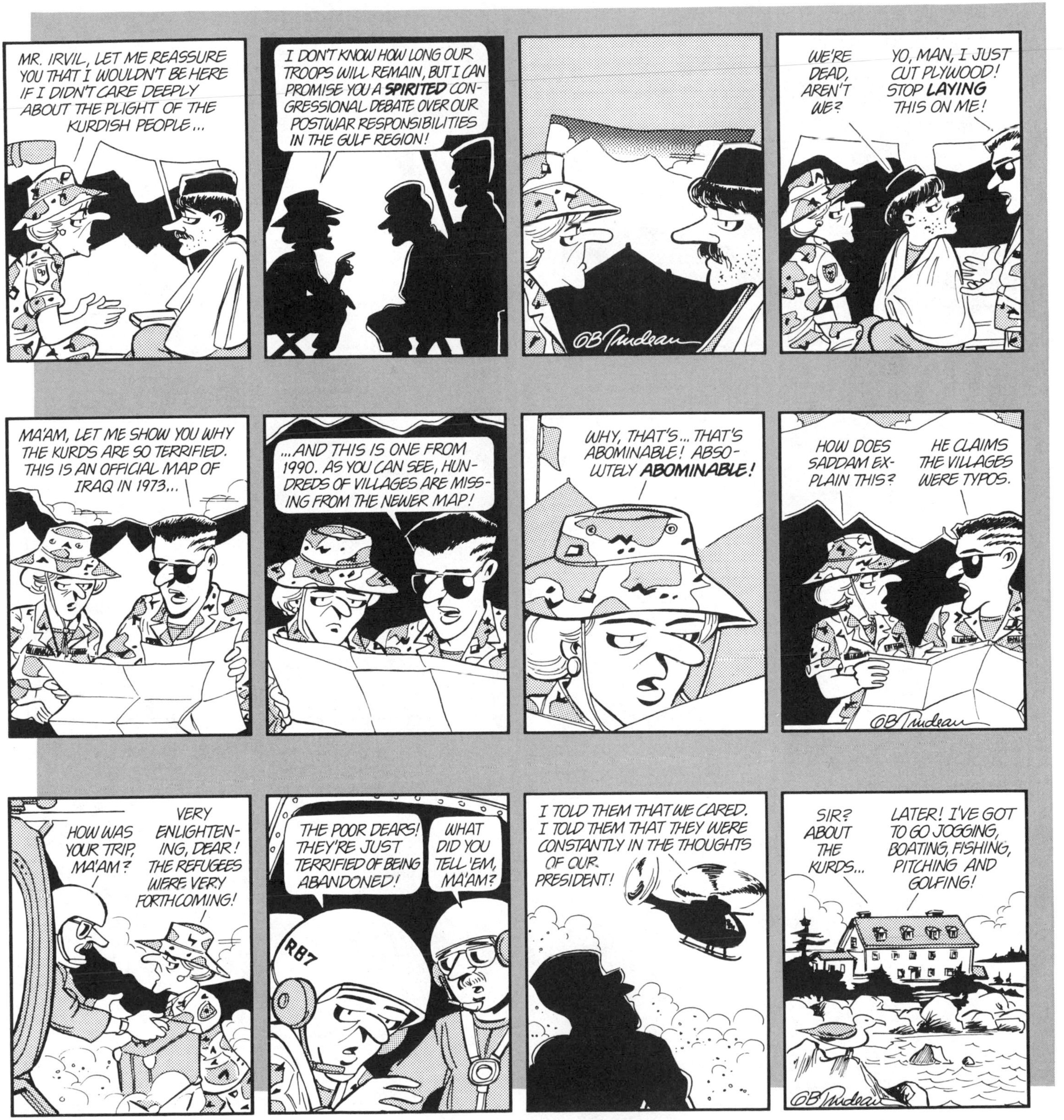
MR. IRVIL, LET ME REASSURE YOU THAT I WOULDN'T BE HERE IF I DIDN'T CARE DEEPLY ABOUT THE PLIGHT OF THE KURDISH PEOPLE...
I DON'T KNOW HOW LONG OUR TROOPS WILL REMAIN, BUT I CAN PROMISE YOU A SPIRITED CONGRESSIONAL DEBATE OVER OUR POSTWAR RESPONSIBILITIES IN THE GULF REGION!
©B Trudeau
WE'RE DEAD, AREN'T WE?
YO, MAN, I JUST CUT PLYWOOD! STOP LAYING THIS ON ME!
MA'AM, LET ME SHOW YOU WHY THE KURDS ARE SO TERRIFIED. THIS IS AN OFFICIAL MAP OF IRAQ IN 1973...
...AND THIS IS ONE FROM 1990. AS YOU CAN SEE, HUNDREDS OF VILLAGES ARE MISSING FROM THE NEWER MAP!
WHY, THAT'S... THAT'S ABOMINABLE! ABSOLUTELY ABOMINABLE!
HOW DOES SADDAM EXPLAIN THIS?
HE CLAIMS THE VILLAGES WERE TYPOS.
©B Trudeau
HOW WAS YOUR TRIP, MA'AM?
VERY ENLIGHTENING, DEAR! THE REFUGEES WERE VERY FORTHCOMING!
THE POOR DEARS! THEY'RE JUST TERRIFIED OF BEING ABANDONED!
WHAT DID YOU TELL 'EM, MA'AM?
I TOLD THEM THAT WE CARED. I TOLD THEM THAT THEY WERE CONSTANTLY IN THE THOUGHTS OF OUR PRESIDENT!
SIR? ABOUT THE KURDS...
LATER! I'VE GOT TO GO JOGGING, BOATING, FISHING, PITCHING AND GOLFING!
©B Trudeau

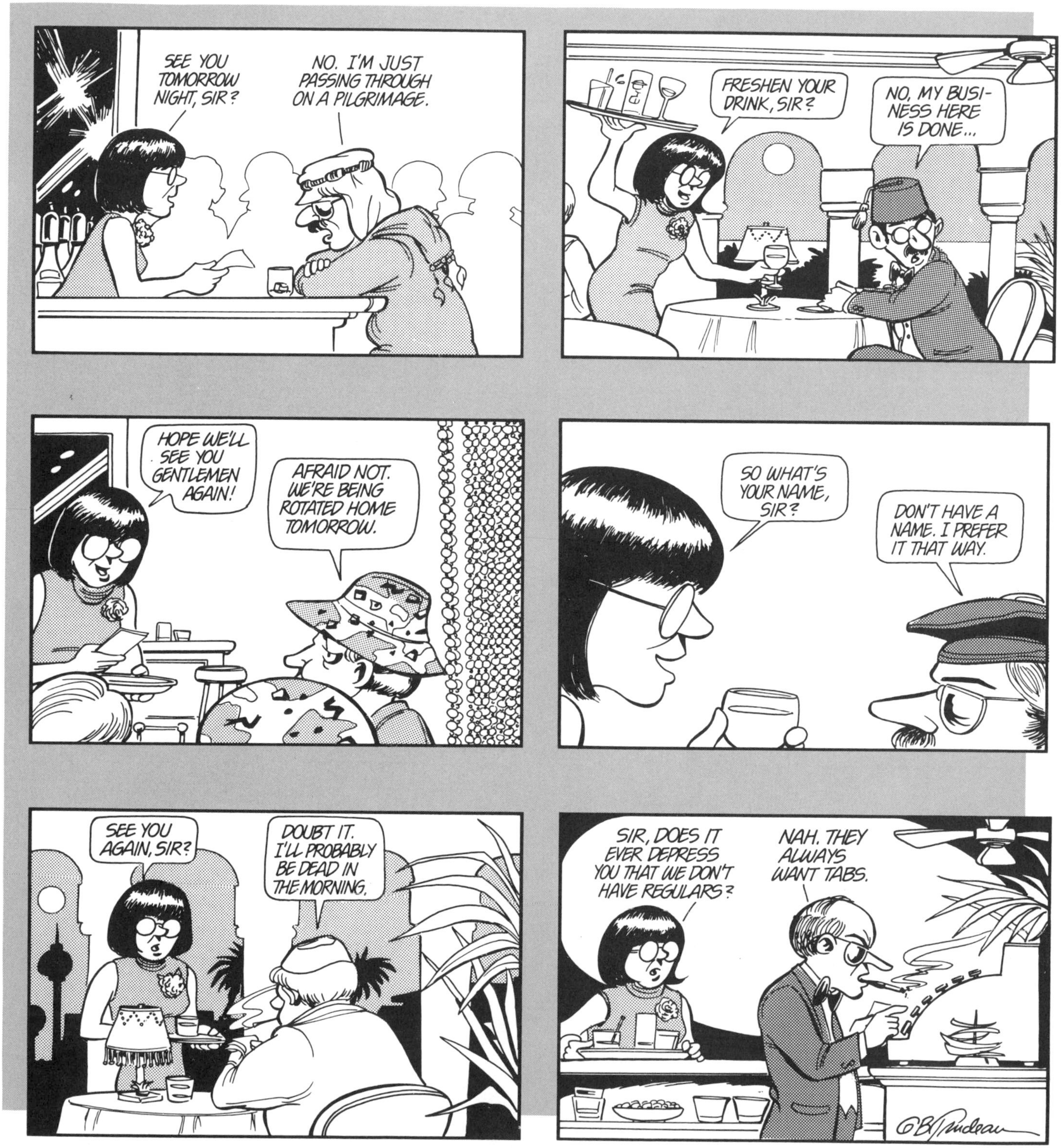
SEE YOU TOMORROW NIGHT, SIR?
NO. I'M JUST PASSING THROUGH ON A PILGRIMAGE.
FRESHEN YOUR DRINK, SIR?
NO, MY BUSINESS HERE IS DONE...
HOPE WE'LL SEE YOU GENTLEMEN AGAIN!
AFRAID NOT. WE'RE BEING ROTATED HOME TOMORROW.
SO WHAT'S YOUR NAME, SIR?
DON'T HAVE A NAME. I PREFER IT THAT WAY.
SEE YOU AGAIN, SIR?
DOUBT IT. I'LL PROBABLY BE DEAD IN THE MORNING.
SIR, DOES IT EVER DEPRESS YOU THAT WE DON'T HAVE REGULARS?
NAH. THEY ALWAYS WANT TABS.
©B Trudeau

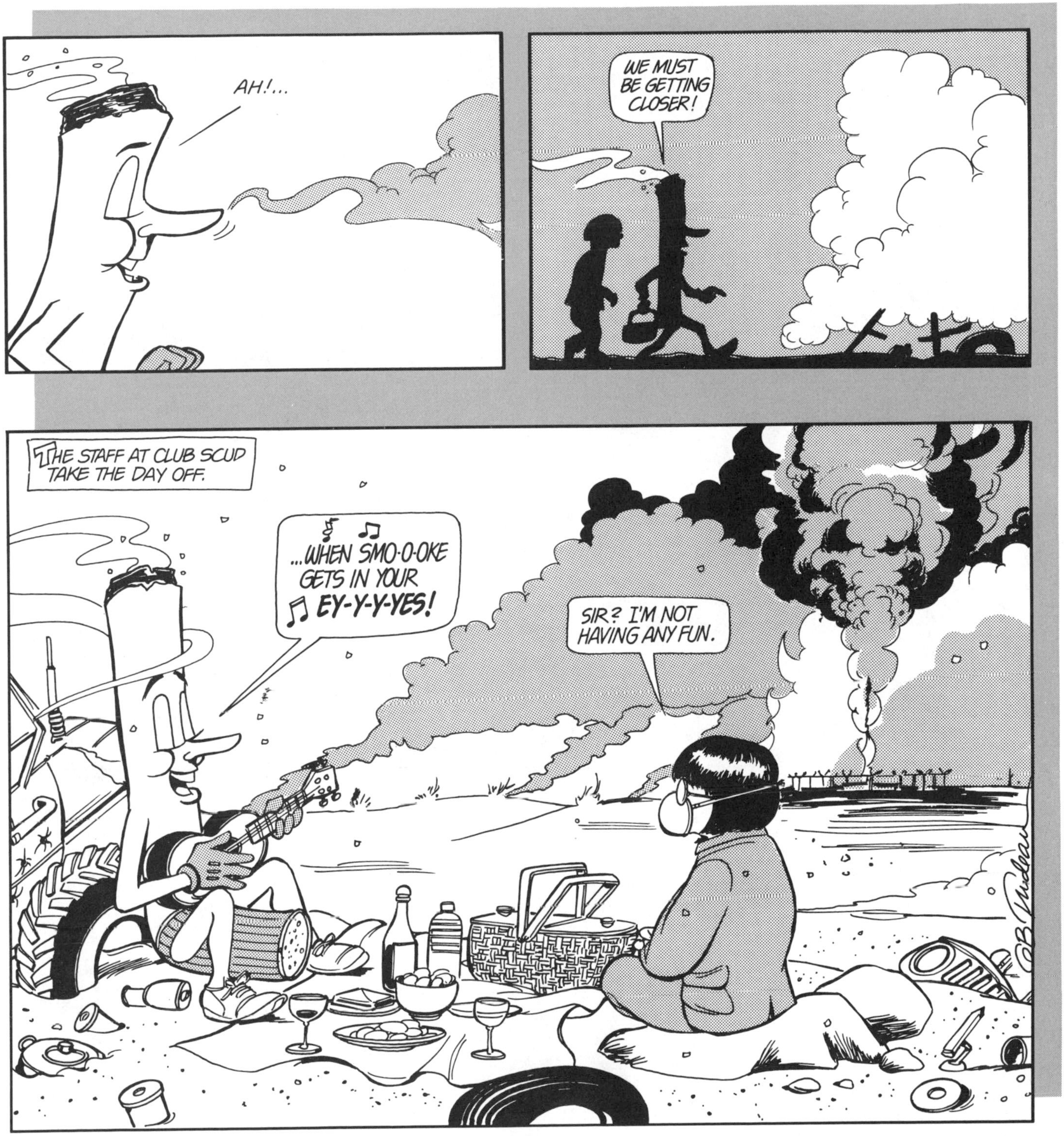
AH!...
WE MUST BE GETTING CLOSER!
THE STAFF AT CLUB SCUD TAKE THE DAY OFF.
...WHEN SMO-O-OKE GETS IN YOUR EY-Y-Y-YES!
SIR? I'M NOT HAVING ANY FUN.

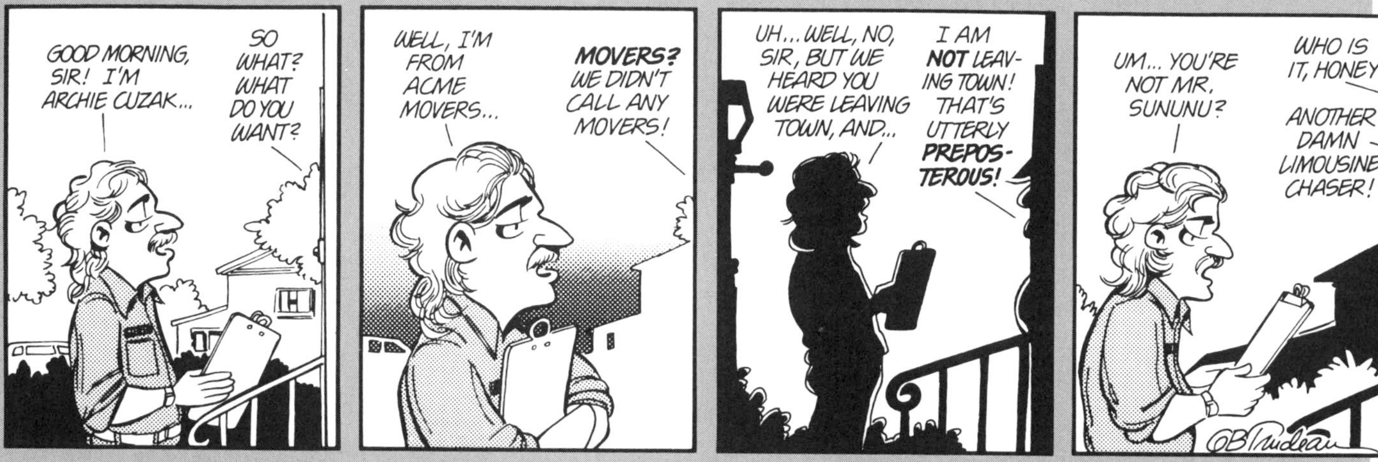
GOOD MORNING, SIR! I'M ARCHIE CUZAK...
SO WHAT? WHAT DO YOU WANT?
WELL, I'M FROM ACME MOVERS...
MOVERS? WE DIDN'T CALL ANY MOVERS!
UH... WELL, NO, SIR, BUT WE HEARD YOU WERE LEAVING TOWN, AND...
I AM NOT LEAVING TOWN! THAT'S UTTERLY PREPOSTEROUS!
UM... YOU'RE NOT MR. SUNUNU?
WHO IS IT, HONEY?
ANOTHER DAMN LIMOUSINE CHASER!

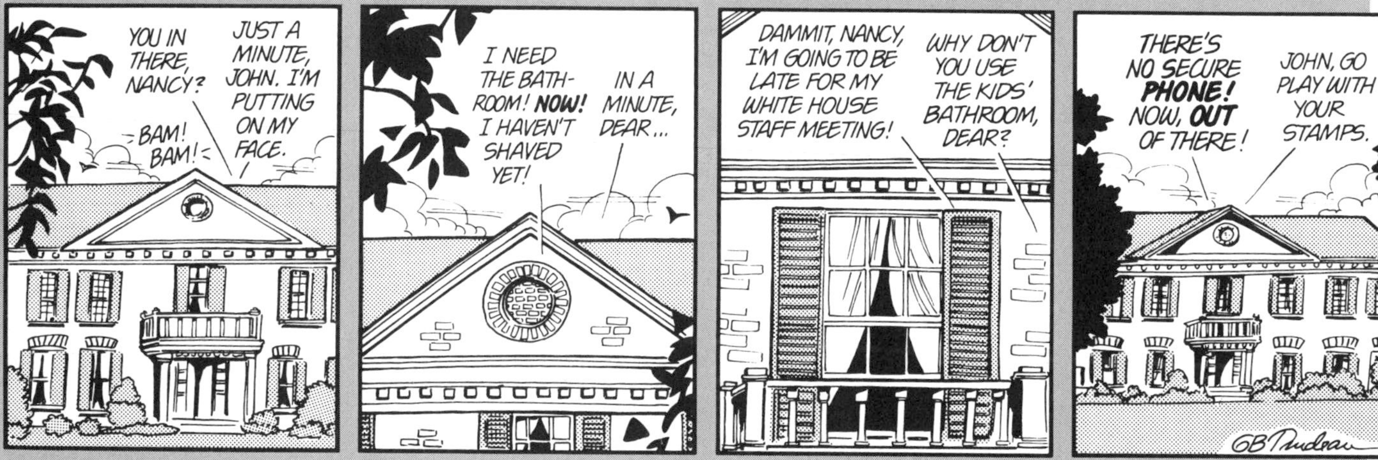
YOU IN THERE, NANCY?
BAM! BAM!
JUST A MINUTE, JOHN. I'M PUTTING ON MY FACE.
I NEED THE BATHROOM! NOW! I HAVEN'T SHAVED YET!
IN A MINUTE, DEAR...
DAMMIT, NANCY, I'M GOING TO BE LATE FOR MY WHITE HOUSE STAFF MEETING!
WHY DON'T YOU USE THE KIDS' BATHROOM, DEAR?
THERE'S NO SECURE PHONE! NOW, OUT OF THERE!
JOHN, GO PLAY WITH YOUR STAMPS.

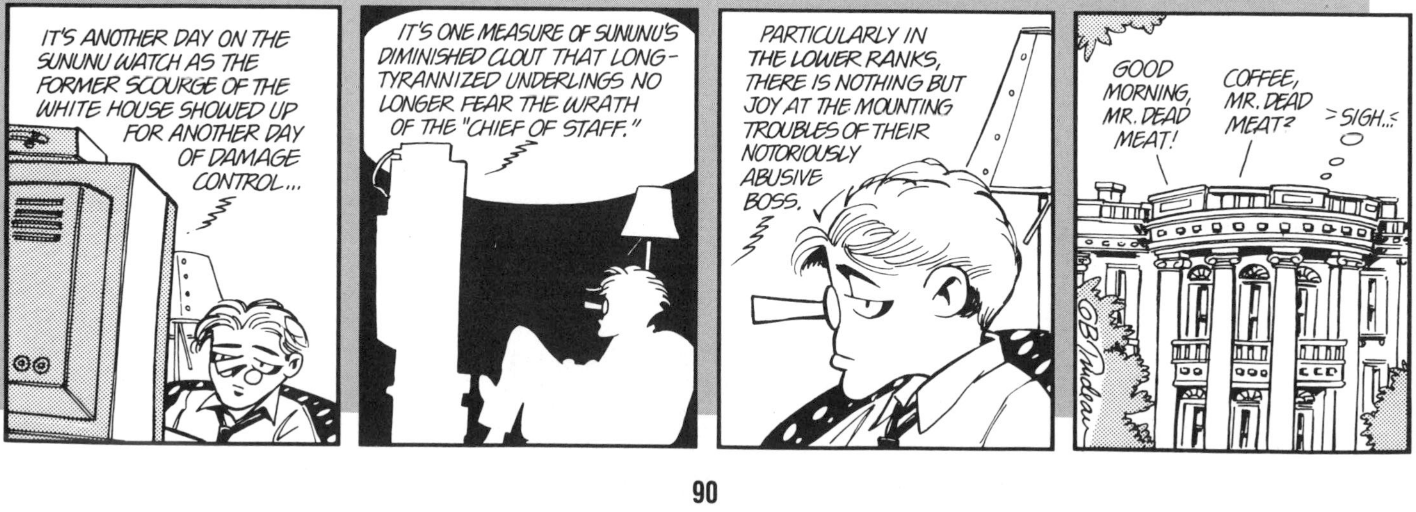
IT'S ANOTHER DAY ON THE SUNUNU WATCH AS THE FORMER SCOURGE OF THE WHITE HOUSE SHOWED UP FOR ANOTHER DAY OF DAMAGE CONTROL...
IT'S ONE MEASURE OF SUNUNU'S DIMINISHED CLOUT THAT LONG-TYRANNIZED UNDERLINGS NO LONGER FEAR THE WRATH OF THE "CHIEF OF STAFF."
PARTICULARLY IN THE LOWER RANKS, THERE IS NOTHING BUT JOY AT THE MOUNTING TROUBLES OF THEIR NOTORIOUSLY ABUSIVE BOSS.
GOOD MORNING, MR. DEAD MEAT!
COFFEE, MR. DEAD MEAT?
SIGH...

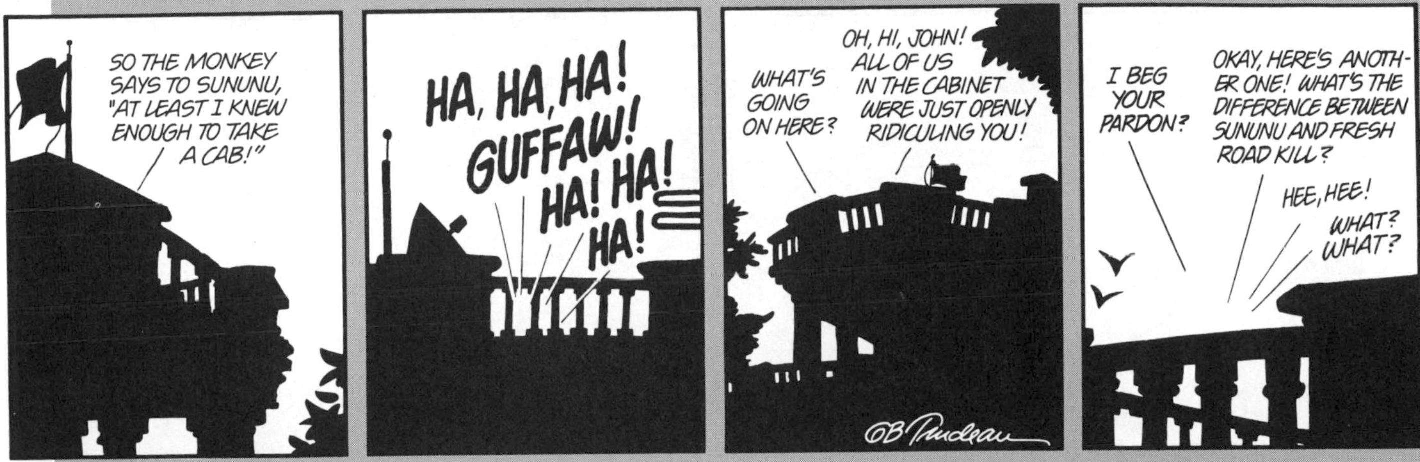
SO THE MONKEY SAYS TO SUNUNU, "AT LEAST I KNEW ENOUGH TO TAKE A CAB!"
HA, HA, HA! GUFFAW! HA! HA! HA!
WHAT'S GOING ON HERE?
OH, HI, JOHN! ALL OF US IN THE CABINET WERE JUST OPENLY RIDICULING YOU!
I BEG YOUR PARDON?
OKAY, HERE'S ANOTHER ONE! WHAT'S THE DIFFERENCE BETWEEN SUNUNU AND FRESH ROAD KILL?
HEE, HEE!
WHAT? WHAT?

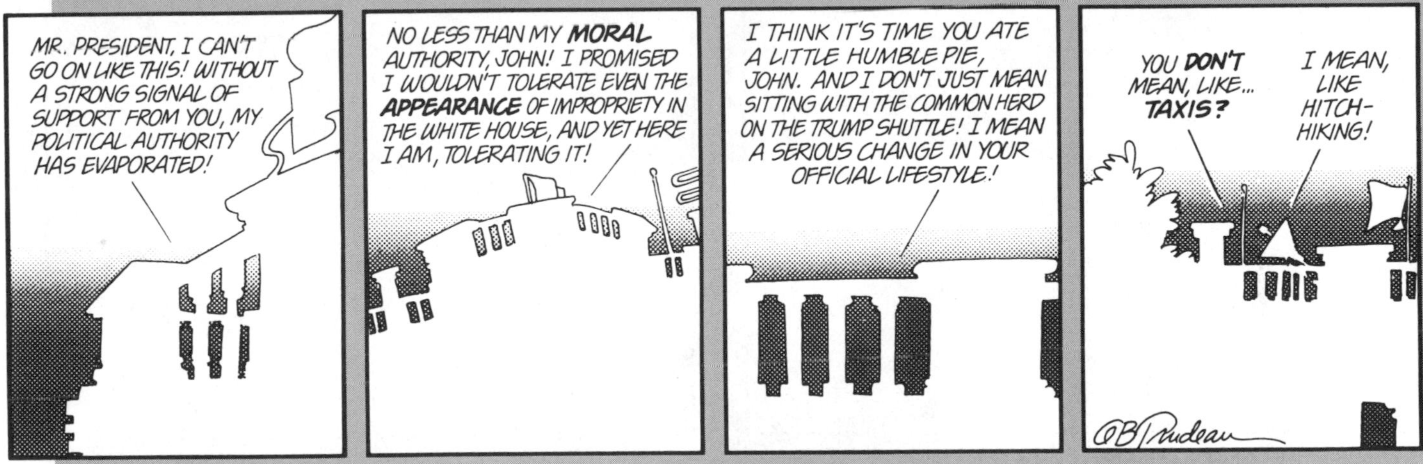
MR. PRESIDENT, I CAN'T GO ON LIKE THIS! WITHOUT A STRONG SIGNAL OF SUPPORT FROM YOU, MY POLITICAL AUTHORITY HAS EVAPORATED!
NO LESS THAN MY MORAL AUTHORITY, JOHN! I PROMISED I WOULDN'T TOLERATE EVEN THE APPEARANCE OF IMPROPRIETY IN THE WHITE HOUSE, AND YET HERE I AM, TOLERATING IT!
I THINK IT'S TIME YOU ATE A LITTLE HUMBLE PIE, JOHN. AND I DON'T JUST MEAN SITTING WITH THE COMMON HERD ON THE TRUMP SHUTTLE! I MEAN A SERIOUS CHANGE IN YOUR OFFICIAL LIFESTYLE!
YOU DON'T MEAN, LIKE... TAXIS?
I MEAN, LIKE HITCH-HIKING!

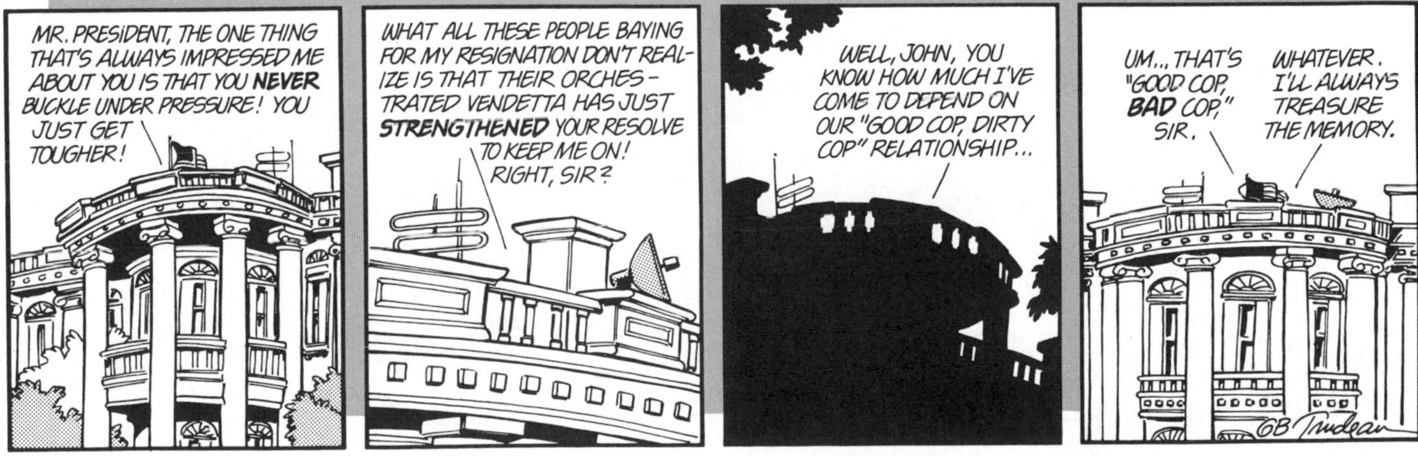
MR. PRESIDENT, THE ONE THING THAT'S ALWAYS IMPRESSED ME ABOUT YOU IS THAT YOU NEVER BUCKLE UNDER PRESSURE! YOU JUST GET TOUGHER!
WHAT ALL THESE PEOPLE BAYING FOR MY RESIGNATION DON'T REALIZE IS THAT THEIR ORCHESTRATED VENDETTA HAS JUST STRENGTHENED YOUR RESOLVE TO KEEP ME ON! RIGHT, SIR?
WELL, JOHN, YOU KNOW HOW MUCH I'VE COME TO DEPEND ON OUR "GOOD COP, DIRTY COP" RELATIONSHIP...
UM... THAT'S "GOOD COP, BAD COP," SIR.
WHATEVER. I'LL ALWAYS TREASURE THE MEMORY.

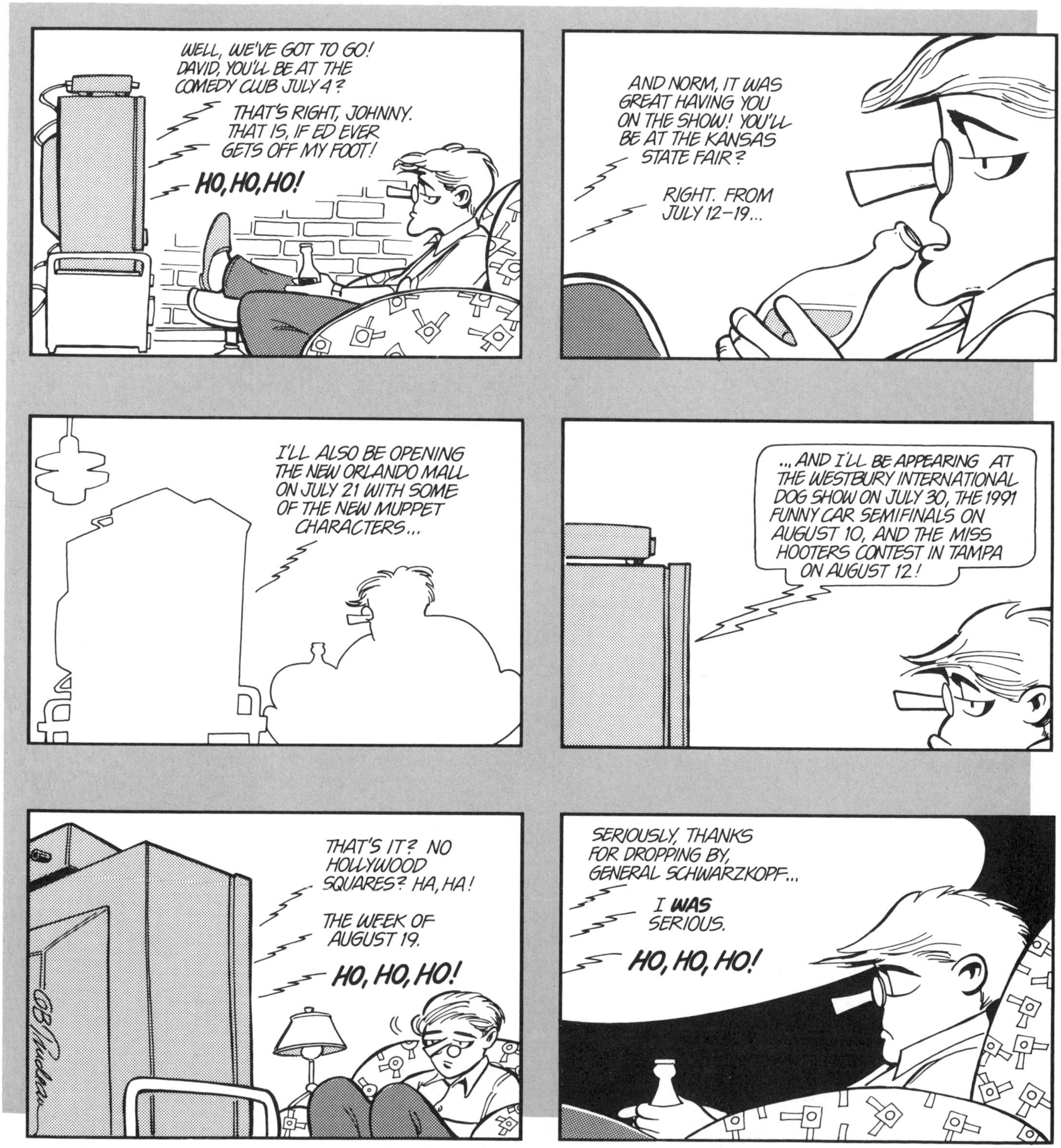
WELL, WE'VE GOT TO GO! DAVID, YOU'LL BE AT THE COMEDY CLUB JULY 4?
THAT'S RIGHT, JOHNNY. THAT IS, IF ED EVER GETS OFF MY FOOT!
HO, HO, HO!
AND NORM, IT WAS GREAT HAVING YOU ON THE SHOW! YOU'LL BE AT THE KANSAS STATE FAIR?
RIGHT. FROM JULY 12–19...
I'LL ALSO BE OPENING THE NEW ORLANDO MALL ON JULY 21 WITH SOME OF THE NEW MUPPET CHARACTERS...
...AND I'LL BE APPEARING AT THE WESTBURY INTERNATIONAL DOG SHOW ON JULY 30, THE 1991 FUNNY CAR SEMIFINALS ON AUGUST 10, AND THE MISS HOOTERS CONTEST IN TAMPA ON AUGUST 12!
THAT'S IT? NO HOLLYWOOD SQUARES? HA, HA!
THE WEEK OF AUGUST 19.
HO, HO, HO!
SERIOUSLY, THANKS FOR DROPPING BY, GENERAL SCHWARZKOPF...
I **WAS** SERIOUS.
HO, HO, HO!

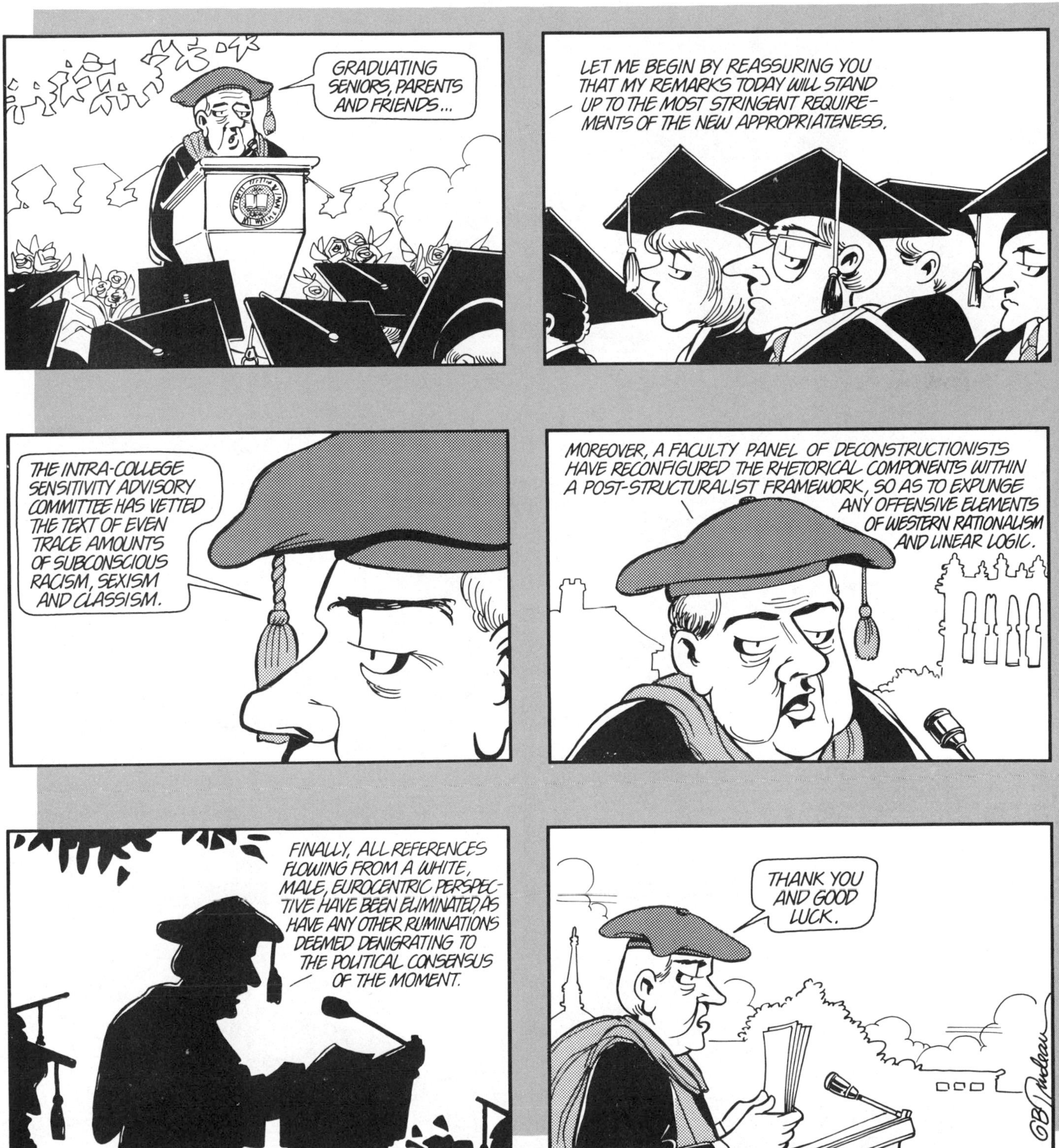
GRADUATING SENIORS, PARENTS AND FRIENDS...
LET ME BEGIN BY REASSURING YOU THAT MY REMARKS TODAY WILL STAND UP TO THE MOST STRINGENT REQUIREMENTS OF THE NEW APPROPRIATENESS.
THE INTRA-COLLEGE SENSITIVITY ADVISORY COMMITTEE HAS VETTED THE TEXT OF EVEN TRACE AMOUNTS OF SUBCONSCIOUS RACISM, SEXISM AND CLASSISM.
MOREOVER, A FACULTY PANEL OF DECONSTRUCTIONISTS HAVE RECONFIGURED THE RHETORICAL COMPONENTS WITHIN A POST-STRUCTURALIST FRAMEWORK, SO AS TO EXPUNGE ANY OFFENSIVE ELEMENTS OF WESTERN RATIONALISM AND LINEAR LOGIC.
FINALLY, ALL REFERENCES FLOWING FROM A WHITE, MALE, EUROCENTRIC PERSPECTIVE HAVE BEEN ELIMINATED, AS HAVE ANY OTHER RUMINATIONS DEEMED DENIGRATING TO THE POLITICAL CONSENSUS OF THE MOMENT.
THANK YOU AND GOOD LUCK.
GBTrudeau

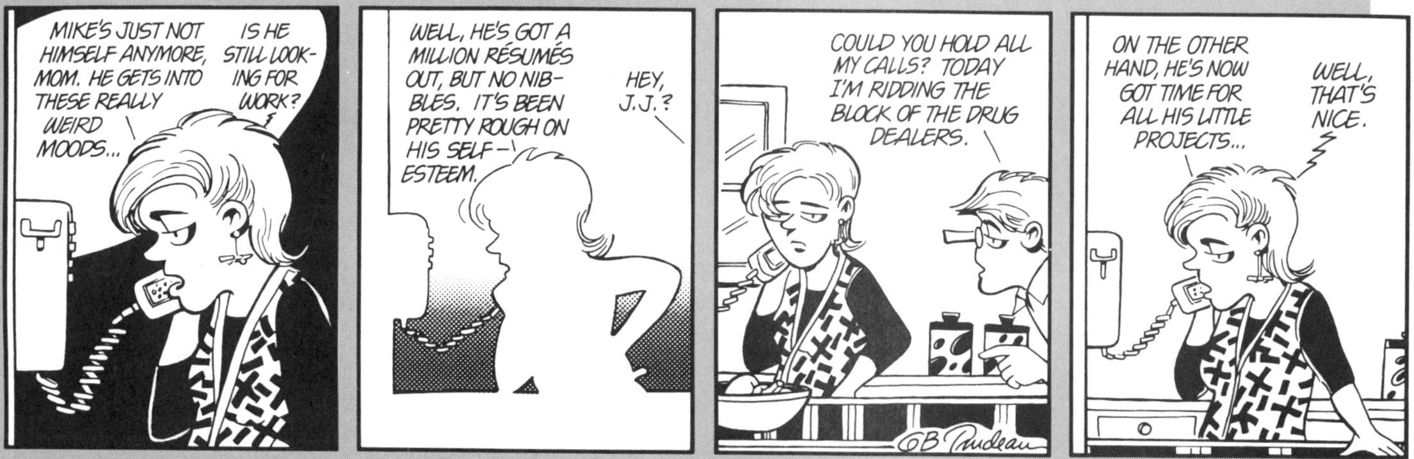
MIKE'S JUST NOT HIMSELF ANYMORE, MOM. HE GETS INTO THESE REALLY WEIRD MOODS...
IS HE STILL LOOKING FOR WORK?
WELL, HE'S GOT A MILLION RÉSUMÉS OUT, BUT NO NIBBLES. IT'S BEEN PRETTY ROUGH ON HIS SELF-ESTEEM.
HEY, J.J.?
COULD YOU HOLD ALL MY CALLS? TODAY I'M RIDDING THE BLOCK OF THE DRUG DEALERS.
ON THE OTHER HAND, HE'S NOW GOT TIME FOR ALL HIS LITTLE PROJECTS...
WELL, THAT'S NICE.

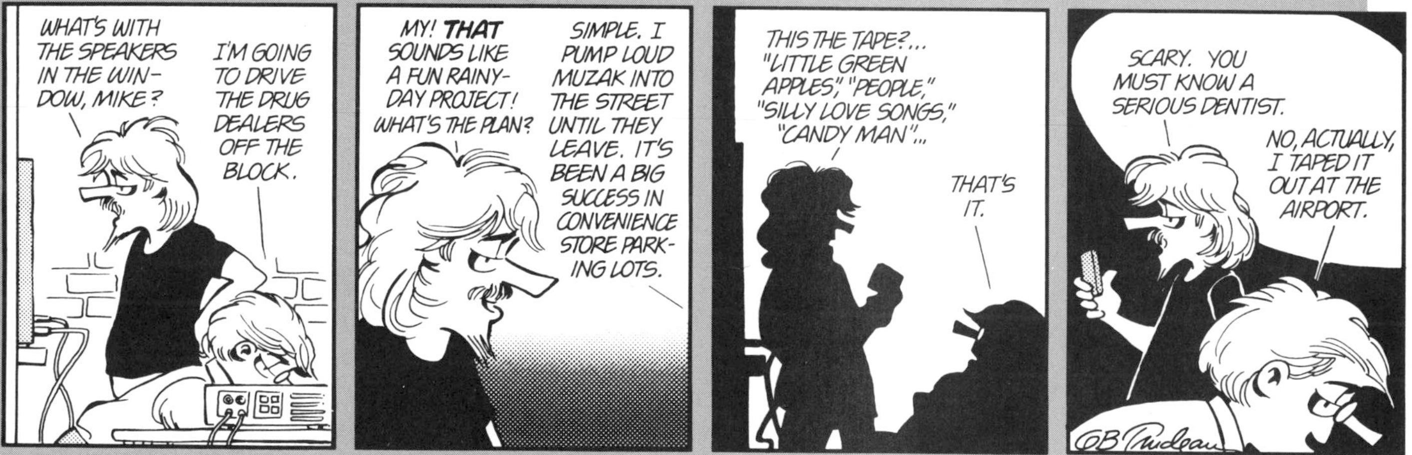
WHAT'S WITH THE SPEAKERS IN THE WINDOW, MIKE?
I'M GOING TO DRIVE THE DRUG DEALERS OFF THE BLOCK.
MY! **THAT** SOUNDS LIKE A FUN RAINY-DAY PROJECT! WHAT'S THE PLAN?
SIMPLE. I PUMP LOUD MUZAK INTO THE STREET UNTIL THEY LEAVE. IT'S BEEN A BIG SUCCESS IN CONVENIENCE STORE PARKING LOTS.
THIS THE TAPE?... "LITTLE GREEN APPLES," "PEOPLE," "SILLY LOVE SONGS," "CANDY MAN"...
THAT'S IT.
SCARY. YOU MUST KNOW A SERIOUS DENTIST.
NO, ACTUALLY, I TAPED IT OUT AT THE AIRPORT.

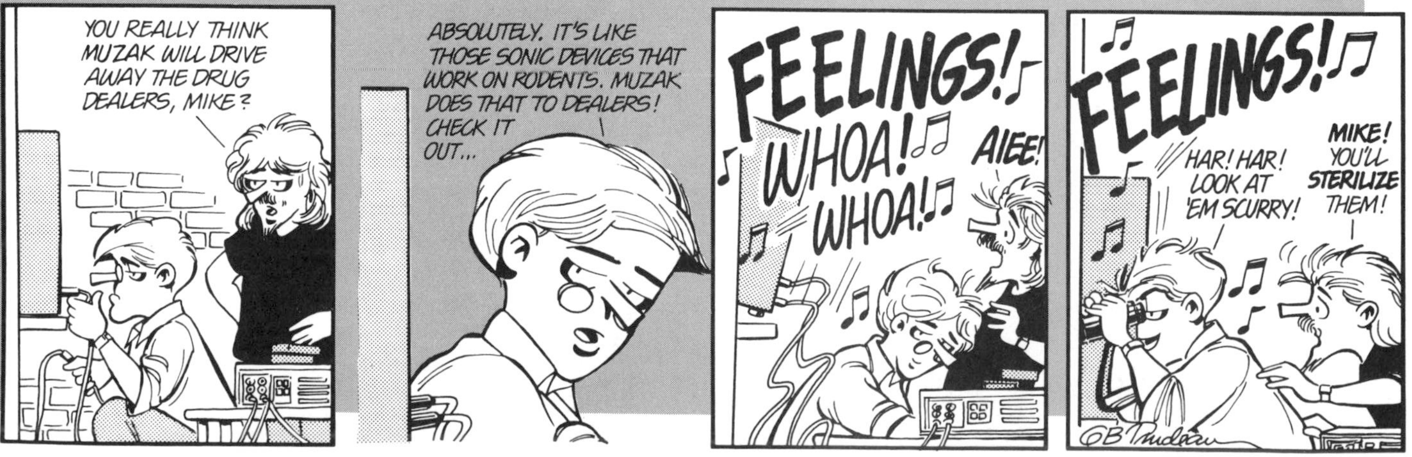
YOU REALLY THINK MUZAK WILL DRIVE AWAY THE DRUG DEALERS, MIKE?
ABSOLUTELY. IT'S LIKE THOSE SONIC DEVICES THAT WORK ON RODENTS. MUZAK DOES THAT TO DEALERS! CHECK IT OUT...
FEELINGS!
WHOA! WHOA!
AIEE!
FEELINGS!
HAR! HAR! LOOK AT 'EM SCURRY!
MIKE! YOU'LL **STERILIZE** THEM!

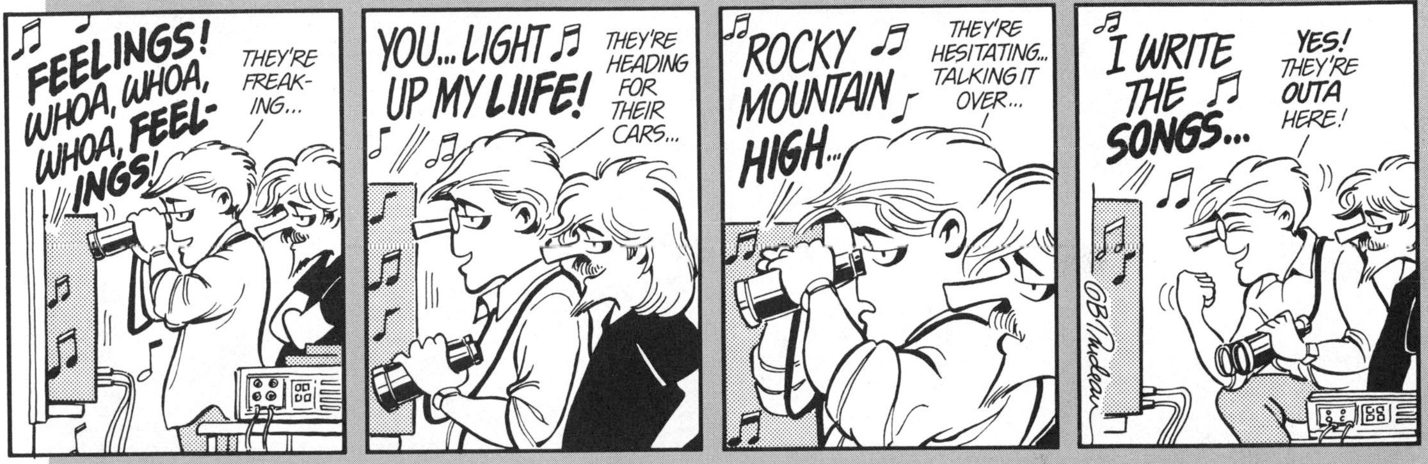
FEELINGS! WHOA, WHOA, WHOA, FEEL-INGS!
THEY'RE FREAK-ING...
YOU... LIGHT UP MY LIIFE!
THEY'RE HEADING FOR THEIR CARS...
ROCKY MOUNTAIN HIGH...
THEY'RE HESITATING... TALKING IT OVER...
I WRITE THE SONGS...
YES! THEY'RE OUTA HERE!

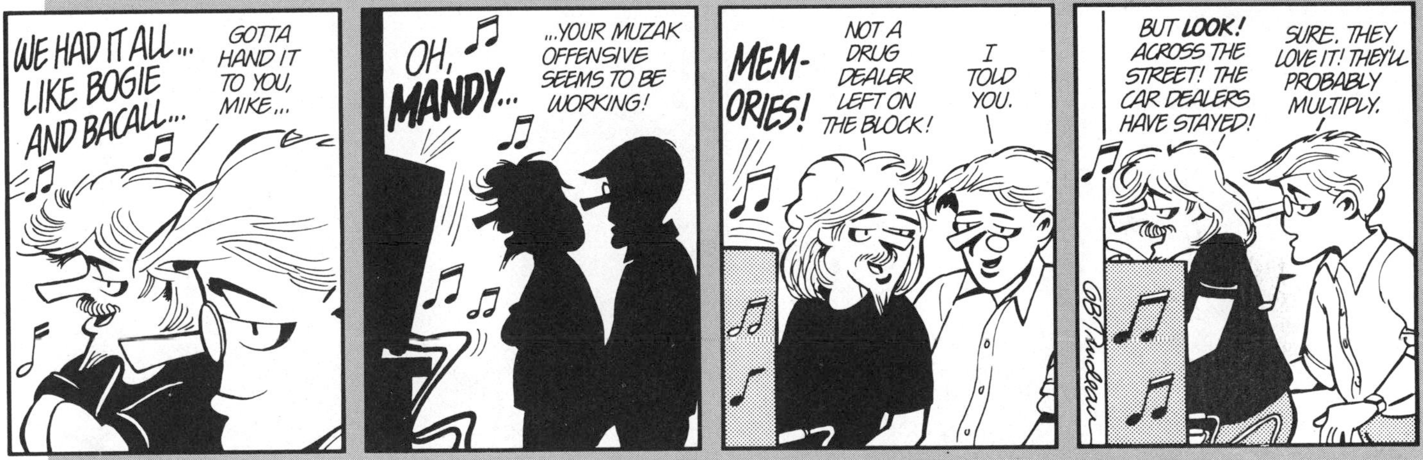
WE HAD IT ALL... LIKE BOGIE AND BACALL...
GOTTA HAND IT TO YOU, MIKE...
OH, MANDY...
...YOUR MUZAK OFFENSIVE SEEMS TO BE WORKING!
MEM-ORIES!
NOT A DRUG DEALER LEFT ON THE BLOCK!
I TOLD YOU.
BUT LOOK! ACROSS THE STREET! THE CAR DEALERS HAVE STAYED!
SURE. THEY LOVE IT! THEY'LL PROBABLY MULTIPLY.

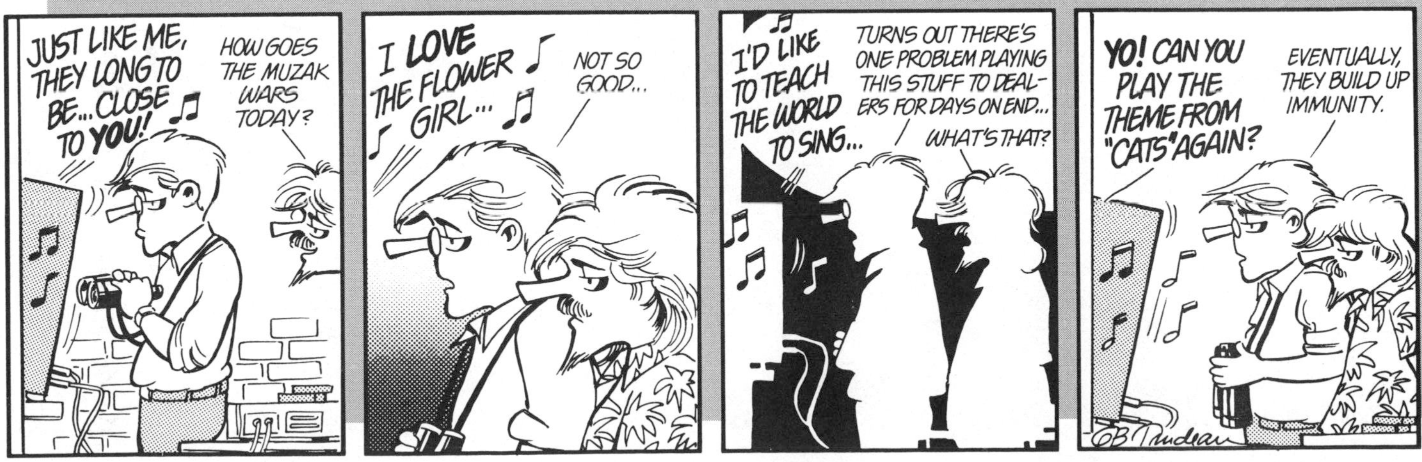
JUST LIKE ME, THEY LONG TO BE... CLOSE TO YOU!
HOW GOES THE MUZAK WARS TODAY?
I LOVE THE FLOWER GIRL...
NOT SO GOOD...
I'D LIKE TO TEACH THE WORLD TO SING...
TURNS OUT THERE'S ONE PROBLEM PLAYING THIS STUFF TO DEAL-ERS FOR DAYS ON END...
WHAT'S THAT?
YO! CAN YOU PLAY THE THEME FROM "CATS" AGAIN?
EVENTUALLY, THEY BUILD UP IMMUNITY.

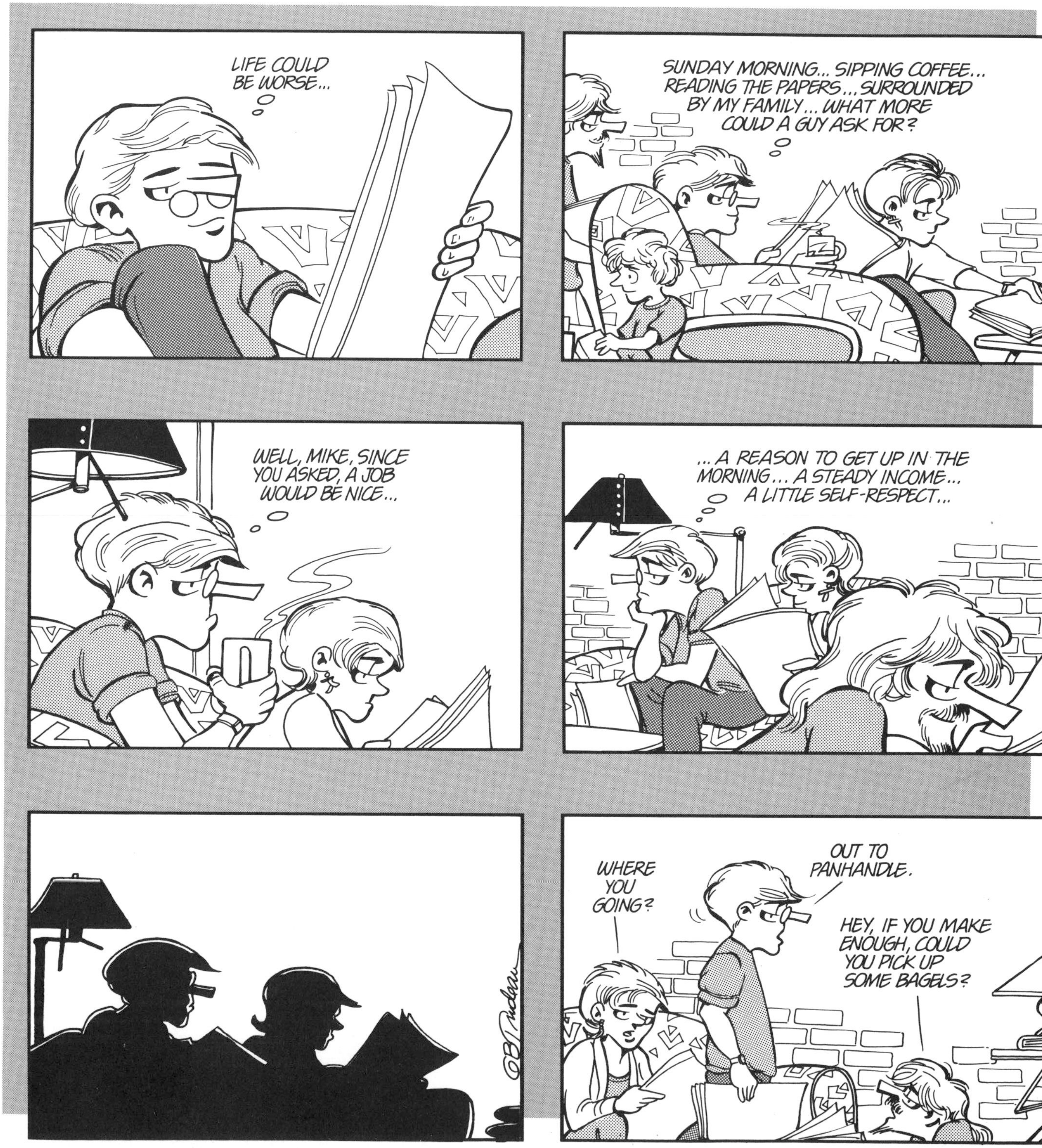
LIFE COULD BE WORSE...
SUNDAY MORNING... SIPPING COFFEE... READING THE PAPERS... SURROUNDED BY MY FAMILY... WHAT MORE COULD A GUY ASK FOR?
WELL, MIKE, SINCE YOU ASKED, A JOB WOULD BE NICE...
...A REASON TO GET UP IN THE MORNING... A STEADY INCOME... A LITTLE SELF-RESPECT...
WHERE YOU GOING?
OUT TO PANHANDLE.
HEY, IF YOU MAKE ENOUGH, COULD YOU PICK UP SOME BAGELS?